MAN UP

MAN UP

Cracking the Code of Modern Manhood

Carlos Andrés Gómez

GOTHAM BOOKS

GOTHAM BOOKS
Published by Penguin Group (USA) Inc.
375 Hudson Street, New York, New York 10014, U.S.A.
Penguin Group (Canada), 90 Eglinton Avenue East, Suite 700, Toronto, Ontario M4P
2Y3, Canada (a division of Pearson Penguin Canada Inc.); Penguin Books Ltd, 80
Strand, London WC2R 0RL, England; Penguin Ireland, 25 St Stephen's Green, Dublin
2, Ireland (a division of Penguin Books Ltd); Penguin Group (Australia), 250 Camber-
well Road, Camberwell, Victoria 3124, Australia (a division of Pearson Australia Group
Pty Ltd); Penguin Books India Pvt Ltd, 11 Community Centre, Panchsheel Park, New
Delhi–110 017, India; Penguin Group (NZ), 67 Apollo Drive, Rosedale, Auckland
0632, New Zealand (a division of Pearson New Zealand Ltd); Penguin Books (South
Africa) (Pty) Ltd, 24 Sturdee Avenue, Rosebank, Johannesburg 2196, South Africa

Penguin Books Ltd, Registered Offices: 80 Strand, London WC2R 0RL, England

Published by Gotham Books, a member of Penguin Group (USA) Inc.

First printing, September 2012
10 9 8 7 6 5 4 3 2 1

LIBRARY OF CONGRESS CATALOGING-IN-PUBLICATION DATA

Gómez, Carlos Andrés, 1981 or 2–
    Cracking the code of modern manhood / Carlos Andrés Gómez.
       p.   cm.
    ISBN 978-1-592-40778-1 (hardcover)
I. Title.
    PS3607.O4876E43 2012
    811'.6—dc23
                      2012016449

Printed in the United States of America
Set in Adobe Garamond
Designed by Spring Hoteling

While the author has made every effort to provide accurate telephone numbers, Internet
addresses, and other contact information at the time of publication, neither the publisher
nor the author assumes any responsibility for errors, or for changes that occur after publication. Further, publisher does not have any control over and does not assume any responsibility for author or third-party websites or their content.

Penguin is committed to publishing works of quality and integrity.
In that spirit, we are proud to offer this book to our readers;
however, the story, the experiences, and the words
are the author's alone.

For Papi.

And for anyone who might
someday call me by that name.

CONTENTS

AUTHOR'S NOTE

Many of the names of people and institutions in this memoir have been changed.

MAN UP

INTRODUCTION

"There are some people who live in a dream world, and there are some who face reality; and then there are those who turn one into the other."

—*Douglas Everett*

When I was in the eighth grade all I ever wanted to be was a professional basketball player. Okay, that's actually not true. I wanted to be Michael Jordan. But I had pretty much resigned myself to the fact that that was impossible. So I was willing to settle for wearing the number 23, leading the NBA in scoring, and playing shooting guard for the Chicago Bulls after my junior year at the University of North Carolina. That was my dream. That was my plan.

In high school I dreamed about becoming a public defender or a civil rights lawyer. I wanted to be like Morris Dees at the Southern Poverty Law Center, suing the shit out of the Ku Klux Klan and fighting for civil rights. I planned on becoming a lawyer for the good guys, on the front line of the right fight, with a shiny Harvard law degree. But then in college I realized that a lawyer's life is one of unceasing homework assignments and busywork. Or at least that's how I saw it. I recognized that I would probably lose my mind, and probably my soul, with all that frustrating paperwork and technical jargon. After a false arrest and the absurd process that led to my acquittal, I decided that the legal system was beyond repair, that it had been built by and for the powerful, to protect those original elite landowning white men and few others.

Then, after college, I wanted to be a social worker. After not very long in Harlem and the Bronx working in social services, I quickly learned that more than just the legal system in this country is in shambles. Neither arena felt like the right venue for me to share my gifts with the world or make my dreams become real. And that's when I found myself at the end of my rope, with nothing but my art keeping me going. Lucky for me, I said yes to the path life had pushed me toward. Art became my savior and the answer to my most pressing question: How do I make the dream become real?

This book is about making the dream real. Every time I have sat down to write, I have wanted to turn "one [world] into the other." To do that I must confront the varied selves I have been and am, and—most important of all—the man I want to be. At each step on my journey, all three versions have appeared in some form. It is often a one step forward, two steps back trek, without regard to chronology or linear progression. But that is the only way to actualize this dream: Acknowledge the full spectrum of who I am.

I am tired of men dying because they feel alone, feeling like they are destined for prison or monotony or gender role-playing or anything less than their most divine of dreams. I am tired of men hurting women and each other and themselves. I know that I am *not* alone in this. The men in my life have told me so.

If I accomplish what I strive to do with this book, I will give some men the license, for the first time, to be everything they ever wanted to be. Not what they feel like they should be or ought to be, or *have to be*, but everything they are. They will be able to open themselves to the possibility of living outside of the all-too-familiar clichéd script they've been handed. This book will give them the permission needed to unlock all of that magic that the world made them hide.

There are so many dreams I have had in my life—foolish ones and shallow ones, profoundly stupid ones and seemingly "deep" ones. And then there are those that I still cannot shake, some that I am afraid to say aloud. I have always been a day-dreamer. But I will not rest until one dream is made real: that we might redefine what it is to *be a man*, that we redefine what it means to say, "man up."

Borrowing a line from my dear friend/poet/rockstar/genius Andrea Gibson, I hope that we might allow men to be more interested not so much in being but in *becoming*. Let us each embrace the full range of who we might be, instead of that con-strained definition imposed from outside of ourselves. Let us not arrive at some stagnant place, but always continue to grow. Each day. No matter what.

Ultimately, I would love to end the need for gender alto-gether. I would love for us to all let go of what we "should be" and finally allow who we are to breathe. Let ourselves dance and sing and move as we might. But I know the bonds of habit and culture and societal practice are so strong. Things cannot completely change overnight or even over my lifetime, but I will continue to push. I will continue to challenge myself and every single man I meet to unlock the magnificent worlds he has inside.

Let me be clear, though: This is not a dream for some uto-pian wonderland. Nor do I imagine this process to be clean and without fuckups and missteps and confusion. I don't imagine it without growing pains and fear and the body fighting against the mind and heart (much like mine has and continues to on frequent occasion).

My greatest dream is to always become, to never stop growing and confronting my flaws, and, more than anything, to admit when I am wrong and make things right. I'd like to catch myself when I am being less than I am and get back on the right track. One story comes to mind that exemplifies what I mean.

Last year while I was in Toronto, I had been on the road doing shows for weeks and was completely run down. I had an early morning flight and a deadline to meet. I needed to use the Internet in my room and the Wi-Fi was down. I was already annoyed. I had wanted to work out earlier to ease my stress and take a swim, but the pool was being renovated. The fitness center was closed as well. I was tired and frustrated and not centered. I was wound up and wanted to take out my anger on someone—anyone. I wanted to project all of the negative energy inside of me onto someone else, make it their problem. I wanted to make my shit someone else's, so I wouldn't feel so alone.

The night manager at the reception desk was an easy target. He was the only person answering the hotel phone and working the late shift, so he had been the one I had been corresponding with through my ordeal. I stomped downstairs in a fury, after a contentious phone exchange with him, and pointed my finger in his face. I called him and the hotel liars for advertising free Wi-Fi and saying they had a pool and fitness center. He seemed livid that I would chastise him so scathingly, and our volatile exchange only built in volume and nastiness.

"How can you *defend* this place?" I challenged him, as though he were wearing a Nazi uniform. "It's disgusting. It's pathetic. You are *unethical*."

His face turned bright red as he started to stammer and fumble with the two phones in front of him, unsure of how to respond to my venom. And then something clicked inside of me. I don't have a clue why, but it did. It was like a switch had been flipped in my body by some merciful force in the universe.

I looked at the man behind the counter in the eyes for the

first time and took him in. I glanced up at the clock on the wall and realized it was almost three o'clock in the morning. I glanced outside and saw puddles building on the sidewalk, another gloomy Tuesday in the coldest month of a ruthless Canadian winter. This man was *working* right now, all by himself. He was proud to have his job, in the midst of a recession, as he should be.

Who the fuck am I? Do I really need to meet this deadline by the morning? Are any lives at stake if I don't just hand it in tomorrow evening?

"I'm . . . sorry, sir. I don't know why I've been so rude to you. I'm not really angry at you or the hotel. I think I'm just tired . . . and lonely. I didn't mean to take it out on you. I apologize," I finally said to him.

He looked stunned. Almost like he wanted to get angry but might cry or laugh instead. It was like I had started speaking an entirely new language. Slowly a smile crept over his face. "It's okay. I understand. I'm sorry too. I was very rude myself. I think I'm tired too. My wife and I just had another baby. I probably haven't had a good night's sleep in a month," he said as a soft chuckle rumbled out of him.

Right there, all of the heaviness and anger and weight lifted. We both smiled, a little embarrassed about who we had just been. It felt like the rain stopped. We knew those weren't really the men we were. They were dark shadows representing the clutter in our chests. We were projecting out the things inside that hurt. That made us tired, and we lost our patience. Or we were just fed up with everything.

I leaned over on that counter and talked to that night manager at the hotel for close to an hour. We laughed and joked and shared stories about our lives. He had come over from India with his wife. He was a trained engineer who was working this job to support his family until he could find a position doing what he really loved. I told him my sister lived for two years in Ahmedabad in Gujarat. He spoke Gujarati. I told him I visited her during college. He giggled like a schoolboy, tickled that I had actually visited his homeland. I told him I was a poet. He told me he'd wooed his wife with love poems by Tagore. I told him I'd visited Tagore's ashram. We both laughed and shook our heads in disbelief at all the unexpected connections we shared.

An entire world opened up that night. But it took both of us adjusting on the fly, catching ourselves when we were being less than we were and being willing to say, "Hey man. I'm sorry. That wasn't me. Let me show you who I am. Let me show you who I want to be."

As I said good-bye, giving him a warm embrace, we shared a final smile—maybe thinking back to the unlikely way we first connected—and he said to me, "By the way, the website is complete bullshit. I agree. It's false advertising. I would have been mad too." And we parted ways, both laughing.

Even a year before this happened, I would have been too proud to apologize to that man and open myself up. I would have felt like I was dug in too deep. I had already disparaged him for close to twenty minutes, on the phone and in person. I had been nothing but vicious to him, tearing him apart with my words and my sharp, intense glare. I would have been way too embarrassed to humble myself and admit that I had been wrong.

I still get too proud far too often in my life and refuse to humble myself to another person when I should. It's something I'm working on. It's part of this man I am becoming instead of trying to be. That night, I embodied that man, in all his fragmented, complex horror and beauty. Each day, I strive to continue to become that man.

I don't aspire to be some perfect man, whatever the fuck that might mean. I aspire to continue to become, to learn from the incredible men I am surrounded by—none of them being perfect either, but incredible examples of men, nonetheless, like my father and my good friends. Like my little brother. Like the men close to me who are not related to me by blood but will always be my brothers.

I have been lucky enough to witness the dream become real on a few occasions in my life. One instance stands out more than all the rest.

Last year at Rikers Island, New York City's infamous jail, I was visiting for an afternoon performance. It was a few days before Christmas, that time during the holiday season when prisons and jails are most violent, that dark time when the pain and solitude of being incarcerated become unbearable for many. This is also when many suicides take place; some men send their pain outward and turn violent on a cellmate, while others turn it inward and kill themselves to end the suffering. I could feel the tension in the room as I walked in, the nearly two hundred young men, ages sixteen to eighteen, staring at me as though I were another added felony charge.

I softened them up with goofy love poems and quirky lines, getting some of the guys to break through and finally chuckle and laugh. Then I read a poem about dancing at the club, approaching a girl on the dance floor and hoping she wouldn't turn me down. Some of the guys were hooting and teasing in obvious empathetic nods to my own insecurities on a Saturday night out. I had one final poem left for them, and I wanted to make it count. As I glanced up at the four separated groups, each of about fifty, divided by burly corrections officers with guns, I suddenly felt like we were in someone's living room, like we were in the ratty, steel-barred gymnasium where I saw my first pep rally at Northeast High School or had prom at Providence Friends School or played basketball for hours when I was in college. I was literally standing near the baseline at center court, about to do my last poem. And all I could think about was childhood and my love for basketball. I thought of all of the ways that the game I loved so much had made me into the man I was. I wanted to pick up a bunch of basketballs right then and there—let us all play a pickup game and laugh and joke and compete and get upset when we lost and try to showboat on a breakaway and miss a layup. But it wasn't time for sports. It was time for a poem.

So I read them my poem "How to Fight." I slowly delivered the lines about creating a new way for us to fight and engage in our lives. I talked about being fed up with the ways we lash out at each other, how I'm tired of seeing all of these beautiful men, especially black and Latino men, die before they are able to even start pursuing a dream that is their own. I looked out on a room of entirely brown faces—black and Puerto Rican, Jamaican and Dominican, mixed like me—with painful stories tucked behind their proud eyes. I stared at Bloods and Crips and Latin Kings and young fathers. I stared at young writers and poets and singers and dancers and basketball players and science nerds and math whizzes and kids as bad at math as I am.

As I went deeper into the poem, the room fell completely silent for the first time. There was not a peep or a whisper, just a room full of thirsty eyes staring down at me as I read them a poem. It talks about the conspiracy against our peoples' beauty and worth. It talks about the trickery of us ever viewing each other as enemies. It talks about the hope shining through out of our chests, in spite of the rigged game of roulette we are forced to play. As I got to the last few lines of my poem, I moved off the microphone for the first time and addressed a pensive, sensitive-looking kid right in front of me in the first row of bleachers. His tight cornrows and deep brown eyes took in my every word as I moved closer to him. My voice choked with emotion as I began saying the last lines of that poem as though they were written for him:

Hermano, we aren't what we call each other.
Hermano, we've lost too many of us already.
Hermano, me llamo Carlos. Ya nos conocemos.

That's Spanish for, "I'm Carlos. We already know each other."
I'm your brother. Tú eres mi hermano.

And I moved even closer, now a mere half step away from him, slowly extending my open palm,

Let's start something.

I knew that if I delivered that line the wrong way, there would be a price to be paid. There would have to be, because respect in jail is everything. If someone disrespects you and is allowed to get away with it, that moment alone could cost you your life. I knew this. But I believed in the men in that room. I believed they wanted the same dream I did.

Who wants to fight and die for nothing? Who wants to not have a father or safe home? Who wants to be treated like an animal and told he's worth shit?

As I leaned forward and put my hand out, I could feel the entire room hold its breath. My heart beat hard against my Adam's apple as though it might break. Before I knew what was happening I felt a hard slap against my palm, as the young man in front of me clenched my fingers, pulled himself up, and embraced me in a long hug.

Everyone clapped. Everyone stood up. None of the corrections officers told them to sit down. I looked up and saw men with tear-swollen eyes and vulnerable smiles. The dream had been made real.

If only for a moment, in that room we had seen that the dream could be made real.

---

* Connext Online: **"How to Fight"** http://www.youtube.com/watch?v=cKMhp7hpYIs

PART I

LITTLE CARLITOS

ALL WE HAVE

by Carlos Andrés Gómez

the only consistency We know is absence
     whether of justice
         or   of food
         or   of opportunity

We live obese on the fatness of grief so We learn
to improvise, move Our hips and hands
tongue-clicks and intonations like the sky is watching
(stars blinking at the beauty)
Our bodies simulating heartbeats, flashbulbs glimpsing
scars out of pitch—
and Our ancestors taught us well

engraved Our souls with rhythm
& fire & pause

(and they were called "slave" when the sun rose)—

but those nights belonged to them
belonged to their dreams, taunting morning twilight
as they danced the *cumbia* on the north coast—
calves cradled in salt water graves
because the dark sky chanted "Freedom"
and they could die there knowing they had been alive
                   calling back

Dance, Savion! Dance! Savion, dance!
Boy—do that tap dance for me!
they shouted at him
in gin-tinted ridicule, their pale faces rose red
with honesty, intoxicating epithets from their mouths

as if hollow banter could be an appraisal of his
worth, breaking his bones down to dust
but he'd broken through walls as thick as silence
& cracked sulfur-spells of pipe hits
and bleeding/chapped lips and when
his dread locks sang they sang in salt water riffs—
baptizing his body with sweat /
the tears he swallowed shot out
heel click like sparks that pinched eyelids

you could almost hear John Coltrane's
knees buckle

bending down from the sky to listen, as the echoes
of his Tenor blasted out of recordings toward a spotlight
on a stage, where a black man's feet made southern white
men's eyes tear with shame

& Coltrane would say,
Dance, Savion, dance . . . dance . . .
do that tap dance for me . . .

and when they don't allow Us to
learn how to read
& teach Us to forget Our languages,
mispronouncing Our names
& lock up Our fathers when they learn to sing,
dragging toxins through Our mothers' spines

stole all of Our possessions & kidnapped Our families

We're forced to build like this—
from Our hips, cradle the innateness of birth
at the source of Our bodies, ball up Our eyes
like fists & fling tears wildly at the stars—
dancing like Our lives depend on it

you can violate women's hips but you cannot break them

and even if you're told you're stupid you can dance—
weaving tidal waves out of soft rain

Our people were never stolen
We were never your slaves

(write it on Our graves)

Black/ Brown/ Indigenous/ Mestizo/ Latino

(carve it in your textbooks)

WE were never your slaves

, just reluctant martyrs / never slaves

and We never lost our rhythm
surviving

so
don't you dare try to copy
this Mambo, Capoeira, Bharatanatyam, Salsa,

this WIndmill, Kwaito, this
Pop'n'lock, this FIRE

We were made to dance like apostles
'til miracles fall back to earth

and you can take everything else because this
is how you get to heaven and We
are the ones
that birthed it & We nicknamed it
God.*

*   Connect Online: **"All We Have"** http://www.youtube.com/watch?v=iZaDJ7BcxZc

CHAPTER 1

"Where Are You From?"

At seven years old I sat on a suitcase in John F. Kennedy International Airport staring at the passersby as if each one was a riddle to solve. We were waiting for the rest of our bags. Our family had just arrived into New York City from Switzerland. After a seven-year absence, I was returning to my birthplace.

I had asked my mother about race. She had made it a point to teach me about it before we arrived in the United States. It still made no sense to me.

"What about her, is she black?" I pointed to a dark-skinned woman passing us.

"Don't point!" my mom scolded, covering my finger. "Yes she's—"

Then the woman started speaking brisk, staccato Spanish to her friend.

"Uh . . . no. She's *Latina*," my mom corrected herself.

"But you said it's skin color, Mommy. She's the same skin color as Victor. And you said if they look like Victor, they're black." I was thoroughly confused.

"*She's* black," my mom said, nodding toward an airport employee.

"But her skin's lighter than mine. Then, what am I, Mommy?" I had finally asked the question.

"You're just you. And don't let anyone tell you otherwise," my mom stated definitively, scooping up our remaining bag while my dad struggled with two more.

It's one of the questions that would haunt me when I was younger. *What am I? Where am I from?* Now I just oversimplify it and say, "I'm from New York." But that's not really accurate, is it? The truth is, I'm still not really sure what is. But I am still asked the question, as Americans, especially, love to inquire: "Where are you *from*?"

To really know where I'm *from* is to learn about what I experienced in the eclectic and crazy mix of environments I was made to call "home," however briefly.

To say I am from New York is partly true. I was born in New York Hospital, which is now New York Presbyterian in Manhattan. We lived on the Upper West Side, where you now find the precious, contentious blocks between the ever-expanding Columbia University campus and west Harlem. When we lived there my mother was doing her graduate work at Columbia, having just finished her master's degree and beginning her work on her PhD. Shortly after I turned six months old, we moved to Brazil.

My father, before living in New York, had worked for the United Nations Volunteers in El Salvador for two years. My parents had lived in Central America during the volatile seventies, and my father had made a name for himself. He was then sent to Brazil for his first official post as a deputy resident representative—as he puts it, the "number two" in the country representing the United Nations. It was a huge honor, and a big career move for him. He was young, ambitious, fresh-faced, and in his mid-thirties.

In Brazil I said my first words. No, they were not in English. Everything around me was in Portuguese, so Portuguese became my dominant language. English was something I was much less comfortable with. To this day I have recordings (on cassette tapes!) of my sister and me playing in Portuguese; me playing a fake sportscaster and her a news anchor. I can tell by the silly voices we're making that we were trying to impersonate what we probably heard on the radio. I listen to those recordings now with nostalgia and confusion—I have no clue what I was saying.

Portuguese was just one of many languages swirling around my head as I grew up. Of course there was also Spanish. As I grew up all over the world in subsequent moves, I would be exposed to a wide array of languages: Greek, Turkish, French, German, and Italian, among others.

I have only a couple of memories from Brazil, but one stands out from all the others. It involved my neighbor, a little boy I would play with under the hedge separating our yards. Why would we play under the hedge? Well, I lived in a house with a pool and well-manicured lawn. He lived next door in an abandoned lot. Really it was a makeshift landfill where poor families built their homes out of the scrap metal they found in the lot cluttered with affluent families' throwaways. It was an unspoken rule, I guess, that we couldn't go to each other's houses, so we'd crawl under the hedge and play.

For Christmas one year I got a bright red fire truck (the first of many) and it was, at the time, the most incredible gift I'd ever received. I immediately ran outside to play with my friend and show off my cool new toy to him. That day, as we met under the hedge, something felt different between us. He didn't seem as excited to play with me as he normally was. He was quiet and aloof. Then, out of nowhere, he slapped me, grabbed my fire truck, and scrambled back over to his side. I was stunned. When I finally realized what had just happened, I went howling and screaming to my mom. I had tried to share and look what had happened—he had *stolen* my fire truck. I will never forget what she said to me that morning.

"Well, now it's his fire truck. That might be the only toy he has. Stop crying; you still have a whole room full of toys to play with."

I was shocked by my mom's callousness. She had no sympathy for me whatsoever. I had done everything she asked of me—been kind and offered to share with my friend—and he had taken advantage of me. It was my first up close and personal encounter with disparity and poverty. Never before had I been forced to grapple with my privilege. Why would my fire truck be his only toy? Why did he live in a yard with garbage? Why didn't he have a pool? Why weren't we allowed to go over to each other's houses and play?

I loved that boy. He was the first real friend I ever made. Unfortunately, our worlds were so drastically different, we couldn't be friends the way we wanted to.

After about three years in Brazil, we moved to Cyprus—an island in the Mediterranean Sea off the coast of Turkey. A partition divided the island in half, a reluctant resolution that formed a tentative peace between the Greeks and Turks, who had been mired in civil war. A mile-wide buffer zone, littered with land mines, prevented anyone from crossing from one side to the other. My father worked for the United Nations as the resident representative, so we were allowed to cross over. The two sides might as well have been on different planets. On one side you'd see topless women and nude swimmers playing and screaming in the water. On the other, women were covered in black from head to toe in the suffocating heat. One side of the island was the Middle East, the other was Mediterranean Europe. When we first arrived in Larnaca, I saw the back of a plane sticking out of the ground and bombed-out hulls of vehicles and other wreckage from war. It looked like a world war had just ended and we were taking a tour through the postapocalyptic aftermath.

In a lot of ways, that country was a metaphor for my parents. They were complete opposites. My mother grew up in a traditional Southern, WASPy American family. She is very pale-skinned with bright blue eyes and light brown hair (which was blonde when she was a little girl). Her dad was in the armed forces, so she moved a lot. My father, on the other hand, is olive-skinned with deep hazel eyes and black hair. He grew up in a strict Roman Catholic family in Colombia. When he was just entering his teen years, his family moved to Miami, where he and his four sisters were put into Catholic school. None of them spoke a word of English and still tell stories about the adversity this caused for them when they first arrived.

The differences between my parents persist. My mother is high-strung and meticulous. My father is laid-back and laissez-faire. My mom likes to be on a schedule and write everything down. My father lives in the moment and relies on his memory or whim. My mom—okay, you get the idea. They're just very different. And, for so many reasons, Cyprus was definitely the turning point where everyone started to realize it.

No one showed up to meet us at the airport when we arrived. My mom sobbed uncontrollably, livid that we had been stood up after more than twenty hours of flying. The way she tells it, my father had (as usual) mixed up the arrival details and was somewhere smoking a cigar at a cocktail party while my mom, my sister, and I sat on our cluster of suitcases, desperately looking for a familiar face. We never found one. We waited and waited but no one came. We couldn't get in touch with anybody, so we hopped in a cab and went to the Hilton in Nicosia. It was the only hotel my mom could think of, so she told the cab driver to take us there. We didn't have any credit cards or money, yet the manager of the Hilton still took us in. (Later on the manager and his entire family would become close lifelong friends of ours.) They had rescued us from our scary situation in this strange, new place. But nevertheless that moment represented a turning point in my parents' relationship, and it would prove to be something my mom was never able to forgive. She felt then (and now) that my dad's job had taken precedence over his family. I know that, even today, my dad wishes he could have that day back. He knows he fucked up. But those are the ones you never get back. That day was a foreshadowing of the strange two years my family lived on that small island.

The school I went to in Cyprus was insane. I don't use that word lightly—I used to work with paranoid schizophrenics and people who were severely bipolar when I was a social worker—so when I say insane, I mean *insane*. This school was completely nuts. I have a few vivid memories from the two long years I spent there and all are pretty horrifying. Most, I look back on now, and think, *How was that shit legal?*

Example number one: We had a toilet in our classroom. I was probably in preschool or the equivalent. There was a sign that hung by the toilet's door. As you went in you would turn it to red to show that it was "occupied." And then, as you left, you would turn it back to green to show that it was "vacant." On this particular day, I needed to pee extremely badly. Like most five-year-olds, I probably realized it as the first trickles were rolling down my leg, so I rushed to the toilet in a desperate sprint. I saw that the sign was on the green side, so I tore open the door and stumbled upon a little girl with her pants down. She squealed, then I squealed, then the teacher grabbed me angrily by the collar.

"You want to peek in on little girls going to the bathroom?"

"No, but the—," I was trying to explain.

" 'No but' *what*? Since you saw her with her pants down, now the *whole school* will see you. Before swimming class today, you're going to stand in the middle of the sandbox on the playground and change into your bathing suit there, so you can really *feel* what it's like to have your privacy invaded," she said, laying down her punishment.

Could you imagine if this whole thing happened in the United States today? I'd probably be driving a convertible Bentley with hundred-dollar bills spilling out of my glove box. That'd be a multimillion-dollar lawsuit, a teacher firing, and, probably, the school being shut down. But no, not in Cyprus in 1987.

I did what the teacher told me: I stood buck naked in front of hundreds of kids at recess who saw my little winky and laughed and pointed and watched me shamefully squeeze into my little white Speedo for swimming class. The story's so absurd that I laugh about it now, but I know a lot of people who think that story's just straight-up abuse. But that wasn't the only crazy shit that ever happened at Cardinal School.

We had recess monitors when we would go out and play. Their number one priority was making sure no children *ran* on the playground. Yes, that's right—*running* was against the rules at recess. On a playground full of little bouncing, energetic kids, who'd been cooped up all day in a classroom, we were not allowed to do anything more than walk.

And then there were the headmaster and headmistress, an adorable married couple, who told us at our weekly assembly that our parents were going to hell if they argued and that we were children of the devil if we parted our hair on the left side of our head. And, trust me, we're just scratching the surface here, but, alas, this book is not about the insanity of Cardinal School (maybe that'll be my next one).

In Cyprus my parents had emphasized that my sister and I should learn English, with no Portuguese or Spanish or Greek or any other languages clouding our minds. We needed to be perfectly fluent in English. If I did speak Portuguese as a child, I was shamed by my parents and told to speak English. (To this day, they both vehemently deny that they ever forbade any language, or demanded that I only speak English, but I remember what I remember.) For a long time I had some bitterness and resentment toward both of them because of it. When I think back, though, to what my dad suffered when he first got to Miami—with the teasing and humiliation and the struggles he most certainly faced—I can't really blame him for wanting me to speak English. Why would he want his son to arrive in the United States and suffer what he went through?

After two years in Cyprus, it was time for my family to go. Our next stop was Switzerland. Bordering France, Germany, Liechtenstein, Austria, and Italy, Switzerland has a unique mix of dialects and languages. We lived just outside of Geneva a few miles from the border with France, so French dominated most things in my life. I was still struggling with learning how to read. All of the languages swirling around in my head, not to mention the reading instruction at Cardinal School (which was based on the British system of word memorization instead of phonetics), seemed to stifle my literacy development.

Our school in Switzerland taught its curriculum entirely in English. It was an international school with students from all over the world, which was very much like the schools I had gone to in Cyprus and Brazil. Up to that point I had understood that all human beings were divided along two lines: sex and nationality. There were boys and girls, men and women. There were people from this country or that country. My father was Colombian. My mother was American. My sister and I were Colombian and American. My friend Yasmin was from Egypt. Victor was from Kenya. Schelumiel was from Norway. Other friends in my class were from China, Bolivia, Ghana, and more than twenty other countries. Switzerland and the United States had the highest number of students represented, with two each.

My mind is so hyper-racialized now from two decades' worth of American brainwashing that it's hard for me to say with accuracy, but I can't remember ever thinking about race before I moved to the United States. That's not to say that it didn't impact the environment I was living in as a kid or wasn't affecting my perspective (as if the brutality of European colonialism could somehow not influence the societies now in place there), but the concept of race seemed completely foreign to me at seven years old.

I didn't understand why it was so important. I had no concept of where I fit into the whole thing. Some people told me I was white. Other people told me I wasn't. Others told me I was "mixed." It was utterly perplexing. Mixed what? With a father and a mother? What the fuck does "mixed" mean? Whatever it was, it didn't sound flattering, especially in the way that they said it.

After two great years in Switzerland, the highlight of my childhood, I returned to New York City. Nothing could have felt more foreign. The utopia I had perceived at my international school, where diversity and culture seemed to be celebrated, did not exist in this new, strange place. It was so different that it made me wonder if I had only imagined that utopia while I was in Switzerland.

I wondered to myself, *Where would Yasmin fit? Would she be black or white? And what does it matter which category someone is in?* After a short stint spending the summer in a studio in Manhattan, the four of us cramped together on two tiny mattresses, we moved out to the suburbs in Connecticut. Starting second grade, I quickly learned the rest of the lesson that my mother had begun at the airport.

"So, does your father sell crack?" he asked me, no malice in his face.

"Excuse me?" I didn't even understand what this strange American kid was saying.

"Your dad? You know, crack cocaine? Isn't that what Colombians are known for?" he snickered and everyone around him laughed on cue.

I didn't understand. *What is this weird kid talking about? Why would my father be a drug dealer? He's a diplomat for the United Nations. He promotes clean water and lowering carbon emissions in developing countries. He has a master's degree from Georgetown University. What does this have to do with anything?*

There was white and then there was everyone else. I was called Hispanic but "fake" since I "didn't really look Hispanic." But I "still was" because of my dad, they told me. The kid they turned on next was American like me but his parents were from China. They made fun of his "chinky eyes." Every single other student in the class was white.

No one else got made fun of for who they were as far as things they couldn't control, unless they were fat. Then they got made fun of too. That was the hierarchy in Connecticut. If you were white and thin, you were at the top. If you were not-white and/or fat, you were not at the top. That's all that mattered. There were those who were haves and those who were have-nots. The white skinny kids had the houses with pools and nice yards. The fat kids and the not-white kids were on the opposite side of the hedge.

By the summer before fifth grade in Connecticut, I had been living in the United States for more than three years. At this point, I had been attending schools in English for more than seven. I couldn't remember a word of Portuguese or Spanish, much less any of those other languages that I had been surrounded by. English was the only way I knew how to communicate.

My best friend at the time and I were having a sleepover. We had been inseparable the entire summer. As we finished brushing our teeth, he looked at me with a warm smile and said, "Carlos, you speak English really well. Seriously. You can barely even tell you're a Hispanic . . . besides your accent," and he meant it in the best way. I knew he did. He was complimenting me from the bottom of his heart. There wasn't one ounce of him that meant to hurt me with those words.

"I don't speak with an accent," I said defensively.

"Sure you do. You just can't tell because it's how you talk. You sound Hispanic," he said good-heartedly, trying to soften the blow.

This was the same friend who called me a "fake" for not remembering any Spanish, who thought I was less than both white and Hispanic, because of the other. Having a Colombian dad tainted my whiteness. Having a blue-eyed, pale-skinned white mother tainted my Hispanic-ness. I felt like I couldn't win. I *didn't* speak with an accent. His perception was being skewed by the lily-white town we lived in. He'd never even met another Hispanic in his life—literally. How the fuck did *he* know what a Colombian accent sounded like? I was learning the toughest lesson about living in America.

I would see how people treated me, then watch it shift when someone said my name: Carlos. During basketball games, at first I would be treated like everyone else, but when the referee heard someone call me Carlos, he would make tighter calls on me and come over to me first and tell me to "calm down" if I and another player got tangled up trying to grab a rebound. I learned that Hispanics were like animals in this new country. They were props and accessories and monsters. They were expected to deal drugs or clean your floors or cut your grass. They were expected to beg and be submissive. They needed to be told what to do, controlled, or tamed.

Simultaneously, though, I recognized how much white privilege I enjoyed in my life. What a testament to how ruthless and insidious the discrimination is that still exists in America, huh? Considering that I could still feel prejudice toward my Latinoness even with all of the white privilege given to me because of my light eyes and pale skin. I have bright green eyes, look like a lot of my mom's Puritan ancestors, am able-bodied, and speak English with years of training from a linguist with a PhD—my mother. How dare I hold it against my dad now for forbidding me from speaking any other language but English when I was younger?

During the seven years we lived in that racist little town in Connecticut, I was reminded of my otherness multiple times. Race, ethnicity, and economic class were the big dividers there. Where you lived in town mattered. What your parents did mattered. What kind of clothes you wore and where you vacationed mattered. Everything was a signifier of where you fell in the pecking order. My parents' education was irrelevant. My father's meaningful work to promote a more sustainable world and my mother's advocacy work for the Yanomami Indians and the Amazon held no currency here.

As much as I criticize and condemn so much of what I experienced and saw while I was in Connecticut, I wasn't immune to the mentality of that place. I may not have joined in while my peers called my Asian classmate, Hamilton, "chinky eyes" or made fun of the South American exchange student by telling her to "clean my house," but I internalized everything I was surrounded by in no less damaging a way. In third grade I had the most profound crush of my life (up to that point) on this new girl from California. She was skinny and blonde, with dazzling blue eyes—the perfect "all-American" girl. I remember the teacher even calling her that when she first arrived. It was like I was being prompted, told what to be attracted to. We were being taught the ultimate lesson of an American classroom—who is most beautiful, most valued, and celebrated. In that process of internalization, I became ashamed of my father being an immigrant, embarrassed by him speaking Spanish and the hint of an accent he still carried in his English. At the deepest level of my being, I was colluding with the hatred that I saw, simultaneously bumping into its dogma and being repulsed by it.

I had only two black classmates over the course of those seven years in Connecticut. The first I was never really friends with. We just weren't into the same things—he was a science nerd; I was an athlete. The second one to arrive, though, was totally different.

His name was Keston and he arrived at our school in seventh grade. He and I immediately connected and were inseparable for the short year he was there. We approached life similarly—we loved basketball and girls, and we were curious about the world. We both had big dreams and big hearts, and were adventurous, with a heavy dose of mischief.

One afternoon, Keston and I were at a pharmacy in our town. We had been walking around downtown (if you can call it that) and went into the store to look for a basketball. It was summer. All they had were those beach balls, so we pulled one out and started playing with it. I got into position, trying to dunk on him and return the ball to the container where we had snagged it and started backing him down dribbling. He partially blocked me and stole the ball. I jumped on his back and started to wrestle with him, playfully, as we both laughed until tears streamed down both of our faces.

"I've already called the police," a security guard declared, leaning back, slightly intimidated.

"What?" I asked, confusion overtaking both of our thirteen-year-old faces.

"Are you okay? Is he bothering you?" the security guard asked me, pointing to Keston without looking at him.

"What are you talking about?" I was baffled. I wasn't sure if he was joking with us or being serious.

"Did he just attack you?" The security guard seemed flustered now.

"What do you mean, 'attack me'? We're friends. We were playing around." Suddenly the pieces were falling into place in my mind.

"Okay, gentlemen. Like I said, I called the police. It's time for both of you to leave," and he abruptly turned and walked back to his stoic post near the entrance.

That's the kind of town we lived in. It was Mississippi in the deep Northeast, with polite white people using coded language to talk around their hate, to just brush away or avoid the things or people they didn't like instead of yelling "nigger!" or "spic!" or shooting anyone with fire hoses. Twice at the mall, Keston was accused of stealing clothes as we perused the items.

Let me say that I met a lot of incredible people I still respect and love from that town in Connecticut. Not everyone was a cold-hearted bigot or a proud racist. In fact, most of the brutal, harsh things that were said or done had no ill intent underpinning them at all, which I think makes it all the more dangerous. There were, however, some amazing people in that town. There are friends I still cherish from those years. I met my best friend, Brent, in eighth grade while I was living in Darien. But, still, you cannot truly know who I am and where I come from without understanding Darien, Connecticut. And to understand it is to recognize the insidious, poisonous, and destructive culture of exclusion in that town. To be anything other than white and rich was two strikes against you, and, according to Darien's standards, I was far from both.

After a tough year in eighth grade, during which my parents divorced and my father remarried, I briefly moved back to Manhattan. My mother had gotten a job in Providence, Rhode Island, as a professor and my dad was living with his new wife in the city. My very brief stint at a Catholic school didn't work out at all, so I moved to the capital city of Rhode Island.

Northeast High School was the magnet public school I started attending in ninth grade. And *everything* about this new school was the polar opposite of the public school in Connecticut. White kids here were the minority. The diversity reminded me of my international school days, with a vibrant collage of every race, ethnicity, and religion you could think of. There were black kids and Latino kids and Southeast Asian kids and Middle Eastern kids and Catholics and Muslims and Buddhists and atheists. A lot of the kids were "mixed" too—just like me. I had a friend who was Cambodian, Nigerian, and Dominican. Another was Laotian and Puerto Rican. Another friend was Italian and Ghanaian.

Unlike in Connecticut, and even as white and green-eyed as I might look, I told everyone in Rhode Island proudly that I was Latino and no one questioned it. Occasionally, my Latino classmates would ask, "What kind?" And I'd proudly respond, "*Colombiano*," and their faces would light up into wide, toothy smiles. I was tired of being "mixed." I wanted to be a part of something big and spirited and magnificent. The more I learned about the history of Latinos, the more it sounded like it was who I was.

All of them were mixed—by definition. They were the product of a violent, complex history of *conquistadores*, Spanish colonizers, intermingling with African slaves and indigenous people and other immigrants who came to the Americas. And when I euphemistically say "intermingling with," that would often mean rape. That's what I was: a strange, fractured mix of American and Colombian. I finally had a proud banner to wave. It took me stumbling into this weird, eclectic mix of people in the hallways of my public school in Providence, Rhode Island, to find it.

Those two years at Northeast were two of the most important and rewarding years of my life, socially. Unfortunately, I never felt challenged there, academically. But there were some amazing kids that went there—they were smart and cultured and dynamic.

When I started dating in high school, I quickly noticed how my identity impacted how people engaged me. At Northeast most people were mixed, so it rarely raised any eyebrows that my mom was white even though my name was Carlos. My basketball teammate and friend, Kartoe, was Swedish and Nigerian. He would get so mad at away games when ignorant people would see him with his mom and ask if he was adopted. And his parents were at every single game: his superpale and petite mom with blonde hair and blue eyes, holding hands with his dark-skinned and broad-shouldered dad with dark hair and eyes.

Not that it really was, but Northeast High School felt like a racial utopia compared with the rest of the world, something I soon realized at a conference I attended my junior year of high school. After being fed up academically, I had transferred from public school to a private Quaker school. Even in just a few short months at the private school, very quickly I had been reminded that, no matter how white I might look, in *this* place I was an outsider. I was definitely not white. I was a student of color—I was Latino. Very much in line with the Quaker tradition, there was an incredible amount of good intention behind how people treated me, what I saw as a sort of self-congratulatory, righteous, patronizing, and flagrant white supremacy that seemed to swell from their auras. If I only had a nickel for all the soft-spoken Quakers I met who offered to help me with their good-natured benevolence. I graduated in the top five in my class—the insinuations were downright insulting.

Something about the prejudice at the new school felt even more severe. Centered and righteous Quakers would visit us each Thursday to convene a weekly meeting with their pretentious tones and eyes that always seemed to be looking down on me. I felt violated by all of them. I felt violated by the culture of Quakerism. All the while, though, much like in Connecticut, I continued to internalize and be taught by what was around me. The school was concerned about students of color feeling left out, so they decided to fund a group of students who were in good standing and involved in the student body to travel to the People of Color Conference in Puerto Rico, which was a conference for students of color attending private schools.

It was at this conference that I first encountered large numbers of students of color who spent very little time surrounded by people who looked like them. This would be replicated when I attended the University of Pennsylvania. In both cases, I wondered why something felt so different about how these folks of color interacted with each other, as opposed to every other black or Latino person I had been around or been friends with growing up. Then it dawned on me. Many of the kids here are the only (fill in the blank) in their entire school—and some have been since *kindergarten*. For some of these kids, their reference point for their culture or identity (as far as they know) is the same one used by the white kids at their schools: MTV, BET music videos, shows on TV. They only know the parody of a caricature. That's their model for blackness or being Latino or Asian identity.

Immediately I felt alienated when I got to the conference. Many of the kids thought I was white and asked me why I was there. I would tell them I was Latino and quickly the interaction would change. Some still pried for more information. And when they found out my mother was white, they'd nod their eyes like "yep, that's what I thought" and walk away. It was a strange social experiment into which I felt thrown. In many other cases, girls wouldn't talk to me or take a second look at me. Then, they'd find out my name was "Carlos" and suddenly I'd be someone with whom they could flirt and joke.

I've felt it both ways—and been exoticized, given a pass, or devalued—either for my whiteness or Latinoness. A few years ago, I was planning to stay with a friend of a friend in Los Angeles. Our mutual friend was close with us both, and we'd only really met each other twice, but she had been adamant that I stay with her for my first four days in town. As I got on the bus, with all of my bags, to travel to her place, I got a flustered and hurried call from her. She said that when she mentioned my name was Carlos, her roommate had freaked out and said she "no longer felt comfortable having a strange man" sleeping in their house. With one word, I had become the worst possible nightmare of a man of color—hypersexual, dangerous, and untrustworthy. At least, that's what I read into it.

Who am I? What am I? Where am I from? I still get the questions. I still feel both challenged and alienated by the prospect of even trying to engage the question. My sense, though, when people ask, often out of habit or just to make conversation, is that they have an inherent need to classify me. The need to classify human beings has been socialized into them since birth. No, I do not think that makes them bad people or bigots or vicious in their intent. How am I different from many of the people I knew in Darien, Connecticut, who I condemned for their prejudice? How am I different from the alienated students of color at the conference in Puerto Rico? All of us are trying to find an identity and a place and a story to call our own, to cling to and know that we are *somebody*. Unfortunately, though, we frequently do hurtful things, often unintentionally, in that complex process.

Recently, I was running very late to an important meeting I had already rescheduled twice. It would definitely be a third strike if I tried to change things again. So I hurriedly pulled on my coat with my right arm, tossed my shoulder bag over my head, and fumbled through my pockets for my keys and MetroCard. As I stumbled down the three flights of steps, I scanned my brain to see if I had forgotten anything for the meeting. I moved swiftly and with impulse and habit more than anything else. I opened the outside door quickly and lost my breath for a second as my eyes spotted something, my body instinctively repelled backward.

The building owner's son was sprinting up the steps. All I

had seen was that it was the figure of a black person moving quickly toward the door I was leaving through.

I had flinched. I had flinched noticeably. I could feel his gentle eyes take in the moment and register what had happened. His name is Brandon and he is thirteen years old. It was 3:47 P.M. on a sunny Tuesday afternoon. He was coming home from playing in the park with his friends. And I had flinched. He had scared me. I had lost my breath. I had felt threatened and afraid, however briefly.

I had become the security guard in the store when Keston and I were wrestling. I had tossed an epithet at him with my actions like my bigoted classmates had done to Hamilton in Connecticut. I had done worse than the patronizing woman at my Quaker school. I had flinched much like the white officer who fired thirty-one rounds at Sean Bell or the four policemen who murdered Amadou Diallo in cold blood in the Bronx while he offered up his ID for proof that he lived at 1157 Wheeler Avenue. I had become what I have been trained to be since I came back to the States at age seven: an American.

Ask me where I'm from and I will tell you that I grew up all over the world but am who I am now via America. I am that unmistakable American that only a place like New York City can breed: a middle-class, racist, light-skinned Latino with a white mom, a guy who is a socially conscious writer and performance artist with an Ivy League degree and big-city dreams living at a Brooklyn address with my black girlfriend, four blocks down from the projects where Jay-Z grew up.

BLACK BOY

by Carlos Andrés Gómez

My friend is afraid that his son will be mistaken
for white,

That's my biggest fear, *he says*, What if he's able
to pass?

And I can't help tonguing the fresh blood
from my bottom lip, as this black man, this
someday father feels the dawn of parenthood
pulling at his torso like a too-tight, too-heavy
suit coat heaving with his asthma. Like a bright-
eyed boy of seven dangling from his neck like rope—
the tousled auburn of his first son—an unhinged laugh
and awkward gait, the only hints of shared blood
between them.

I guess you can't relate, he says, finally.

The unspoken weight of things neither of us
wished to inherit, only his thin shoulders
hardened and chiseled by the burden.

My words sift clean as apologies disguised as honesty.
Trying to put my finger on a cloud 43,000 feet above
me and 392 years too late.

The sentence pours from my mouth like a fresh wound, like
an artery I can't close, the breath stolen from between the hasty
syllables,
I am afraid of raising a black son.

The fractured, incompatible, poetic symmetry
of what trembles in our hearts.

Honestly, I say, *I never really thought about it until now.*

And I have visions of being startled by the sight of my own
face. By the same brash walk I borrowed from my father.
The overbearing song of that rhythm planted and re-planted
into my chest, a stag's galloping hooves against it, late at night
when I see a black face I do not know moving in too close.

No matter how much Brooklyn I swallow. No matter how much
West 118th Street I breast fed into these bones. No matter
how much I remember my high school best friend, the love
of my life's father, my future brothers-in-law, the director who
believed in me, the man who coaxed tears from my eyes with the mere
rumble in his throat before I even realized I had a heart I was allowed to love.
That this heart was a doorway I was allowed to move through. The mentor
I will someday raise a son with. The black boy who might someday
startle me—
the way my landlord's 7th grade son did last week.

I have already colonized the children I hope to one day raise.

And I do not know how to give back things I cannot yet hold. How to unsteal
things that arrive already kidnapped by history but cannot yet be cradled in the soft,
fragile nook of my right elbow.

I am afraid of raising a black man in this unforgiving world, I tell him,
I am not enough of a man. I do not know if I will ever be. *

*   Connect Online: **"Black Boy"** http://www.youtube.com/watch?v=dgoi_PmFcFg

CHAPTER 2

Fear: Beneath the Façade

Men are not allowed to be afraid. Or we have to qualify it by saying we were just "startled for a second," but never "afraid." We play with semantics and history and memory when it comes to fear. Whenever I got scared as a kid, I was told to buck up and be strong and be tough—oftentimes, to "man up." Fathers tell this to their sons, uncles to nephews, and Little League coaches to their players. Every day I watch men around me struggle with the burden of concealing their fear, like I did for so many years. Men puff up their chests and curse and yell and fight and even die to avoid being called afraid, as if it were a mortal sin, the worst one of all.

As a little kid, I worried that I might never earn the right to call myself a man because I was so afraid of everything. And by everything, what I mean is *everything*. I was afraid of the dark. I was afraid of my dad. I was afraid of not having friends. I was afraid of monsters under my bed. I was afraid my parents would leave me, that they'd die, that they'd never come back when they left us with a babysitter. I had flat feet and I was worried that someday I wouldn't be able to walk or that I would have braces put on my legs that would prevent me from running and playing sports and that it would make it harder to make friends—which I was afraid I couldn't make otherwise. I had buck teeth and was worried that someday I would have to get braces (which I did), or that I would have to get headgear (which I did), and that *that* would make it impossible to ever go on a first date. Both of my parents were blind as bats, so I worried that someday I might need to get glasses (which I did). And how was I ever going to have a girlfriend with flat feet, braces, headgear, and *glasses*!?!

Because I had problems learning to read, I was scared I wasn't smart. I was afraid that I'd never fit in when I wore my cousin Mauricio's hand-me-down clothes. I was afraid that I might never get married. Afraid that I would set goals and fall short.

I moved so much during my childhood that I often felt like I was sleeping in a foreign place. My room felt more like an incubator for ghosts and goblins than a safe haven where I could play and that I could call my own. My parents still joke about how I was the "thirstiest little boy who ever lived," because multiple times each night I would wake them up and ask for a glass of water. One time my mother said, "I just got you a glass of water a little while ago. Are you really *still* thirsty?"

"No. I just missed you," I said.

So that's how it went. I would spend entire nights convinced something would take me away while I slept. Hours went by as I manically surveyed my room with the covers pulled tight beneath my chin, poised and ready for anything that might spring up.

One day I felt this powerful shift in my body. I was six years old and had just moved *again*—this time to Switzerland. I was in a new country, in a new room, with new sounds and smells and sights. I had spent so much of my life worrying about every-thing, overwhelmed by the most paralyzing fear. *I can't do this anymore,* I thought to myself. *My heart will just give out one of these days. It's just too much.*

I had had enough. I needed to make a change. I made a bold decision that day. First it was a small but very big step for me: I turned my night-light off. *No more night-light. I can't sleep with that on forever, so why not turn it off today?* Then I decided to close my bedroom door while I slept. Then I decided to stop hiding under my covers as if they were a shield. What were those covers going to protect me from anyway? Each small step was proof to myself that I was bigger than my fear, that I was not a hapless prisoner to the plethora of phobias that consumed my every thought, proof that what terrified me could be made into fuel—used to propel me toward my dreams.

Killing all of the fears inside me became an obsession. It became a way for me to dare myself into not being the little boy I still was and prepare myself to one day become a man. The way I saw it, I couldn't have any of these fears inside of me if I was to ever become a man, so I might as well get rid of them now to save myself the trouble later.

If I felt scared riding a horse, I'd make sure I galloped on that horse until the earthquake in my chest subsided. If I got nervous standing on a roof, I'd go to my friend's house and climb on the shingles of his garage. If I got nervous at the end of a basketball game, I'd demand that the coach give me the ball to take the last shot. This was my ritual. My trial by fire, the gauntlet I threw down for myself.

I was taking control of making myself into a man.

My mom had always fostered this idea in me that I was brave, which actually created a lot of anxiety. For years I was daunted by the expectations, as though I had to live up to her idea of who she thought I was (although I knew that I was any-thing but). She was like self-esteem central and—like me now—

she's so damn convincing that you *have* to believe her. She looks you in the eye, without one ounce of hesitation, and just tells you how it is. Or at least that's what you believe: "You're brave. You were born brave."

One thing I never had any fear about was my parents splitting up. It was the one anchoring constant throughout my childhood. My fears were many, but my mommy and papi would always be there, and they would always be together. With the constant moving that we did, losing friends and struggling to make new ones, they were the unshakable foundation of the family. My faith in my parents' union as the cornerstone of our family gave me an added sense of confidence as I continued to challenge my lingering phobias. *As long as my family is strong and healthy,* I thought to myself, *how bad can anything be?* Our rock-solid household was like a bunker I could always retreat to in times of need.

And then one day, just before I started junior high school, I walked down our stairs and heard my parents having an argument. It was the first and last argument I would ever see them have.

I peered around the wall into the kitchen where they were and watched my mom washing the dishes. My father's back was to me but I could hear angry, whispered venom firing back and forth between them, occasionally escalating into full-throated talking and even yelling. My mother looked down into the sink the entire time, neurotically washing the same four dishes and slamming them into the drying rack and then doing it all again.

What was happening? I had always believed that my family was exceptional. I thought we were immune to this American trend of marital problems. It seemed as though most of my friends' parents were divorced or split up. Everyone had constantly told me how lucky I was to have such a perfect family, with both parents together and happy—with two parents who *never* argued. I honestly cannot remember them having even one minor disagreement in my entire life up to that point. As an adult, I can now see why *that* in itself might be problematic and symptomatic of greater communication issues, but at the time this singular argument seemed to come out of nowhere.

"Carlitos, let's go," my sister whispered into my ear. She had been standing behind me listening as well.

I grabbed my basketball and we walked out the front door.

For about ten minutes we walked side by side in silence. I bounced my basketball as she looked up at the trees lining the road. There were so many questions overloading my brain, I had no idea where to start.

"Why are they arguing?" I asked.

"I don't know . . ." my sister began, her voice trailing off.

"It's not like they're going to get divorced or anything, though, right?" I surprised myself with the question, anxiousness and desperation cracking in my voice.

"I don't know . . ." My sister looked upset, panic creeping onto her gentle face.

For the first time in my life, my perfect family might be in jeopardy. The model life I had lived might actually be a complete fraud. Had I actually misjudged and misperceived everything around me so badly that I had not seen things for what they were? Had problems been brewing between my parents for years that I had overlooked? Had I *caused* their problems with all of my crazy acting out?

Shortly thereafter, my parents separated. I'll never forget the day the announcement came. My father had been sleeping on the couch in the living room for a few weeks and both my sister and I were very worried about our parents. He seemed to be spending more and more time away from my mom. We would do more things with just one parent at a time, rarely having the four of us together on any outing.

My father called up to my sister and me, "Sarita and Carlitos, can you please come downstairs?"

I knew something bad was about to happen. I didn't want

to hear whatever it was that he had to say. I didn't want anything else to fall apart around me. I just wanted to hit the reset button and go back to how things were before, to be able to go back and undo the times I had acted crazy or misbehaved, to be able to stop the whining I'd done ever single time my parents were about to go out on my birthday, which also happened to be their anniversary, to get some time together with just the two of them. I wanted to go back and fix everything that had broken, glue it back together and make it beautiful again.

I sat in my room. I could feel my eyes filling up, a massive knot caught halfway up my throat. I didn't want to hear whatever was about to be said.

Quickly, I grabbed my basketball, sprinted down the stairs, and headed out to the driveway in front of our house. I had a basketball hoop that had been set to six feet so I could dunk on it. I ran and jumped and dunked on that rim harder than I ever had. Each time I swooped in toward the basket all of the pain and loss and anger rose up in my arms and legs. I wanted to break that hoop. I wanted to splinter the pavement with my dribbling. I wanted to destroy everything I had once trusted and loved that I felt had betrayed me. Everything I had believed in, the core of what sustained me when I was afraid of everything else, had all along been a lie. My world was breaking apart, so I wanted to break everyone else's world too.

My father came out the front door and down the steps to where I was playing.

"Carlitos," my father called out to me, emotion and hurt in his voice. "Carlitos, please . . . come here."

I could hear a man's voice, as lost as I was, pleading with his son. I ignored him, as best I could, only dunking harder—feeling a release each time the ball tore through the net and the rim wailed and screamed as I pulled it beneath my chin.

I stepped back again for another thunderous drive, another merciless slam dunk on the rim I had spent so many hours perfecting my game on. This would be the one to destroy the last thing I loved: my basketball hoop.

Suddenly I felt two arms around me. They were firm and loving and desperate. They were my father's arms. I dropped the ball as the tears finally came pouring out of me. It was like everything unspoken, smoldering just beneath the surface, was finally being released.

"I love you so much, Carlitos. I will never leave you. I will never hurt you. I promise you, everything will be okay. I love you." My father was more emotional than I had ever seen him. Maybe he was saying whatever he could to try to make his heart hurt less. I knew he loved me. I knew he would never willingly hurt me, but he was leaving. And just like that, my biggest fear came to life.

He moved to a town about ten minutes away. I don't know too much about where he lived or what he did when he wasn't with us. I think he wanted it that way. I think he wanted to try, as much as he could, to not disrupt our routine. We would spend time with him, but my mother would never be there. Or we would spend time with her and he would be off doing his own thing.

Over the next two and a half years, my parents did marriage counseling and we went to family therapy together, doing everything to try to save a marriage that had already been too far gone. My father had fought to keep up with the rigorous demands of his incredible and meaningful work with the United Nations, which required him traveling up to a quarter of a million miles per year. He was gone from home a lot. My mother was trying to raise two children, often in strange countries, hold down the household, and finish a PhD. My mother and my father were different people, growing in different directions. Both were still trying to define who they were in the world.

By the spring of eighth grade, my parents were divorced, my

father was engaged to be married to his coworker, and my high school future was up in the air. Just to clarify one detail: My father was faithful to my mother. His whirlwind courtship, engagement, and wedding all happened in the course of a one-year span when it was clear that my parents were finished and both were moving on with their lives. As far-fetched as that may sound, I actually believe that story.

Nevertheless, it didn't make the transition from separated parents to remarried father and pregnant stepmother any easier. I was tired of moving. I had asked my father, at the height of the contentiousness and complexity of the split, to promise me that I would never have to move again. I told my parents that I was so tired of having to continue to make new friends. After all they had put both my sister and me through with the divorce, the one thing I asked for was stability in my life on the friend front. I wanted them to let me stay in Darien, Connecticut, where we lived, to let me keep the friends I had made at that pivotal time in my life.

My father, trying to juggle the multiple pressures, confusion, and alienation he was struggling with himself, made a promise to me. He made a promise to me now that I know he regrets making—he promised me I would never have to move again. For years—almost a decade—I could not forgive him for making that promise to me. Finally a man in my own right, I realize how difficult it must have been for him with what he was coping with. Sure, he wasn't the best communicator with my mother, he traveled too much, he was probably too ambitious for his own good, and he was just a very different person than his wife, but my father never meant to betray me.

He never lied to me with any intent or malice. I believe that he meant the promise he made that day. Unfortunately, it was a promise that couldn't realistically be kept.

My sister was leaving for college. My mother was struggling to try to find a way to support herself in the midst of a very ugly divorce battle (is there any other kind?). My mom had been awarded her PhD at Columbia University with her thesis on documenting endangered languages of the Yanomami Indians in the Amazon. She worked as an adjunct professor at SUNY–Purchase and had just gotten a job working at Rhode Island College. My father was living in Manhattan at this point. I was trying to figure out where I would be for high school.

My father wanted me to go to the United Nations International School (UNIS). I wanted to stay in Connecticut and go to the public high school where all of my friends were going. Ironically, I thought of the UN school as a nerd-filled, yuppie school with a bunch of corny kids. Not that there weren't great friends that I made in Darien, but I doubt those Fairfield County kids were that different, especially socioeconomically, from the kids at UNIS.

I did not want to go to UNIS. I *definitely* didn't want to end up in some dead-end state like Rhode Island. And I wanted to make sure that wherever I went had a great basketball team. I had played AAU basketball for a regional all-star team in eighth grade, and one of my teammates had suggested I look into Southern Christian Prep School. It was only about forty-five minutes on the train from the city and was the next town over from Darien. It seemed like the perfect compromise.

My dad wasn't quite so sure about it. We argued and fought back and forth about the decision. I called him childish for refusing to compromise. He accused me of being a fourteen-year-old who "thinks he's a man but isn't." Finally, he gave in and agreed that I should go to Southern Christian Prep. They had been state champions multiple times over the past few years and I was recruited to play shooting guard. It seemed like my destiny had been set in motion.

Having struggled through such a difficult year with my parents' divorce, my dad being remarried, and leaving my friends, I relished the challenge of this new school. It was another way to confront my remaining fears. I became obsessed with this martyr-riddled narrative I was beginning to build for myself. I planned to use all of the uncertainty and fear in my path to transform myself into something great—a high school basketball star.

So that first day I started my new routine: Each day I would have to wake up at five o'clock in the morning. I would do push-ups, take a shower, make myself breakfast, and then get dressed. I would walk from Waterside Plaza, just across the FDR Drive where we lived in Manhattan, to the 6 train at 28th Street. From there I would take the subway to Grand Central. Then take the Metro-North train to Stamford, Connecticut, where a shuttle van would pick me up and take me to Southern Christian Prep School, where, if I was lucky, I would arrive by quarter after eight.

I had this grandiose story built up in my head that I would tell to *Time* magazine and *The New York Times* when I was seventeen and the number one recruited shooting guard in the country. I would hit the game-winning three-pointer and be carried off the court at the state championships. Then I would get a full ride to the University of North Carolina (just like my hero, Michael Jordan) and lead them to the Final Four before going on to the NBA. This was what I believed was my fate. I believed all the trials and tribulations I had overcome and continued to encounter would only enable this dream to become real. And it would all be accomplished by me facing down my fears and conquering them.

Of course, I never really factored in my quick mouth or my intellectual curiosity in school, or the fact that my dad had never really taken care of me all by himself before. He took his clothes to the Laundromat. He ordered Chinese takeout food. He was not my mother. God bless my father's strengths and talents, but washing clothes and making healthy meals, at that time in his life especially, were not among them.

Things were not going according to plan. The triumphant story I had laid out in my mind quickly evaporated. During orientation at Southern Christian Prep, everyone was asked to sit in a circle and say who they thought was an example of a good Christian. About two-thirds of the kids said "Jesus." When they got to me I said, "Malcolm X."

And, sure, during orientation I might have tried to act tough, but this new school completely scared the hell out of me with its strict rules and ominous Roman Catholic architecture. I couldn't let this place intimidate me, though—right? Of course not. So I decided that I would fight back. What I needed to do was stare this strict Catholic school right in the eyes and say *I'm not afraid!* (just like my mom had always told me to do with a bully). I imagined myself heroically standing up for what I believed in at Southern Christian Prep and my parents and friends applauding me. Well, in theory it looked a lot more heroic and inspiring than it actually was.

My first day of actual classes was a fiasco. After showing up late to my first class, I called one of the nuns a "savage" after she referred to indigenous people as "primitive." I went on to *clarify* that what I had meant to say was that I thought the beliefs of the Catholic religion were primitive. As you can imagine, I got thrown out of class. The same happened in my next class: religion. I think I could have predicted that one. As we sat down, the teacher passed out a sheet that said "The Ten Commandments to Reading the Bible." The first commandment was "Thou Shalt Not Question Anything In The Bible, As It Is The WORD OF GOD."

I raised my hand. "How can we not question what we read? Isn't that the point of education?"

She told me to go to the office. And I got kicked out of math for getting in an argument with my teacher about standardized tests being culturally biased, Spanish class for taking off my tie before the end of class, and English class for cursing accidentally. I even got in trouble at *lunch* for cutting the line. I didn't, but when I got confronted by one of the nuns and got into an argument, I was given another detention. After all was said and done, I got six detentions the first day of high school.

And so I did what any other rational, unruly, wiseass teen would have done—I skipped all of them, caught a cab to the train station, and went home. That night my dad got a phone call telling him that the school and I "just weren't the right fit." Finally, here was something my dad and I could agree on. It was a cripplingly close-minded Catholic school. All the walls were painted light green, a massive crucifix hung down from the front of each room, and a prayer would begin each and every class. The first minute I walked in, I knew I would never have survived there.

I had thought, up to that point, that my decision to go to Southern Christian Prep was the first adult decision of my life. After the catastrophe that it turned out to be, I realized how much pride and foolishness had informed my hardheaded choice to try to split the difference and live with my dad while staying as close to my old friends as possible. My decision had not been inspired by courage; it had been driven by fear. I was afraid to leave my middle school friends. I was afraid to start from scratch in a new place with only one parent by my side. I was being broken by the fear in my gut, not made great by it like I had planned.

Crying in my room, I sat down and pulled out my journal from religion class. All of the pages were completely barren. At first, all I wanted to do was burn that book. Then, I decided to do something unusual for me: write down what I was feeling. I needed something potent enough to let me scream everything inside of me out, so on sheer impulse, I wrote my first real poem. The first one that was completely my own. And then I did something else surprising: I decided to make my first *real* grown-up life decision, a decision that required a renewed sense of courage and maturity in me, the kind of difficult, imperfect decisiveness required in hard times. I loved my father very much, but I couldn't stay where I was. I needed a drastic change. I needed to move on from the hurt and the pain and all the toxic energy still lingering between New York and Connecticut. I needed to do the unthinkable: move to Rhode Island.

That night I packed a suitcase full of clothes, got an Amtrak ticket, and told my mom I was arriving the next day. I'll never forget arriving in Rhode Island, looking out at the meek skyline of Providence and thinking, *What the hell have I done?*

She enrolled me in the magnet public school called Northeast High School. Immediately I liked the energy of the school, a diverse mix of kids from all parts of the world, mostly working-class, who seemed to have style, grace, and gusto. It was everything Darien, Connecticut, was not. It was the exact opposite of what I had hated about the WASPy town I had lived in for far too long. This school reminded me of my first seven years going to international schools, being surrounded by kids who were cultured, multilingual, and cosmopolitan.

Once again, though, I was the awkward new kid. I could feel that familiar fear of not being able to make any friends start to creep in again. I wore corny plaid button-down shirts (I still get teased about that by old Northeast friends!) and had a haircut that screamed *suburbia*. As with each new place at which I had arrived in my life, I felt like a square peg in a world of round holes. Nothing I said or did seemed right. I remembered first arriving in Connecticut and having the wrong clothes, the wrong haircut, the wrong accent. I remembered asking a classmate who the "yellow, spiky-headed alien" was on his T-shirt. "You don't know who Bart Simpson is?" The kid squealed and ran off giggling, pointing at me and whispering to his friends.

Here I was again. Through so much of my childhood the fear had been similar: What if no one likes me? I worried about a life by myself, defined by solitude. Through much of my youth I saw it as a strength. I could empathize with anyone because, ultimately, I had intimate, firsthand knowledge of what it felt like to be alone, to be left out and excluded. Many school years had started with me coming home trying to find ways to keep myself busy, distracted, and entertained without anyone to call or play with. Before she left for college, my sister had usually been the way I kept myself distracted—most times, like many little brothers, by bothering and harassing her.

This was one of the darker periods I can remember. Just a few weeks earlier, my mother and I had been talking about my transition to the new school. Typical of my mom, she was brainstorming ways to help me fit in at Northeast. She's never been one to sit and wallow in her pity or sadness; she wants to find a *solution*. Our apartment had two floors—she and her boyfriend, Dave, lived on the first floor. I lived up in the attic. I sat on the stairs as she looked up at me from the bottom, her eyes full of concern and love.

Then, the phone rang upstairs. She had gotten me my own phone line so I could keep in touch with my old friends. As I sprinted up the stairs to answer, the phone downstairs began to ring. As I answered the phone, I could hear the strained voice of my recently *ex*-girlfriend on the other end.

"Carlos, has anyone called you yet?" she asked me.

"No. Why?" I answered.

"You don't know anything? Like, no one has told you anything about this evening?" she persisted.

"What's wrong with you? Why are you acting so weird? What the *fuck*?" I was mad now. *Did one of my friends die? Is she fucking with me?*

"Oh, okay . . . well, I guess this is kinda weird but I wanted to say congratulations."

"Lena, what the fuck . . . ?" I felt like the world was playing some sick practical joke on me when I was most vulnerable. A joke everyone was in on but me.

"I saw your dad and Karin on News 4 New York. They were being interviewed at a fertility clinic. They're . . . having twins." I could hear her struggling for how to say it all.

"Fuck you. You're sick," I said hanging up the phone.

Then my phone rang again. It was my best friend, Brent.

"Carlos." I could hear the concern and hurt in his voice.

I immediately hung up the phone and left it off the hook. My heart tumbled into my sock. My mouth muted with shock. Wow. My father wanted to build a new family. My sister and I weren't enough. He wanted to make a new family because his old one was broken.

"Carlitos," I could hear my mom calling me from the bottom of the stairs.

Great, I thought, *one of her old friends just told her the news. Now we'll have to talk about it.*

I could see she was already devastated. Tears quietly rolled down her face as she looked at me, trying to hold her composure.

"I'm so sorry, Mommy," I said, feeling the hurt in her eyes as if it were my own. "I don't understand. I wish we had found out some other way."

"Who told you?" she asked me.

"Lena," I answered.

"Lena? Wait . . . what did she tell you about?" I could see my mom moving into confusion and panic.

"About Papi and Karin having twins," I said.

"*What*?! Wow. Well, I can't say I'm surprised, but that's interesting," she responded.

"What was your phone call about?" I asked, now very concerned about the tears in her eyes.

"Your uncle in Colombia was killed this morning," she said.

My lips went numb. I felt my whole face beginning to buzz and vibrate as if bees had flooded my veins. One of my favorite uncles had passed away. My father was building a new family to replace us. My ex-girlfriend had a new boyfriend. I wasn't making any new friends. My world was falling apart. All of my biggest fears were flooding back into my life, one by one.

When I used to cling to the pain in my life as an identity I often said that my childhood was defined by two things: death and divorce. My other uncle died in a car accident. My aunt killed herself. My best friend in Switzerland died in a car accident shortly after I moved away. And those were the unexpected deaths. My grandma died of cancer. My grandpa, Doc, who my grandmother had married shortly after my grandfather passed away, died shortly after grandma. I will always remember, probably more vividly than I'd like, going to funerals and seeing a person I loved lying in a casket, all done up with that creepy funeral parlor makeup. And now my parents were divorced, and my dad was remarried with twins on the way.

Going to funerals made me think that everyone I loved was destined to die before me. When my best friend from Switzerland died, I was convinced that I was cursed. I stayed up nights afraid that my dad would be next on one of his many long flights, or my mother, with months in the Amazon doing fieldwork, cut off from all contact. Or what if it was my sister, my best friend in the world? Was there some tough-love God up in the sky, dead set on trying to teach me everything I needed to know the hard way?

I channeled my remaining fears into my work ethic. I had been reminded, more times than I wanted to acknowledge, that life is, as my mom so eloquently puts it, a crapshoot. I might die tomorrow or become paralyzed, it might even happen today, but in *this* moment that I have *right now*, whatever I'm doing, I want to be remembered as being great.

After that fateful talk with my mom on the stairs, I became

more focused than ever on my studies. I never wanted to get an A-minus ever again. I practiced basketball every moment I could, waking up early in the morning to jog before school to get my endurance up. I began doing push-ups and sit-ups to refine my body into the well-oiled machine I wanted it to be by basketball season. I thought more and more about what my legacy would be if I died the next day. Would anyone remember me? Would anyone even care? Who would show up at *my* funeral? It had been building like a giant storm in my body—this urgency, this drive—ever since I moved to Rhode Island.

The night before I left New York City for Providence, my dad had asked me to take a walk with him. By the way he said it, I could tell it was going to be one of those life-defining talks. That "grown man" walk a dad takes his son on to welcome him to manhood. I thought to myself, *Maybe this is the talk that brings it all together—sex, relationships, growing up, being strong and taking on the world! Maybe this is the night he ends curfews and babysitters and chaperones. Yeah, this is the night.*

I knew my dad must be proud of me for making the difficult but mature decision to go to Rhode Island. I could feel it in his tender embrace as he casually smiled and rubbed my shoulder, anxious butterflies doing somersaults in my belly while we waited for the elevator. In that moment, my shoulders felt a little bit broader, my voice was an octave deeper, and my walk was a little taller and more proud.

As we walked down to the steps overlooking the East River, I couldn't help but marvel at how gorgeous the water looked. It was one of the most perfect summer nights I have ever seen, with a soft, gentle breeze and the glowing lights twinkling across the river in Brooklyn. We each plopped down on a step to take in the view, me half expecting my papi to pull out two fat Cohiba cigars to celebrate and muse on life, wish me well on my entrance into adulthood, and talk to me about women and being a man.

"I was going to save this for later, Carlitos," my papi said, "but since you think you are a man and want to make man decisions and walk out of my life, I am going to treat you like a man. And there are a lot of things that are wrong with you, Carlitos, so I wanted to make sure that you knew about all of these problems that you have, because if you do not fix them, you are never going to succeed in your life."

I was stunned. Fat tears were swelling in my eyes.

"You have no discipline, Carlitos. You are selfish and self-centered. You never follow through with anything you say you will do—never. And you cannot accomplish anything in life when you do not follow through. You think you are a man? You are a boy. You cannot take care of yourself. And you think you are strong? And look at your face! You keep picking at those pimples and your face is going to be all scarred up, but *don't say I did not tell you*. And that little potbelly you have that was cute when you were six? It is not so cute anymore. But that's the problem—you have no discipline. You have no drive. You have no manners. You do not hold your fork correctly. You are not thoughtful. You keep this up, and you are not going to succeed in life."

I felt like I was dying.

"What? I'm just telling you how it is. So you'll know. . . . Do you have something you want to say to me, Carlitos?"

And in that moment, I knew there was only one weapon I had left that could hurt him the most. Even more ruthless in its power because it was still the pure, raw truth—"Yes, Papi, I do. . . . I love you."

For nine years, that talk was the driving force behind my discipline and insatiable desire to succeed—and not just to do well but thrive, far and above everyone else I might be measured against. That is not to say that I did. But I would beat myself up, ruthlessly, when I finished anywhere lower than first place. In that talk it was like my dad had pulled back the curtain on my façade of being exceptional and revealed to the world what I actually was: mediocre. This was my defining fear throughout my high school years, as I started to move on from the fear of death to the fear of being average.

In basketball I never really became what I would have hoped. I was five foot eleven, not a tremendous ball handler, with feet much too slow for a two guard. I didn't have a very realistic chance at playing Division I basketball. I had a diligent work ethic and was a standout three-point shooter, but besides that, I slowly realized that I wasn't destined to become a professional basketball player. Or I lost interest around my junior year in high school. I wondered to myself, *If I do become a professional athlete and make millions of dollars, who cares? What impact will I have on the world around me?*

Through everything, I still cared deeply about having a positive influence on the world I lived in. I didn't know how to make that impact, but I knew it was important to me. The more I lived and the more I read, the more I recognized disparity in the world. I couldn't live with myself knowing I was doing nothing to actively address what wasn't fair. Or I would be a bystander like everyone else. I would be mediocre. I would be average.

A lot of my teachers in high school would suggest that I get involved in peer tutoring. I was smart and good at explaining things. One teacher once told me that she thought I was a good listener and sensitive to kids who had learning challenges, since I could relate because of my own troubles with reading. I began tutoring classmates after school and getting involved as a peer counselor. I noticed that I was someone my friends felt like they could confide in. I was the guy people felt like they could trust and open up to. This led to me volunteering to help second graders with homework after school, and that was the first time it happened.

She was a tiny Dominican girl with a long black ponytail

trailing all the way down her back. She was playful, unguarded, spontaneous—like most second graders one might meet. Immediately when I arrived, she jumped in my lap and I helped her with her math homework. It was as she finished her worksheet that she looked up at me, with those full hopeful brown eyes of hers, and seemed to gently ask and mostly tell me, "Papi," as a huge smile broke over her face.

And that was the first time it hit me. I was a sixteen-year-old high school junior and someday I would be someone else's papi. Someday there might be a little boy I raised turned man writing a memoir about manhood talking about the times that he and I shared. I broke into a cold sweat and pulled away from that little girl. *Wow,* I thought (a million ideas flooding into my brain at once), *someday I will be* Papi. *Someday I will be a father.*

So many of my intimate relationships with women, whether driven by love or lust, have been impacted by my revelation that day: I want to be a great father. I can only be a great father if I have a baby in a stable relationship and the pregnancy is planned. I have to be certain to not get anyone pregnant before that.

I have slept with only six women in my life. Believe me, there have been a lot of situations where I wanted to have sex and resisted. With all six women, we were in a relationship. With all six, we used a condom each and every time we had sex. My fear of people I loved dying before me transformed into this strange fear that I would impregnate someone I didn't really love, that she would have the baby against my wishes. I worried that then I would be an absent father and a horrible dad, despite my best intentions. I would have the most shameful legacy any man can have: being a deadbeat.

I thought about how hard my father had tried, how much he loved me and my sister. He would travel all across the world for his remarkable work with the United Nations, literally *changing* the world for the better, and then he would give us every moment he had when he was back, no matter how exhausted he was, even if it was thirteen hours later for him, arriving from China or Australia or some other far-off place. I'd wrestle with him when he'd sleep in and then we'd play catch in the backyard or basketball, or he'd play goalie when I wanted to practice my shooting in soccer. I thought back to everything I thought of my father before the divorce: He was my hero. He was Superman, He-Man, and God rolled into one. He was everything that I wanted to become.

Ever since the divorce, his legacy had been tainted for me. My adolescent angst associated everything to do with my father as being shameful and false and negative. Now I look back and realize that he was neither Superman nor this villain he temporarily became; he was a man, one who grew apart from his wife and lost his marriage, one who *was* an amazing, loving, generous, supportive father who tried to cope with hard times as best he could, maybe loved his work too much, said things he wishes he could have taken back and didn't mean. He tried to do it all.

I try to do it all as well. I have said things so hurtful to people I love that I would be devastated if they held it against me still. I know my father didn't mean what he said to me that night before I left for Providence. I now know that he was hurting inside and felt like his entire world was crumbling, so much that he barely still knew who he was. My father and I are not that different.

I am passionate about what I do. Last year I performed at fifty colleges and universities across North America and at festivals in four countries. I sip from the same well he does. We both eat, breathe, and live what it is we do. We both need to be reminded about what is most important. As I get older I notice his mannerisms in me more. I glimpse his jawline when I look in the mirror, catch myself reminded of his brisk strut when I walk. I wonder sometimes, *Am I my father?*

In those times I feel the double-edged sword of the implications involved. I am scared to death of becoming my father in the ways I do not want to emulate. I don't want to love what I do so much that I lose track of my marriage or my family. I want to communicate even when it hurts, when the truth is something that makes my throat choke up and my eyes water. I want to live a life where I do not regret the choices I have made with my family, especially my kids.

On the other hand, I am scared to death of trying to live up to my papi's legacy as a father. I feel daunted even thinking about trying to be half the father he was to me and my sister. In the times he was there, he *was* the greatest dad who ever lived. There are memories I still cling to and will never forget—spending a week in Los Angeles with him in sixth grade, going swimming in the ocean while sitting on his shoulders, eating hot dogs together at Mets games, watching him cheer me on during basketball games at the YMCA, taking me to an awkward "puberty talk" in fifth grade. How lucky could I call myself to be a father with all of the aforementioned experiences just being a glimpse of what I could share with my son?

I am scared to become him and scared to become anything less than him.

Right now I stand on the precipice of confronting two of my biggest fears: marriage and fatherhood. Each will require a life-altering leap of faith. Either one demands a plunge into the unknown, without guarantees or shields or certainty. But I've learned to no longer view fear as a burden.

Each and every time, just before I go on stage to perform, I am scared to death. I am so filled to the brim with fear, it is almost spilling out of my mouth. I can literally *feel* the energy of the world trying to crush my body with its expectations and doubts and judgment. I can feel the weighted purpose and urgency of the stories I am about to tell, and the hopes and hearts of everyone who has ever seen me perform before, each person who ever called me "raw" or "vulnerable" or "fearless." I frequently think of that last tag especially—"fearless"—as if it could ever even *be* a compliment, and I laugh.

Fear is what makes us great. It's what makes us commit to the leap and dive in, full-bodied, and risk and dig and push. Fear means something really important is on the line. It means the stakes are highest when you're shaking, about to walk out in front of two thousand people and strip open your story in front of them. And courage is never the absence or avoidance of fear; it is the deep inhalation of it—a frightened, shallow breath turned into a powerful shout or belted song note.

Fear is the fuel behind everything great that I have ever done. It is the symptom of my passion and my sensitivity. And I have made it my life's work to take all of those quivering vulnerabilities in my body and turn them into those resonating stories and truthful poems that make the broken parts of me heal. And I thank God for discovering that I am only as strong as those fears I am willing to confront. Thank God for my mother pushing me to be brave. Thank God for my insane obsession with wanting to face off with my fears, staring each one down, as if it were a bully.

Fear, ultimately, is the reason I have survived.

3 AM

by Adam Falkner and Carlos Andrés Gómez
(Edited by Jeanann Verlee and Geoff Kagan Trenchard)

My mother always says, "Nothing good
ever happens after three o'clock in the morning."
So when I refer to a man on TV as *beautiful*,
shirtless and glistening beneath a thick row
of white stadium lights—I'm not surprised
when the friend I am meeting for the first time
since his deployment darts his eyes towards a sticky
neon corner of the bar. I watch as the panic in his chest
becomes its own person. Leaps from his mouth
like a bedspring, *What are you now, a faggot?*

> The bar is a fever pitch, a mob of testosterone.
> Bones writhing in our moat-flanked bodies,
> the paradox of trying to stay a safe distance
> from each other while craving to be touched.
> My shoulder brushes the chest of another man,
> *Bitch, you fuckin' crazy? I will fuck you up,*
> stepping forward. His fist is a cocked revolver,
> brandished with the safety off. My eyes swell up
> like overused sponges, the bruise in my chest
> spreading across my body. Four tears fall
> in one gasp down my face. I am about to fight
> eight men in a dark New York City nightclub
> and I am crying.

I remember wrestling with a friend in the leaves
behind my parents' house, our rock hard centers
mashing into each other's thighs.

> I remember punching my cousin in the face
> when I couldn't think of anything else to say. Stutter
> in my mouth turned earthquake-jumble of sound.

Or when he and I shared a torn *Playboy*
to masturbate in the woods behind his parents' house
then accused each other of being gay for weeks.

> I remember Malik in high school breaking up a fight
> then getting shot in the parking lot.

The sweet smell of other boys' sweat
after basketball practice in middle school

Wilson's brother shot in a drive-by,
wanting to stab Elana's ex-boyfriend
in the face after he beat her.

Remember the feeling of power the day I realized
I was stronger than my best friend, holding his arms
as I made him say he was my bitch I a faggot.

An hour ago all I wanted to do was tell him I've
missed him [Iso], that I've thought about calling
and wondered about his family [Brent], his son.
[Eric] I wanted to ask how many years he has left
in the service [Maurice], when his next tour ships out.
[Chris] I want to ask if he's seeing anyone [Warren],
if it's serious [Eli], if he still keeps in touch

with Gene or Micah or Ray.

The crowd jumps backwards
like an impulsive gasp for breath.

I have pulled a grenade.

I want to tell him I still wonder about his jump-shot. I want
to laugh about things that made us laugh when we were kids.

I want to tell him, "We have been dying.
Right here. For years."

But I'm not even sure those memories
are the same as they were eight minutes ago
when we hugged each other so hard and so long
in the entrance to this bar, people stared.

---

* Connect Online: **"3 AM" (with Adam Falkner)** http://www.youtube.com/
watch?v=97lqLhkykJQ

CHAPTER 3

Guys' Club: No Faggots, Bitches, or Pussies Allowed

At six years old it seemed so simple to me. I was visiting my family in Colombia for the summer and bored on a sleepy July afternoon. My sister and aunt were painting their fingernails. The colors were dazzling, mesmerizing, almost *delicious*! And I wanted to get my fingernails painted too.

My aunt tried to laugh off my request. Then she calmly explained to me that this kind of thing was only for girls. And then she started to scold me when the volume of my whining became unbearable. Finally, she gave in.

"Okay," she said. "I guess you'll have to learn the hard way."

And thus, the lesson began. I wanted one hand of each color. Both looked stunning. I wanted to be made pretty as well. So I sat there in my chair, like a king, as my sister thoughtfully painted my left hand with the color she had used and my aunt carefully put two coats of whatever hue she had chosen.

I remember them finishing my nails, and feeling so proud I could barely contain myself. I wanted to run all over town and show everyone what they had done to my nails. They were beautiful!

I heard the rising cheers and laughter from the courtyard outside. A soccer game was breaking out, so my sister and I bolted full speed down the stairs to join in the fray. As usual, I was one of the more athletic kids for my age. I sprinted and screamed and dove all over the cobbled square like a madman, trying hard to keep up with the older and bigger kids. There must have been about twenty of us, all huddled around the ball like bees over honey.

Then one of the big kids trapped the ball with his foot and grabbed my hand.

"You can't play," he said quickly, in his gruff Spanish. "Why are your nails painted? What are you, a *faggot*?"

Suddenly everyone came running and giggling and pointing at me. They called to siblings and friends who were still inside their houses to come see. I had become an attraction, an oddity, something to be laughed at and made fun of. I dashed home as fast as I could, hiding my hands in my shirt, hot tears drenching my cheeks in confusion and horror. I had become the neighborhood freak, all because I had painted fingernails.

That's the first lesson in masculinity I can recall. It's pretty hard to forget being called a hurtful word (one I didn't understand at the time) and then have everyone point and laugh at you in unison. It seemed so strange to me then. My aunt just carefully and tenderly removed the paint from my nails and said, "I tried to tell you, Carlos Andrés, but you wouldn't listen."

I thought to myself, *Tell me what? What did I just do that was so wrong?*

Manhood is something that is enforced. Growing up, my friends and I would always tell each other to stop being a bitch or a pussy anytime someone showed weakness or vulnerability. Staying within the acceptable boundaries of this enforced masculinity (or being "man enough") was a huge issue for me as a kid, especially because I've always been *very* sensitive. I get it from my mom. She's like me: supertough and very vulnerable. As an adult now, I think it is an incredible combination. But when I was little, only the supertough part was an asset.

I remember a back-and-forth teasing exchange that happened on the bus in second grade. An older kid was picking on a younger one. The older kid called the younger kid a faggot, and the younger kid in his defense said, "You don't even know what a 'faggot' is."

The older kid responded, "Yeah, I do."

"Okay, then what is it?" the younger one challenged.

"You. You're a faggot," he said as it quickly became obvious that no one really knew what the epithet meant.

That's how it is when you're that age. By someone's reaction to a word, you intuitively learn its power. And that power is a currency, even if you have no idea what the word means.

That day after school, immediately when I got off the bus, I asked my mom what "faggot" meant.

"It's not a nice word," my mom began, after a thoughtful pause. "It's like calling someone retarded. It's very wrong."

I know my mother was trying her best to condemn and try to unpack the word to a seven-year-old—a word that still might be the most malicious epithet you can hurl at an LGBT person—but there was so much in what she said that bounced around my head. I can't imagine how to explain that word to a seven-year-old myself, but I remember thinking, "Oh, okay—so 'faggot' means 'retarded.'"

That was how I interpreted what my mother had said. I know that's not what she *meant*, extrapolating on her answer as an adult, but to a second grader *that* was what her answer meant.

Think about it for a second. If "faggot" was the same as

"retarded," it implied that there was something wrong with that person. Not something to be mad at them for, or hold against them, but it was paralleling a "faggot" with someone who was disabled. And the implications that carried for me at seven years old was that a "faggot" was to be pitied and looked down upon. The whole world could have told me otherwise, with their politically correct bullshit, but I *watched* how people with cerebral palsy were treated. I noticed how a woman in a wheelchair was often ignored or overlooked as though she was invisible. Unintentionally, my mom had made "faggot" and "retarded" the same word.

I don't remember when I learned "faggot" referred to someone who was gay. What I do remember is having friends and classmates who talked about gay people as though they were all pedophiles and molesters. A friend in sixth grade once told me, "Be careful at the pool. That faggot lifeguard might jump on your back while you're not looking."

Even at twelve, I didn't understand the correlation between someone's sexuality and some association with deviance. My friend tried to sell me some story about a guy at the lake one summer who kept trying to climb on his back. Whether or not he believed any of what he was saying, like so much that is about being masculine, I now understand that he was merely signifying to me that he was "safe." He was just proving that he wasn't "one of them." I'd be curious to see who he's dating now.

When I think back to my childhood, there are so many examples and stories of people enforcing my masculinity that I don't know where to start. And in most cases it's a fleeting moment, a passing glance, or an under-breath comment. It's my dad making sure I'm staying in shape and going to the gym. It's friends freezing up and not knowing what to do whenever I get emotional. It's me, caught off guard by my best friend telling me he loves me, and being surprised at the homophobia creeping up in my own chest.

In fifth grade, two of my best friends and I used to play strip poker at our sleepovers. Our bodies had just started exploding into puberty and our hormones were going crazy. I remember the rush I felt doing something I knew was completely taboo. Something inside my chest told me, *This is wrong. You should not be doing this,* and I found it exhilarating. I was breaking the rules, and not just my parents' rules—I mean everything the three of us were supposed to be doing as blossoming men. Sure, we'd cover ourselves up with a pillow or T-shirt, but I've thought back often to the rush I felt. I was curious and intrigued by this phase of our lives we were all embarking on together.

An outsider could simplify what was happening and characterize it as merely homoerotic, three guys playing strip poker until they were completely naked (with something slight covering each person's privates). But it was more than that. Only with my perspective now as an adult can I see it for what it was: We were curious, we were becoming sexual beings, and we were testing where the boundaries were. I wanted to know if what I was going through, especially physically, was normal. Was I the only one who had hair growing in weird places? Had any of them had a wet dream yet? I needed to know if I was just an outsider again, or finally part of the crowd.

I remember taking a shower after swimming at the gym, right around this same time, having just started puberty and peeking at my friend to see if his body looked like mine. As I glanced over, I realized he was doing the same with me. We both had little hints of pubic hair at the base of our penises, hair starting to emerge from underneath our arms. I'm sure we both giggled and accused each other of being gay, and then kept sneaking peeks when the other wasn't looking. We were curious and young and didn't know yet how high the price could be for breaking this rule among others.

In my first year of high school, one of the kids in my gym class got caught doing much less and almost paid a high price for it. He was checking out one of my teammates on the basketball team as he changed. Just in the longing of the glance, I could tell that this awkward, reticent kid (who I actually had never spoken with) was infatuated with my friend, who turned abruptly and said, "Yo, faggot, don't fuckin' look at me. Unless you want your ass beat." The message was clear and impossible to misunderstand.

Shortly before that incident, when I was fourteen, I first went to a nightclub. It was the night after my father got remarried. My cousin Pilar and her boyfriend saw how emotionally spent my sister and I were after the wedding and were looking for any way to get us to cheer up. My father certainly wasn't arguing with that, so he let them take us into the city and sneak us into the Palladium, the most incredible nightclub in all of New York City. I wore sunglasses and strolled past the bouncer arm in arm with my beautiful cousin. The bouncer took one look at her and couldn't care less if she was bringing an infant or a miniature horse into the club. I marveled at the lights and dancers in cages above the dance floor and the energy and unhinged excitement; it was like nothing I had ever seen.

A few months later, while I was briefly living with my dad in Manhattan, I convinced him to let me go out again with my best friend, Brent. It was just the two of us, on our own. I'm still not sure how I talked my father into that one. I'm sure I used my powerful persuasion skills and some healthy doses of post-divorce guilt, but regardless, he gave in. I can't remember what we told him but he agreed to let us stay out much later than I had expected. I told Brent the plan: I was taking him to the Palladium.

Brent at the time was fifteen but looked like he could have been in his mid-twenties. He was already six foot three and well built. I remember him, just a few months earlier, walking around with his girlfriend at the mall (who was actually *older* than him) and people glaring at him like he was some sleazy, shameless pedophile. If only they knew he had actually snagged an older woman! Anyway, Brent had no trouble passing for eighteen (or even twenty-one for that matter), but I was the wild card. I was good at acting older and walking up to a doorman with swagger, but eighteen was *definitely* pushing it.

I'll never forget waiting in that line to get into the Palladium. My heart was beating so hard I was worried everyone could see it pounding through my shirt. Brent and I had gotten fake IDs on Eighth Avenue near Times Square. We thought we should have *something* just in case. We had also both dressed up—as sophisticated and cool as we knew how—which wasn't saying much: Brent wore a brightly colored Tommy Hilfiger rain pullover and I wore a bright blue high-collared sweater with "Nautica" written across my chest in huge letters. As we walked out of my dad's apartment, though, no one on earth could have possibly convinced us we weren't the best-dressed guys this side of the universe (instead of rolling up like two fools who got lost on their way to a Wu-Tang concert!).

In front of us was a group of three, two girls and a guy. We had finally made it to the front, where the drag queen at the door was checking everyone's IDs.

"Yeah, nice try. Go back to Eighth Avenue and get your money back. Next!" the door person called out, throwing the ID back at the man in front of us.

Oh shit. We literally got our IDs on Eighth Avenue. Fuck. What the fuck? Why did we think this was a good plan? What are we going to . . . okay, we'll just hand over both of our IDs and . . .

"Just the two of you boys?" the door person asked flirtatiously.

"Yeah, just us," Brent finally answered after my throat almost closed up because I was so scared.

"Try not to have too much fun . . ." the drag queen said, winking with a smile, opening up the velvet rope and checking out Brent's ass on the way in.

Oh, New York, I thought. *There's room for everybody here. Whatever or whoever you might be into, you can find it at any club on any night.* As we ascended the lighted steps and went into the main room, Brent and I exchanged looks—we knew we were about to have the night of our lives.

We snaked our way through the crowd, checking out who was there and what was happening and something felt . . . off. We made a few laps, both of us trying our best to put our finger on it. What was it? Something was not what we expected.

"There are no girls here," Brent finally blurted out, our minds finally catching up.

"No . . . ," I said, glancing around the room frantically, "it's just because it's early, don't girls usually . . ."

Then I realized, no—he was completely right. There were only two women in the entire place. And they were in the corner making out with each other. Besides that, every single person at the club was a man.

"Huh . . ." I could see Brent continuing to process as we climbed the stairway to the second floor. We both noticed a number of guys check us out as we passed them.

On the second floor—same thing. We couldn't even find a lesbian couple on this one!

"Oh fuck . . ." I was finally putting it all together. "I can't believe this shit."

We listened to a couple more songs and took a cab home. I will never forget breakfast with my dad and his new wife, Karin, the following day.

"Aren't Fridays gay night at the Palladium?" Karin asked, with a smirk on her face.

A brief flash of panic flitted across my dad's face.

"Yeah, apparently. We found that out last night," Brent said with one of his infectious, wry smiles. Everyone laughed, cutting through the tension.

I suppose everyone was convinced we had had no idea. I still wonder how my dad and Karin would have reacted if they thought we went on purpose. It takes me back to a conversation with my mom.

Having just spoken on the phone to my sister, then a college freshman, my mom's eyes beamed proudly—she had a daughter in college and a son starting high school.

"I just feel like I have the two most amazing kids. I got the ultimate that any mother could ever ask for: You're the ultimate son and Sarita's the ultimate daughter." My mom was so happy.

I don't think she was trying to demean anyone with what could have come off as a hurtful statement about gender binaries but—good ol' me—that's how I interpreted it.

"What does that mean, Mommy?" I challenged. "If I was gay or not a 'guy's guy,' would I still be the *ultimate* son? Or would I be a letdown?"

"No, Carlos, that's not what I meant," my mom protested.

"Mommy, I'm gay. I can't hold it in anymore. I just wanted to tell you. And I thought it'd be better to let you know now than to let you down later," I said with a straight face.

"You're not gay," my mom dismissed me. "You're being a jerk. That's not what I meant."

My mom knew me too well. But I remember seriously thinking about what she had said. Even though I don't believe any part of her was consciously disparaging anyone who doesn't fit the heterosexual, gendered norms, it's impossible to not make that inference. Or, at least, it was impossible for me to not make the jump. What if I were gay? Or didn't like playing sports and lifting weights? Would I have been a disappointment to my family? Would I have let my mom down? How would my father feel about me?

My dad is funny. Come to think of it, so am I. He is one of the most cultured and open people I have ever met. And yet he is still a human being. Aren't we all? He'll quietly encourage and enforce all of these masculine norms but still tell me to love and appreciate everybody. I look at the seeming contradiction there and I am reminded of myself. I am reminded of how beautiful and complex all of us human beings are.

I have never felt consciously homophobic about same-sex anything—relationships, affection, marriage. Following the lead of my parents, I've just never really cared who someone dated or was attracted to, nor did I ever feel threatened or put off by it. To me it was just another characteristic that helped tell the story of who a person was. As I headed off to college, I'd read and dialogued and discussed so much regarding homophobia and heterosexism and all the gender-related theory socially conscious kids love to ponder.

Then one day I found out about what was really brewing underneath my open-mindedness. It was the first semester of my freshman year, and four of my girl friends wanted to go to a gay club to go dancing. I did feel turned off by how they were fetishizing gay culture as though it were an accessory (see *Sex and the City* for more), and I was seriously on the prowl for girls most of that year, but I still felt surprised that I didn't want to go with them. It wasn't just that I didn't want to go, I felt very *uncomfortable* with the idea of going to a gay club. And despite my seemingly valid justifications to myself, I had to accept the truth: I was homophobic.

My friends laughed at me when I said I didn't want to go, a couple of them raising their eyebrows in surprise.

"I thought you were different, Carlos. . . . Wow. I didn't think you'd feel like that." I could hear the disappointment in my friend's voice.

"I just don't want to lead anybody on," I blurted out in my defense. "It'd be like colonizing the space," I said proudly, trying to challenge them back.

"Oh, come on," she shot back. "That's bullshit. You're just scared and homophobic like every other guy."

And I was. Those are the moments when you really learn

about who you are, when something comes up that cannot be planned for, when you can't prepare or put your best foot forward, and you just stumble into who you are. I had a similar experience when I spent two months in Zambia after my junior year in college.

In the township where I worked, Mtendere, men frequently would walk the streets holding hands. It had no sexual connotation whatsoever (believe me, not in East Africa!), but it was just how people did things. It was so strange for me to see two muscular, maybe even superhomophobic guys with their pinky fingers interlinked walking down the street.

I remember being in college and seeing this girl I had been hooking up with at a party. We would hook up late at night and not really see each other otherwise. At the party, while I was flirting, at one point, I interlinked my fingers with hers.

"Whoa, what are you doing? We're not married, Carlos," she scolded me, pulling her hand quickly away from mine.

I had never held hands with her. And I never did. She had literally sucked my dick probably twenty times, swallowed my cum every time, but holding hands was too intimate? Yep. That's America for you.

And it may sound strange, but I actually understand it on a certain level—there is something so beautiful and intimate about holding hands (and sex is just whatever, right?). I wish most guys in the United States could be granted more permission to enter spaces like that with each other, not necessarily in a sexual way, but to develop some kind of emotional literacy among us, especially with each other. As much as I might hope for that, though, that's not to say my handholding experiences in Zambia were any easier.

My good friend Andreas would wrap his pinky around mine while we'd walk. When he would stop and talk to a friend he would keep our fingers interlinked. Sometimes while we talked and joked he would rub his hand against the small of my back. And he wasn't the only guy who did this! In the United States that would be considered flirting by pretty much anyone. But in Zambia it was just the way friendships were signified. I was painfully awkward with Andreas. He probably just thought it was some cultural difference with me being American, or maybe didn't notice it at all, but I was so uncomfortable with all of this handholding and intimate physical interaction among men.

On so many levels, though, I loved it. I thought it was beautiful and powerful and refreshing. I loved how rarely men in Zambia got into conflict or fought when they were out. Unlike when I go out in Brooklyn, I didn't see one fight when I partied with Andreas and Japhet and my other friends in Mtendere. I believe that the language of intimacy and connection that occurs between men there, with handholding and eye contact and listening, prevents violence from erupting so easily. As a man in the United States, I often feel alienated and aloof around my fellow brothers. It's kind of hard not to, with so many rules and boundaries constantly keeping us apart.

Although I consciously may have loved the differences in how men interacted physically in Zambia, my subconscious was screaming. My body was petrified stiff most of the time. As I walked around the township with Andreas I suddenly felt like I no longer knew how to move. My body was no longer my own. When we would stop to talk with someone, I forgot how to stand. My cool, calm aura was completely upended by the simplest detail: two pinkies being intertwined.

My visit to Zambia helped me drop some of my socialized defenses, especially with other men. I now had an easier time embracing my friend Leila's Iranian father when I would visit her family, following the Middle Eastern custom of embracing arms and touching both cheeks. I thought back to my time in Thailand when I was in high school and how easily men embraced and often held hands there as well. On the plane ride home, I thought about how drastically differently people interact and exist outside the United States. As I headed home, I craved that connection I'd discovered in Zambia, arriving back to the "man hugs" and formal handshakes of before.

I don't know how much it was related to the revelations I had in Zambia or not, but something strange and beyond explanation happened that fall. I was visiting Brent during our final year of college. Both of us were struggling through a very tough semester. Brent had just suffered a very painful breakup with his long-term girlfriend, and my mother had just been diagnosed with congestive heart failure and awaited emergency open-heart surgery.

I traveled up to Brent's school, Bates College, for a typical weekend for us: parties, long talks, Mario Kart on his Nintendo 64, and a few drinks. It was our chance to get our feet under ourselves again and do what we always did for each other (and had since we were barely thirteen): pick each other up when we fell.

My first night there we drank like fish. Both got sloppy drunk, hooked up with random girls (whose names and faces remained a blur), and finally stumbled back into his room— where he fell into his bed and I collapsed onto a half-inflated mattress on the floor. I remember being mesmerized by an intense dream. In it, I was talking with my high school sweetheart, Vanessa, and she was stroking my head and kissing me. At this point, she and I hadn't spoken in a year and a half after abruptly breaking off communication when I began briefly dating another girl. For so long she had been a stabilizing support system in my life. Both she and Brent had been my rocks. With my mind swirling with the uncertainty of my mother's health, I needed their support more than ever. I remember how sensuous and soft each kiss was, as we started to kiss some more.

"Carlos." I looked down and saw Brent looking up at me as though he'd seen a ghost. "Carlos. Are you okay?"

I was hovering over Brent, just inches from his face.

"What . . . ?" I looked around the room, trying to get my bearings.

"What were you doing?" Brent asked, as if trying to piece it together himself.

"I . . . have no clue. I was just having a dream. And then I was over you." I had no way to either understand *or* explain myself.

"Were you just . . . *kissing* me?" Brent tried to ask, as neutrally as possible, his huge, generous heart doing everything it could not to accuse or shame me.

"I . . . have no idea. What just happened?" I still felt caught in a haze.

God bless Brent for his heart and humanity. He very gingerly brought up the subject the next morning, trying to give me permission to open up about my sexuality. Give me the forum he thought I might need to talk about what I had been hiding from everyone, and him, for so long.

"No," I said, "it's weird. I have no way of understanding or explaining what happened. I don't feel any attraction to men at all. At least, not that I'm *conscious* of. That's the best explanation I can give," I told Brent plainly.

He knows when I'm lying. I know when he's hedging on something. He knows when I'm withholding. As he studied my face, I could see his perplexity only grow as he realized that everything I was saying was the truth. Regardless, I started some soul-searching that morning. Was I gay? Did I have something inside of me that was trying to break free? Had I been lying to myself about my sexuality my entire life?

I didn't feel like that was the case, though. Sexuality is just one of those things. It just is. It's an impulse, a moment of kinetic energy in your body. It's not found in a textbook nor can it be explained by a scientist. It just is. That's what's so beautiful about sexuality. And I didn't feel anything romantic or sexual toward my best friend, nor had I toward any other man that I could recall.

Then I considered something even deeper and more powerful—did I just kiss my best friend while I was sleeping as an expression of something else? Was that kiss symbolic of a closeness I craved that I had tasted in Zambia? Was it my desperate attempt to connect to my other best friend, Vanessa, who I had lost? Was it an expression of desperately reaching out, when I felt like I was at risk of losing everyone?

I have no idea what that kiss was about that night. Brent and I rationalized it as me craving intimacy and connection during one of the lowest points of my life. I can't say definitively what it did or did not mean.

There is a writer I very much look up to and respect. He is seventy years old and has been an out gay man since his twenties. One day recently while we were having drinks and talking he told me: "I'm in love with a woman."

"Really?" I asked with genuine surprise. "Who?"

"This twenty-eight-year-old girl who helps me," he began. "Can you believe it? Fifty years all I wanted was dick. And now this woman has climbed into my heart."

I tell that story to say, "Who the fuck knows?" Sexuality is a fluid, changing spectrum of experience and impulse. Who knows? Maybe when I'm seventy I'll be gay. Or bi. Or who knows what. I hope that when I'm his age, I have the same courage to follow my heart. I think we can all learn from his story. Which brings me to another example closer to my own experiences that challenges not just sexuality but also gender.

While living in New York just after college, I developed a friendship with a woman. I always thought she was gorgeous but knew that she was into women. Everything about the way she dressed and moved and acted reinforced my own stereotypes about where she landed on the sexuality spectrum. Over time we got closer and more open with each other. She told me that she had dated one guy in her life, briefly, while she was in high school and still figuring out her sexuality. Besides that lone exception, she had only been with women.

Finally one day she confronted me. "You're not into me, are you?"

I was thoroughly confused. My kinda butch, lesbian friend is attracted to me? And I had to admit, what fucked with my head further—I was *very* attracted to her. This woman who said "fuck gender" and spoke and moved like men I knew. Like *I* did! Ultimately, though, it didn't matter to me. I had always been attracted to her but, long before this talk, I had accepted the fact that she wasn't into guys.

"Uh . . . I'm confused. I'm *definitely* into you. But I thought you weren't into guys?" I asked, trying to get some footing.

"Fuck it. It's beyond gender. I like you," she said smiling, as though she were reluctantly conceding something.

In the months we saw each other, I felt challenged by her in how I saw gender and sexuality. Friends and classmates of hers at her university viewed her as "queer," many of them identified similarly, so you should have seen the looks we got when she told them I was staying over for the night. Suddenly she was breaking the rules. She was the Latino with the white mother tucked away somewhere. I could see the nods and betrayal in people's eyes. They didn't like seeing the walls they knew breaking down.

Sexually, things between us were amazing but complex. I could tell that she was the one who was used to being in control. Some of our hook-ups were like wrestling matches, as I struggled to submit and receive, while she became self-aware, and maybe even self-conscious like me, of her own need for dominating. There were so many narratives and energies playing out every time we took off our clothes. I felt both daunted and exhilarated by the explorations that we shared.

Our times together made me rethink what I took for granted in terms of sexuality and gender. I wondered why I was always the one to initiate in my relationships with women. And I mean *initiate* in terms of everything—first contact, sex, the relationship. I wondered why I postured and doted and acted in ways that, after the revelations with my friend, had seemed contrived and programmed.

On the bus ride home after one of my visits, I had the realization that straight men strategically use certain words to police who we are. And three staple words at the center of that enforcement are the ones included in the title of this chapter: faggot, bitch, and pussy. All three of those words share something in common: Men use those words to devalue the feminine.

That day I first recognized how homophobia, although it is usually directed toward other men, is, ultimately, an indictment and an attack on women. Gay men, accurately or not, are often called "effeminate" or "girly" or other names that connote femininity. In a world in which gender is socialized to exist in drastic binaries—with tough guys on one side and dainty ladies on the other—where is there room for any of us to be who we are? Furthermore, and more to the point, where do we see anything associated with women given value?

To have the power of patriarchy and then to surrender it is a threat to all men. When I am not the overbearing, all-powerful man, who am I? When there is a fluid, changing spectrum of sexuality and gender, where actions aren't prescribed and roles aren't all but scripted, how do I know what to do? The truth is, we have no idea what to do. The truth is, only when we move away from what we've subconsciously learned can we ever truly find and know who we are.

That's why I felt lost in Zambia. I felt lost and confused, and then saw a change in myself. It's why I felt liberated and opened up and craved the connections I made while I was there. It may have been why Brent and I woke up mid-kiss, both of us confused, flustered, and embarrassed.

Masculinity is a choke chain. It is a suffocating bar that can never be met. How can every man alive be the toughest? And the most stoic? And the most brave? And the most powerful? And the most "manly"? I realized with my once-lesbian friend that my aspirations toward manhood had been a riddle for my own destruction. I was willingly playing a game I was destined to lose. We all are. By buying into the illusion of power afforded by patriarchy, we as heterosexual men do far more than just oppress women and gay men—ultimately we are oppressing ourselves.

I want more than this narrow slice of humanity I've been given permission to taste. I'm tired of not being able to show affection to my brothers and friends. I'm tired of feeling self-conscious when I kiss or hug my father. I'm tired of feeling like I have to hide my emotion and my sensitivity. I'm tired of being stigmatized for wanting to communicate and express myself. I'm tired of needing to throw hurtful words like "faggot" or "bitch" or "pussy" around to prove that I'm a man.

More than being just tired, though, I wish I could speak to that six-year-old version of myself with beautifully painted nails, that I could be standing in that square in Toledo where my aunt, uncle, and cousin Mauricio used to live in Bogotá and hear those kids yell "¡Maricón!" (which means "faggot" in Spanish) at the top of their lungs. I wish I could circle up the group, like they were one of my classes at Drew Elementary School in west Philly, where we had a thirty-minute conversation about why the word "faggot" was wrong. I want to ask those kids questions and challenge them, try to break down some of the growing, still-forming hate in their chests, force them to ask the questions their parents and siblings and teachers are allowing them to gloss over, to make sure that they don't live in a world like the one we do now.

Just today, I read an article about the president and creative director of J. Crew, Jenna Lyons, sharing a cute picture of herself and her young son in which she painted his toenails hot pink, his favorite color. The story got massive press coverage and sparked a heated dialogue about sexuality and gender that drew passionate statements from think tanks and politicians and political pundits and celebrities and scholars from all across the world, all because of a picture made public of a loving mom and her cute, giggling son, as they sat in their bathroom and she painted his toenails. Over painted *toenails*! When will that six-year-old version of myself, of Jenna Lyons's son, of my own future son be allowed to be whoever and whatever he is? When will we stop the shame and policing that forces people into the closet or prevents them from being all that they have inside, whether that be a gay football player or a straight ballerina or a bi-curious bar bouncer or transgender construction worker?

I want a different world for my children than the one in which painted nails create a public outcry.

PART II

ON THE PRECIPICE

Written and performed by Carlos Andrés Gómez
Directed by and developed with Tamilla Woodard

"I Wanna Fuck More vs. the Health Care Worker"

The only consistent piece of advice married men have given me:
fuck as many women as possible . . . before marriage.

And the truth is, I *do* wanna fuck more women. To keep it really real, I wish I could be fucking the better part of every single day.
Here's the problem:

I used to be an HIV educator. And I'd spend the *better part of every single day* staring at pictures of genital warts and herpes outbreaks and trichomoniasis and scabies and syphilis ulcers and lymphogranuloma venereum—

do you have any idea how that shit affects your psyche? And I'm a hypochondriac as it is. I'd be at the clinic every other fucking week—
"Doctor, what the fuck is *that*?"
    "Carlos, it's a hair follicle."
"Okay, you sure? What about *that*? That *can't* be normal."
    "Carlos, trust me there's nothing abnormal on your penis."

A lot of times, I kind of wish I didn't know all of this. It seems like everyone else is pretty relaxed and they seem to be living healthy/fulfilled lives—most people I know only seem to use condoms *occasionally* or whatever. I can't reconcile it. Constantly, it's like

the nympho-freak vs.
                the health care worker

and I can't ignore the shit I know. It's kind of like taking that pill in *The Matrix*—I'm fucked—no pun intended. Now that I know all this shit, I can't pretend that I don't.

And besides all the health shit—there's all kinds of emotional stuff that comes along with hooking up.
I'll be so clear. We'll have the talk, you know,
"Okay, we're just fooling around? That's it. *Nada* else. Right?"
    "Yeah, Carlos, cool—we'll just fuck around."

And then, she's petting my face and has that look in her eyes and wants to cook dinner on a Tuesday night and gets mad I'm calling her at eleven thirty P.M.—
I'm like:
"Yo, we're just hooking up."
And then they're in love. It happens. Seriously. Every time.

And then if I don't want to fuck them.
It's:
"Wow . . . Carlos, you don't trust me?"
        "No, I don't trust you."
"Oh, you don't think I'm clean?"
        "No, not if you wanna fuck me without a condom."
"Just put it in for a second. Let's just see how it feels."
        "A second!?! What—is it gonna feel bad!?!!"
"Have you been tested?"
        "Yeah."
"Okay . . ."
        "I didn't even tell you what the results of my tests were!"

So, the woman thinks I'm arrogant. Because I don't want to. Without a condom. When she's just told me she wouldn't ever have an abortion *and* we still don't have a condom.

What the fuck is the plan?!?

But at the end of the day, I still wanna fuck more. I've had sex with six women in my life! SIX!!!

Find a twenty-five-year-old guy who's had sex with six women!! Find a twenty-five-year-old guy with my opportunities that's had sex with six women!!! I don't give a fuck if that sounds arrogant!!

To fuck or not to fuck?

The question.

And, too often, unfortunately, it's *not*.

CHAPTER 4

Sex: Fucking, Making Love, and Fucking Up

There is no way to recount my sexual coming-of-age in a way that is clean, palatable, and graceful. Like most men, I viewed sex as a measuring stick for my manhood—a way to perform the most Neanderthal, unresolved parts of myself. It was a way to cope with insecurity and loss, signify and find my identity, and prove to the world that I existed, prove to anyone who would listen, especially women, that I mattered.

Ever since I was a little kid, I was fascinated with sex. I'm not entirely sure why, but I was. When my mom recounts one of our earliest conversations on the topic, she always says with a laugh, "Yep. I wasn't planning for *that* conversation for another five or six years—at least." I was six years old.

At the time we were living in Switzerland. My sister and her best friend, Caroline, were playing in the backyard. As usual I was bothering them, wanting to hang with the big kids. I heard Caroline say the word "sex" and then giggle. For some reason, the word seemed vaguely familiar . . . and forbidden. I asked her what it meant and she just laughed and tossed back her head, intriguing me even more. To me she was practically an adult, but as I look back now I realize she was barely ten years old! Who knows if she even knew what the word meant?

So I did the only thing I could think to do. My mother always told me that I could talk to her about *anything*. So I came inside and asked my mom, "What is sex?"

You should have seen the look on her face. My mother is normally very poised, and there's not a lot that throws her for a loop. But she regained her composure, grabbed an anatomy book, and sat me down on my bed. She calmly explained to me how babies were made, that the man's penis goes into the woman's vagina and a baby starts growing in the woman's belly.

At the time, I thought about my little, floppy penis. How the hell was that thing supposed to fit inside a little girl's thing?

"Mommy, how does the penis go in there?" It literally made no sense. More questions followed: Is it just stuffed in there? How does it stay in? And is it just putting it in there that makes the baby grow?

These were all very fair questions from a six-year-old's point of view. My mother's brow furrowed and she explained that it was just how it worked and that it was time for bed. She definitely earned her "Greatest Mom on Earth" title that night.

After that conversation, I had only two other exchanges about sex with my parents.

Once when I was eighteen years old, my mom walked into the den while my girlfriend and I were completely naked. We weren't having sex at that precise moment but were about to. I quickly threw a sheet over my girlfriend and sat up abruptly, peering over the back of the futon.

"Mommy, please go upstairs."

Her expression shifted from stunned to embarrassed.

"I give you and Dave privacy. Please give us a second."

Dave was her boyfriend. I think she was just happy that I gave her an escape from the awkwardness. When I look back on some of the crazy shit I said growing up . . . damn, was I a handful. As my mom told me at different points as a kid, often while she jammed soap into it, "You have a smart mouth"—and, no, she wasn't complimenting my intellect.

When I finally came upstairs, fully clothed, after my girlfriend hurried off in her flustered and mortified haste, my mom was waiting for me at the kitchen table.

Here is the entirety of our conversation: "Carlos, if you get her pregnant . . ." my mom began, about to tear into a manifesto.

"Mommy, am I stupid? I'm not an idiot," I interjected, cutting her off.

"Okay . . . I'm just saying," she said, relieved.

And that was the end of it.

My parents were all-stars at avoiding certain things and then having very minimal, awkward communication about it when they did. Which brings me to another exchange about sex, this one with my dad.

I was in fifth grade and we were living in Connecticut. The school had organized a special night where everyone was supposed to come to the school for a meeting run by a visiting health counselor. I'm not sure if it was required, but it was definitely recommended. The boys went to one room with their dads. The girls went to another with their moms. As we walked in we got a little brochure titled "Puberty: What Is Happening With Your Body."

The brochure talked about both boys and girls. It had pictures and descriptions of body changes and the pituitary gland triggering it all. It talked about breast development, pubic hair, wet dreams, periods, and just about everything my dad would have preferred not to talk about with me on a Wednesday night.

The so-called health professional who facilitated our session was a character, and not in an endearing way. Maybe it was just my adolescent perception of the whole thing, coupled with the awkwardness of it all, but there was something creepy about him. He seemed to enjoy himself throughout the night, maybe a little bit too much. When he started talking about "hair growing in strange places" on our bodies, his eyebrows excitedly rose as he looked at one of the boys next to me. I remember thinking to myself, *Is this shit serious? What the fuck is wrong with this dude?*

On the drive home my father didn't say a word. He didn't touch the volume knob on the radio and drove without looking over at me. As we pulled into the driveway, he abruptly turned the car off and looked down thoughtfully. My insides were doing somersaults as I thought to myself, *Oh no. Here we go. I thought it would never happen with Papi. I thought I would be spared but here it comes.*

His face scrunched up and he tightened his lower lip, focusing his eyes intently on the dashboard as though he was about to summarize the Theory of Relativity.

"Carlitos," he began, "you know that . . ."

What was he about to say? Do I know what? "That . . . ?" I said after he trailed off.

"Well," he began again, "you know."

And that was it. That was the whole talk. Looking back on it now, I laugh. A classic Colombian talk about sex. In other words, a non-talk. Not that my American *gringa* mom was any better. We only had those two brief sex talks twelve years apart. I guess it's tough for any parent!

Strangely enough, though, shortly after the talk at school, I *did* notice changes in my body, like a little Hitler mustache growing above my penis. It may sound strange, but that's what went through my mind when I first saw it. When I would walk through the halls at school, I thought everyone knew about it somehow. I'd sneak into my parents' bathroom and borrow the first razor I could find to shave the hair off. That hair scared the hell out of me. It was a symbol that I wasn't a kid anymore. It meant that I finally had to grow up.

I had my first wet dream the next year about Becky, a character from the television show *Full House* played by actress Lori Loughlin. I woke up soaked in sweat and thought, *Wow. I guess that creepy dude was right. This is really happening.*

My body was exploding with hormones. Everything became sexual to me. We had a woman who cleaned our house once a week and I would run naked through the hallway to the bathroom hoping she would see me. That's just about the only time I would come out of my room, where I'd spend hours obsessively trying to figure out how to ejaculate.

When I thought I had finally done it, a clear fluid appearing on the top of my penis, I was so excited I ran to my sister's room, barely realizing how inappropriate this was.

"Sarita, is this sperm?" I asked, covering up everything but the top of my penis with a T-shirt.

She looked slightly horrified and responded, "I don't know, Carlitos. Ask Mommy. She knows better than me." And that was pretty much the end of that.

Thanksgiving Day in sixth grade was the first time I ever saw semen. After about an hour of humping my bed, I finally saw the white fluid I'd heard about at that talk. I felt like I was a god that day. I was finally no longer a little boy. I mean, I could make a baby now if I wanted!

One thing that had thoroughly confused me throughout the puberty discussion was this notion of me "finally" liking girls. There was this whole piece about how girls and boys would no longer be grossed out by each other and finally want to hang out. *Who is this guy talking about?*

I had never been grossed out by girls. I remember kissing my girlfriend Natalie on the playground when I was in the first grade. In third grade I had a crush on the new girl in school and gave her little gifts and left love notes in her cubby. Was I just a romantic from the beginning? Or did I just feel like I was supposed to woo and romance the girls in my class? Was I just mimicking what I saw adults do? I don't know. But I do know that I never went through two phases I was told little boys go through. The first was being grossed out by girls. The second was not wanting to hug or show affection in public. Since I can remember, I have been two things: a hopeless romantic and a great hugger. Some things never change.

In eighth grade I had my first real girlfriend. We went to see the movie *Babe* on our first date. Or, I should say, we met in front of the movie theater after our parents dropped us off. To this day, I still haven't seen one second of that film. I put my arm around her during the opening credits and we sloppily kissed and sucked each other's faces for the better part of two hours. Over the course of the next year, we fumbled around each other's bodies, thoughtfully and curiously exploring what we had only caught a glimpse of in the sterile pages of health class textbooks.

High school to me was all about sex. I knew I wasn't ready for it yet in ninth grade, but as I looked around the hallways, everything seemed to ooze with sex. At Northeast High School, where I was at the time, everyone flirted and teased, and sensuality was everywhere. I'd marvel at the junior and senior guys with their girlfriends, who I knew they were having sex with, as they'd hold hands and make out up against the lockers between (and, oftentimes, during) classes. A whole new world was opening itself up to me.

I had just moved up to Providence from New York and

would typically head back down to the city on weekends to visit my dad. I relished these weekends away from the more structured environment with my mom because they were chances for me to experiment and find out about this completely new world that now existed. My father was juggling a new marriage and residual guilt from the divorce so I knew I could manipulate him into letting me go out in the city. I think some nights he probably appreciated the time with his new wife, so I took full advantage. Sometimes I would hang out with my cousin, who was in college at Columbia, or go out with Brent.

Brent and I had the most fun. We got cheap fake IDs and did everything we could to get into whatever we thought was the hottest spot in town. Usually it was whatever Funkmaster Flex or some other big DJ was hyping up on the radio at the time. Once, I snuck into the Tunnel with Brent when we were fifteen years old.

It was like nothing I had ever seen. There was smoke and endless strobe lights and two women and a man in a cage above the dance floor. Or at least it seemed like two women. I wasn't so sure as I took a second look. Whoever or whatever, they were totally naked and it looked like the three of them were having sex. Or something close to it. Or wrestling. Or doing both. Everything in the club was totally out of control. Women were dancing topless. I walked into the bathroom and saw a guy snorting something off of the bathroom counter. People kept walking up to me offering me X.

Brent and I were both trying to play it off as though we did this every day. I don't know about Brent, but I was scared shitless in there—and equally enthralled by the whole thing. As freaked out as I was, there was something about the energy and the possibility in that room that absolutely captivated me.

I suddenly felt a hand on the small of my back. As I turned around I saw this gorgeous woman, completely topless, leaning in toward my face. She had a massive set of boobs that looked like they were about to pop out of the strained skin on her chest. Without a word exchanged, I started to make out with her as she grabbed my hands and put them on her breasts. Something about them immediately felt really weird. They were hard and stiff. I suddenly got this strange feeling like something was wrong. She put her hand near my mouth as I smiled, nervously, until I realized she was trying to put something in there! I think she wanted me to be on the same eight-hour ecstasy trip she was currently rolling on.

My brush with having an ecstasy tablet dropped in my mouth gave me a brief sense of overwhelming soberness. I hadn't even had anything to drink but quickly pulled myself out of the intoxicating aura of that club. Now I looked at this woman and realized she was completely gone. She was on another planet. I could have taken her anywhere, done anything and she would have done it. I was no longer feeling so special that she had picked me. Then I looked at her body and her face again and started to break into a cold sweat.

I'm still not sure, to this day, if that person was a man or a woman. I was sure she was a woman then. Now, I'm pretty sure he was a man . . . but a voluptuous, damn sexy one!

I always find it funny when straight guys, especially, have this life-altering reflection, severe embarrassment, and heightened defensiveness when it comes to someone who is either trans or a drag queen or whatever that turns them on. Like, "Oh shit, that person may have been born with a penis. What does that mean about my sexuality that I was into them?"

My usual feeling is, who gives a fuck? Beyond that, though—and I know plenty of women who openly acknowledge this—a lot of drag queens, especially, have the gender role-playing down better than anyone. Being able to pass as a woman is a top priority, and never with higher stakes than when they go out on a Saturday night. So, no, I do not feel weird about making out with someone who might have been transgendered, or a drag queen with bad implants who probably still had a dick. Not that there's anything wrong with that. (How homophobically straight I am, huh?)

Nights out on the town were often where I tested the boundaries of what I could get away with. Like, how far will this woman let me get with her? Will she believe me when I tell her that I'm twenty-two (and I'm really fifteen)? Another time out at a club with Brent, I hooked up with this woman on the dance floor and fingered her in the bathroom. She asked me if I wanted to go home with her, and I felt both excited and totally out of my element. I knew I wasn't ready for sex, and I was pretty scared to leave a club with a stranger, so I said no.

A little over a year later, though, I thought I was ready for sex and I *almost* lost my virginity. I had always had it in my head that I would be in love with the girl I first had sex with. As silly and incongruous as it might seem with everything else about me at the time, I had this big romantic vision of how it would happen. Being in love with the person was a huge part of it. Then, as more and more friends went ahead and had sex, I started to feel the pressure. I started to feel like I was falling behind, and all I wanted to do was just get it over with.

It was the fall of my junior year in high school. I had just transferred to a private school, and I had my eye on this senior girl in my math class. She was gorgeous. She was also eighteen years old. We were probably only about fifteen months apart, but to me she was a full-grown *woman*. In class we had this incredible rapport. We would flirt and joke and play around every single day. She made my knees tingle. There was a chemistry that was undeniable.

I invited her over to my house to watch a movie. In my head I thought, *If I'm lucky maybe I'll get a kiss at the end. But who knows? Just play it like a gentleman, Carlos, and see what happens . . .* and so I did. As the movie started, she sat an awkward distance from me. It was as if she was waiting for me to get up the guts to put my arm around her or pull her over to my side.

"Why are you so far away?" she teased.

I gently grabbed her hand and we started kissing. Before I knew it, both of our shirts were off. I unlatched her bra and started sucking on her breasts and gently kissing her stomach. Suddenly her pants were off. So were mine. All we had between us were my boxers and her underwear.

She straddled me and we started dry humping, the back of my old futon creaking in protest. Yes, my mother was directly upstairs as this was happening. Yes, I grabbed the remote and turned the volume up on the movie, hoping it would drown us out. She began moaning and breathing heavily. Was this really happening? It was like my body was so far ahead of my mind that my brain would never catch up.

"Do you have a condom?" she asked.

"Yeah," I said, as if I did this every day. "Hold on."

I had been playing around with condoms, just masturbating lately, to practice for whenever the big day might come. Of course, I only had the nerve to buy a six-pack, and I guess I'd been practicing a bit too much, so I had only one condom left. *Shit*, I thought to myself, *I sure hope I can make the most of this. I don't even know how to put it in!*

I was so nervous I could barely breathe, much less talk. Sweat was pouring down my face like we were in a sweat lodge. I was trying to play it off like I was turned on by her but I was actually scared to death. I was so scared I could barely get the condom wrapper open.

I tried to remember the whole process: *Okay, don't tear the condom taking it out. Check. Make sure it's not dried out or ripped. Check—*

"Carlos, are you okay? Are you good?" she asked impatiently.

"Yeah, I got it," I responded.

Back to the process: *Pinch the top. Okay. Roll to the base of the* . . .

"I need you to fuck me," she demanded.

Okay, I thought. *Here goes.* But I was having the hardest time getting it in. *Is she too small? Am I too big? Is this the right hole? Do either of us have a fucking clue what we're doing?!*

It was taking so much brain power to try to get this thing in that I felt like I was doing trigonometry instead of having sex. Instead of being in the moment with this voluptuous, completely naked eighteen-year-old *woman* on my futon, I was focused on *getting it right.* And any adult knows how that goes when it comes to sex.

My penis shriveled up and the condom fell off. I tucked it in my palm and asked her for help. She went down on me and started using both hands and suddenly I was back in the game.

"Quick, grab another condom," she said.

I went back over to where I was before and pretended to get another one, then slid the only one I had back down over my penis. This time I felt good. I was ready to lose my virginity! Yes, this would be the day. I would no longer have to be the only one left who is still a virgin.

This time she grabbed my penis with her hand and directed it to where it had to go. I could feel myself about to go inside her. My body tingled with anticipation and excitement, fireworks erupting from every pore in my body. I was about to become a man!

And then it happened.

No, not losing my virginity. I ejaculated. And, of course, my penis was not inside of her yet. I got so excited *thinking* about what I was about to do that I actually ejaculated before I had even *started* having sex. *Oh no,* I thought to myself. *Is this serious? For real?!*

"It's okay," she assured me, "we'll just wait a little while and then try again."

Of course, she had no idea that was the only condom that I had, or that I was so emasculated and embarrassed by the whole thing that I could barely look her in the eye again. It's something I laugh about now, but it completely devastated me at the time.

I told her I wasn't feeling well and drove her home, and we never dated again. She must have felt so confused by the whole experience. I never got the chance to explain the whole plotline she had missed, as we pretty much ceased all contact from that point on—no more flirting, joking, talking in class. She would still make the effort, clearly wanted to connect and hang again, but I felt so overwhelmed by the humiliation of that night, I couldn't even talk to her. *What a waste,* I thought. And how unfair to her. Regardless, I was still a virgin. I had tried to lose my virginity and it had turned out to be a fiasco.

I viewed the whole experience as a sign. The universe was trying to tell me something. *Listen to it, Carlos, or you will be sorry.* I still get superstitious about things to this day and will alter my plans if I think the universe is trying to steer me in a certain direction. I decided that my initial impulse was correct: I had to lose my virginity to someone I love.

As my junior year of high school drew to a close, I felt the pressure mounting. I wanted to be sexually experienced but didn't want to have sex with some random person. I was torn between the competing things I felt compelled to be. I wanted to be a good guy. I wanted to be sexually experienced. I didn't know how to reconcile the two.

And now, in the midst of that conundrum, I found myself without a date for prom—not a move in the right direction toward finding love *or* losing my virginity. I had already set up my two best friends, Vanessa and Brent, as dates for each other.

I ended up going to the prom with a girl friend of mine, who happened to have a boyfriend, and we quickly parted ways as the dance portion of the night drew to a close. That night I started to sense a different energy from Vanessa. She had been there to support and comfort me recently when a situation with another girl had fallen apart, so I thought it was just pity. A short while later, though, I learned that what I had mistaken for pity was actually something else.

After the prom Brent, Vanessa, and I went to an after-party at the lavish house of one of our classmates. His Italian family was infamous in Providence, the kind of family where you don't ask how his dad paid for their multimillion-dollar home.

By the time we rolled up in our rent-by-the-hour limo, I was feeling more lonely and unwanted than ever. I walked into the basement and grabbed a forty-ounce bottle of beer and began chugging it. *Fuck love,* I thought to myself. *Fuck my romantic notions of sex and dating; I don't know where I ever got all that bullshit in the first place.*

Before I knew it I was downing shots and the room was spinning. Things blurred between dream and reality. I started kissing one of the girls next to me and feeling her up. She walked me over to a little cubby where we could be tucked away in the corner of the room. It was a storage space or something in the basement, with some blankets tossed on the floor. Somewhere in our drunken make-out session, another girl came over. Both girls took their tops off, as the three of us sloppily continued to kiss and grope and rub.

I was so drunk at this point that there were blank spots in my memory. I looked up and there was only one girl left. She was sucking my dick like her life depended on it. There she went up and down, passionately, with gusto, with heart. It was like nothing I'd ever seen before. She dragged her nails from my chest to my stomach, making direct, seductive eye contact the whole time. It was like something I'd seen in a porno. I had done this before, but I'd never done *this* before.

I came in her mouth and she wouldn't stop. She just swallowed and kept going, as though she would never stop. She sucked and sucked and sucked. Until I ejaculated a second time in her mouth and she tried to keep going.

"Okay, okay, okay . . ." I slowly lifted her head up.

A sudden, tremendous shot of oxygen went into my brain. I looked into her eyes, filled to the brim with insecurity and wanting, her expression asking me if she was enough, if what she had done had made me like her, if the past half hour had made her beautiful. Her eyes asked if she would be remembered in this life for what she could do with her tongue.

My heart sank. I felt dirty and sleazy. I felt like I had betrayed everything I was. I had never exchanged two words with this girl in my life and I had ejaculated in her mouth twice. And she had swallowed my semen both times as though they were sacred promises. Who was I tonight? Who was this cynical, reckless ghost of a person I was becoming? How had I become this caricature of a Latin lover at my all-white private school?

I got up and stumbled outside to the limo. Brent met me outside the door, his playful smirk simultaneously prying for a story and congratulating me on whatever I was about to tell him.

"Talk to me," he demanded.

As I glanced inside the car, I saw Vanessa. Our eyes met and it felt like a horse had kicked me in the chest. Like I was pleading guilty to the most despicable crime with my whole family looking on in horror. She was holed up against the far door with Brent's tuxedo jacket draped over her shoulders. Her expression seethed with hurt. Was she in love with me? Had I betrayed her? Did she know what had just happened?

Later that summer Vanessa and I fell in love. We finally revealed all of the feelings we had both been hiding for years. We became each other's teachers—taught each other about love and sexuality and relationships. We became high school sweethearts as we entered our last year of school before college. Right when I had given up on it, I had stumbled into the fairy-tale relationship. The exact circumstance I had imagined for losing my virginity.

That fall, we both lost our virginity, on that same old futon where I had almost had sex barely a year before. This time, however, was perfect. I had a six-pack of condoms. We both wanted to do it, and we had talked about it. We knew nothing about what we were doing. But we knew one thing: We loved each other. I stumbled as before, but I finally got my penis in and had the most glorious fifteen or twenty seconds of my life. It was practically over before she knew what was even happening.

The rest of that school year together certainly wasn't a fairy tale. I realized how complicated it can be to date your best friend and be on the verge of leaving for college. Both of us seemed very aware of this entirely new world that we were about to dive into. The ways in which we dealt with this impending change were polar opposite: Vanessa clung to me tighter than ever, as the inevitable closed in, and I, typical of a guy, began to drift away.

We both went to the University of Pennsylvania. The July before we left home to go to school, the pressure was beginning to wear on both of us. She wanted more and more promises from me that I couldn't give. I wanted independence. We ended up breaking up that summer as I took off with Brent to go backpacking around Europe for three weeks. I can barely admit it to myself now, but I broke up with Vanessa because I wanted to be free that summer. I wanted to start college fresh, free to indulge in all of the new opportunities with girls. I thought this three-week graduation trip with Brent would be my warm-up for the wild times of college.

But when we arrived in Greece, I was lovesick. Even when I'd go out and get completely drunk, it would just make me miss Vanessa more. Every night we'd go out and meet girls but each one would make me think one thing: *You are not Vanessa.* My inconsolably romantic heart was strangling this vacation. I was trying so hard to be a player and hook up with girls but every time, my heart would ache and I couldn't.

The only night I hooked up with anybody that trip was our first night out in Mykonos. Someone had given us a flyer about a foam party at a nightclub in town. Foam party? Brent and I wondered what that meant.

After taking a taxi up the hill to this chic nightspot, we soon found out. There was an open bar, after paying the cover, and foam slowly crept and snaked its way across the entire dance floor. As we continued to down drinks, the foam started to rise like a bathtub filling up. By the time it was at our waists, clothes started coming off. I made out with this topless woman who straddled me in the middle of the foam. I sucked on her tits and kept kissing her. Before I knew it, hands were groping at my crotch. Then there were multiple hands. I suddenly noticed that both of her hands were on my shoulders. In my drunkenness, I remember thinking, *Well, if it feels good—a hand's a hand.*

Don't let that story mislead you, though. Besides that wild night of debauchery, I spent almost every other night during that trip thinking about Vanessa. The debauchery of the first night in Mykonos was my way of trying to prove to myself that I could still do this, to prove to myself that I could hook up with girls and not care, that I wasn't this incurably romantic fool and nothing else.

When I got to college, I thought things would be different, but the problem persisted. Vanessa and I were both living in the freshman quad, so we would see each other all the time. We still hung out and had meals together. We may have been just friends on paper but quickly became friends with benefits. During the difficult transitional time of freshman year in college, Vanessa and I became each other's crutch. That's not to say we were both living by the same rules.

I still loved Vanessa, but she was possessive and jealous. And I knew I couldn't make any new friends or build a new social network with a girlfriend like that. So we both did our own thing. Over time the meals became less and less frequent and the late-night hook-ups were the only times we ever saw each other. More and more often it was when I was drunk. Every time I visited her, she was completely sober.

During my sophomore year, she found out that I had been hooking up with other girls. In fact, she found out mostly because I told her that I had, and that I was interested in starting a relationship with one of them. Reality finally set in for her—she was losing me. Never mind that the girl I was planning to date turned out to be a smoker and drove me up the wall (and our short-lived week-long relationship ended), Vanessa and I were officially done.

This was a defining moment for me. I had finally let go of my high school love. I was finally ready to move on.

I was most certainly not looking for a relationship at this point. For the first time in my life, I felt like I was sexually mature enough and completely unattached. Every night out was a new experience. I felt responsibility to nothing but my whim and what the moment dictated to me. I made it a point to embody one of my lifelong mantras: "carpe diem," or "seize the day."

That's not to say I was having a lot of sex. In fact, I had sex with only one person during this stretch, an older woman I dated for about a week. That was it. But I certainly played around with a lot of people. So many times, I deflected the thoughtful eyes of the person I had been hooking up with. And each and every time, I'd reach for my banner phrase, "I'm not looking for a relationship. Let's just keep it simple." I know, I know—it's a classic phrase so many women are used to hearing from men. But when I was twenty years old, I thought those words were revolutionary . . . and original.

Going into my junior year, I had my eye on this one girl. She was a stunning beauty who made me feel something in my body that I hadn't felt in years. My stomach hurricaned when she was around, my throat dried up, and my palms got sweaty. Besides being gorgeous, she was smart and sensitive and just so raw and open.

She was never afraid to say what she really felt. She told me when she was uncomfortable or acknowledged when she'd made a fool of herself and would laugh at it. She embodied so many things that I wished I could be. I still wanted to look cool and collected at all times, be that guy who had everything together, despite the chaos clouding my brain.

We started to hang out pretty regularly. I guess we can call it that. We actually never went on a proper date, come to think of it. One time I was visiting her at her house and we just started kissing. One thing led to another and we were both naked in her room. She asked me if I had a condom but I told her I just wanted to hook up but not have sex. She said she was cool with it, so that's what we did. It became a ritual. I'd visit her late at night, we'd hook up, and then I'd go back to my place.

At the beginning things were relatively harmless. I would suck on her tits and we'd dry hump a lot. I felt like I was back in high school, making the most of things without having sex. She seemed concerned that if we took our pants off again, without a condom, that we'd make an impulsive decision, one we'd regret. I assured her that I still didn't want to have sex. "Trust me," I told her. "If I wanted to—I would bring a condom. I don't want a pregnancy or anything else as much as you don't."

Even before we started hooking up, we'd spend hours talking

with each other. We'd share stories about our families and growing up and our dreams. She was just so easy to talk to and be open with. Her eyes would gently rest on mine while I talked and thoughtfully take in each new story or anecdote.

Before long, though, our pants did come off for our make-out sessions. I remember the first time we got completely naked again. She started to play with my penis and then stopped. Her eyes dropped pensively toward the ground.

"My uncle used to make me do this." She dropped the words like a bomb. "And then he'd make me suck it."

I can still feel my blood running cold as she told me this. My whole body went dead, my breath trapped somewhere deep down in my throat.

"I'm so sorry," I said. "That's horrible."

Who could ever do that? For years, when she was a little girl, he sexually molested her. I felt angry that she had to go through that. I imagined myself meeting her uncle someday and punching him in the face over and over again. But that day never came. I was just in this room lying naked on her bed with my arms around her.

We stayed like that for a while. Without saying a word. I decided at that moment to never hook up with her again. It would be like taking advantage of her. It would be wrong. I needed to be her friend. I held her as if my arms were an impenetrable shield that could protect her from the world. Against every bad man and dirty uncle who might be out there. And we stayed like that, neither of us saying a word.

I don't know how long it had been but suddenly I felt her hand on me. It was rubbing the inside of my leg and slowly moved onto my stomach. And then between my legs and onto my penis. I still felt this huge painful ache in my chest from the story she'd told me. I thought to myself, *Okay, this whole situation is not cool. I can't casually hook up with a girl whose uncle used to make her do what we're doing.* And then I thought, *You can't*

hold it against her. If she wants to hook up, why not? Is she no lon-
ger allowed to be sexual because she survived abuse? The words and
ideas cluttered my body. My mind went blank. My heart
throbbed in my chest. Then all the thoughts were quickly gone.

I looked up and realized she was sucking my dick. Something felt strangely familiar about the way she did it, as her lips
slid up and down my penis like her life depended on it. Her
whole body involved as she kept going—passionately, with
gusto, with heart—*almost* like nothing I'd ever seen before.
Then she dragged her nails from my chest to my stomach, making direct, seductive eye contact the whole time. As I came in
her mouth, she swallowed and looked up at me, seeking my
approval.

My heart shattered through my rib cage. Those were the
same eyes I had seen that night after my junior prom. I had
become a dirty uncle. I felt like I had just molested this beautiful girl whose heart had been handed to me the first moment I
walked into her apartment. *How could you do this, Carlos?* I was
horrified at what I had just done and still conflicted about
whether or not it was wrong.

Regardless, I continued to make late-night visits to her
house. The ritual was the same. We'd kiss for a bit, I'd finger her
for a little while, she'd suck my dick until I'd come, and then
I'd leave. Our relationship seemed less and less human as it went
along. I knew she wanted a relationship—she had told me so—
but I placated her. And then I stalled. And then I fed her lines
about how I "wasn't ready" and "needed more time." And she
nodded and listened. I kept us in a holding pattern because it
was convenient for me. And she trusted me and gave me the
benefit of the doubt as I used her like a cheap prostitute that I
never paid. I barely even gave her the most minimal respect as
the visits became shorter, the motivation more and more clearly
cut-and-dried.

Why did I do that? I really *liked* this girl. I was attracted to her and even enchanted by her but I could never commit to her. Sure, I valued our friendship on some level, but, in the most chauvinistic, shallow, and despicable of ways, I used her. To make matters worse, I had found someone else but continued to hook up with her. It all came to a head when she saw me one night, strolling down the walk with my new fling. She wrote me a painful, angry email, telling me how much I had hurt her and how much she felt betrayed.

She was right. I still don't know why I treated her like that. Maybe deep down her history of abuse made my heart ache but also gave me the convenient excuse I needed to not enter into a relationship. Maybe I used that history as my license to treat her like a whore while cowardly hiding behind words like "respect" and "beautiful" when I was with her. Regardless, I have neither excuse nor explanation. I took advantage of her and I took her for granted, quickly moving on to a new girl.

This new fling turned out to be my college sweetheart, my first serious girlfriend after Vanessa. Her name was Melanie. Whenever I would see her around campus I'd think, *Damn. That is the most beautiful woman I have ever seen in my life.* She was a radiant dark-skinned Sri Lankan woman with a dancer's body and big expressive eyes that captivate a room. I was swept off my feet. The first time we spoke was in a math class we were both in. She noticed the om symbol on my necklace (a gift from my sister when she lived in India) and we started talking.

For months we just hung out and talked. She kept telling me that her parents would disown her if she ever got together with a guy like me. She came from an incredibly proud Tamil Hindu Sri Lankan family who had relocated to northern California after leaving home. Despite living in the United States, her parents were adamant about both her and her sister remaining connected to their heritage. A big part of that was finding a husband from the same background and culture. And, of course, finding someone with the same *religion*.

I say "husband" because her parents didn't really believe in dating. They probably didn't believe in anything that the two of us were doing with each other during that year. As time wore on, we became more passionate about each other and inseparable. Before I knew it, I was completely in love.

Unfortunately, she was a grade above me, planning to graduate and move back to California in May. For the first time in my life, I was in a relationship where I thought about the real possibility of marriage and kids down the line. Despite the huge possibility that her family would never approve of me, she seemed ready for a lifelong commitment. She talked on and on about how she didn't plan to get married or have kids until her thirties, but then she'd ask me what I thought she should do next year. It blew my mind that she would consider changing her life plans for me.

Once again, similar to what occurred during my relationship with Vanessa, I started to feel suffocated by rising pressure and expectation. Once again, I felt the dread of being trapped, of having my individuality and my freedom constrained by being in a relationship. Who knew where I'd be in four months, much less after I graduated college? I was scared to death that she might stay in Philadelphia for my senior year of college. *If that happened, we might as well be married with kids,* I thought to myself. I pictured a sad, boring life for myself as a married man with a white picket fence going to my job in a cubicle.

After my parents' divorce, the idea of commitment— whether marriage or in a relationship—felt tainted to me. I don't trust in it, and it is as though I am always waiting for it to fail. As I grow older and watch marriages of friends and family fall apart, I wonder if those fears are justified.

The closer we got to May, the more Melanie pressured me for a decision. I would constantly tell her, "Let's just enjoy the moment and cross that bridge when we get to it."

And then May arrived. Melanie wanted to do anything to

make it work. She even told me that she was willing to risk her relationship with her family for me.

"I don't want you to risk losing your family for me," I said. "That's not a choice I want to have any part in supporting."

The reality was that I was scared. I was confused. I was conflicted. I loved this woman. I was worried the pain would be unimaginable later, if we had to break up years down the line because of my cultural and religious background. A big part of me was protecting myself against that. I was also twenty-one and curious about being single again. And afraid to lose her. And scared she might be the last woman I ever slept with. I was a cluttered, confused mess.

As she left to fly back to California, we crumpled into each other's arms and sobbed, kissed, and, finally, said good-bye. If only it was. Over the next year, we'd continue to hook up each time we'd see each other, putting off the inevitable.

Then one day she told me she had met someone. He was a family friend, came from the right background, family, and religion, and she had been hanging out with him. She said she was attracted to him but would stop seeing him immediately if I wanted.

"No," I told her, "we're not together. I want you to be happy. Do what you gotta do."

Inside I was dying. I knew that the only way to stop the inertia of what had already been set in motion was to commit to her again. Even then, I worried she might still be seeing this guy out in California. I mean, he's a *family friend*. This guy might as well be her future husband that her dad handpicked for her.

Then came my birthday that winter. I was visiting my father in Germany and I had been trying to call Melanie every day while I was there. Because of the time difference, I told myself, it had been quite difficult to get hold of her. I emailed her twice and didn't hear back. On my birthday I moped around the house, trying to be cheerful as I played with my little brother and sister, feeling as though I had been kicked in the chest. I felt ugly. I felt unwanted. I felt forgotten.

A few days later, the phone rang at the house. My father answered and said it was for me. I took the phone and finally heard her voice. It was Melanie.

Something felt off in her tone. She said she had been in Las Vegas and that the battery had died on her phone while she was out there.

"You couldn't borrow someone else's?" I snapped at her.

The phone went silent, a brief calm before the storm. Before I could even pry, Melanie told me that she had hooked up with that guy who was the family friend while she was in Vegas. It had happened the night of my birthday. While I had been sobbing in the guest bedroom, Melanie had been sloppily hooking up with *that* guy. Not just any guy. Not some random fool at a club I could have forgotten about in an hour—the one person I never wanted to hear about again. I pictured his hungry paws all over her naked body and wanted to throw up. *That body is mine,* I thought to myself. *How dare he think he can touch it?*

When I look back now I think, *Who the fuck did I think I was? What was she, Carlos, your property? She begged you to be with her—and you said no. How can you be angry at her for that? What, should she have remained a nun until I was finally ready to commit? As far as she knew, I was out fucking half of west Philly. How could she ever know that I hadn't even kissed anyone since I got back to school?*

For years, though, as patriarchal and illogical as it was, I held on to the hurt of that night. The bitterness of feeling betrayed and lied to bubbled up in my throat. It became my license to hook up with women ruthlessly, without accountability or concern, and justify it to myself. Everything I loved and cared for in the world seemed jeopardized by my cynicism. Nothing was pure anymore. As I walked around the world, everything seemed stained and heavy and broken.

After graduation I decided that I wanted to move back to New York. Of all the places I had traveled and lived, New York is the closest thing to home I have ever known. It embodies everything I am and aspire to be. Brent and I had decided we would be roommates and hustle to find jobs and try to make a life for ourselves in the big city.

After finding an apartment in Brooklyn, Brent and I quickly learned how crazy the dating scene in New York can be. And I mean *crazy* because it's complete chaos. Just because of the sheer number of people and opportunities afforded by those numbers, anyone can be anything. People lie without any thought to consequence. People have multiple girlfriends. Some people have boyfriends in the day and girlfriends at night. You can almost do anything in New York and be protected by the anonymity of living in such a big place. You can fuck a trans dominatrix, get a hand job in a nail salon, and dress up like a cartoon character and dry hump someone at a party while sipping a pomegranate martini. That's just how the city is built. And I'm talking six in the morning on a Sunday or lunchtime on Good Friday. You can do anything at virtually any time . . . and no one's going to stop you.

That kind of freedom and opportunity is a slippery slope. I remember visiting my friend, who was still in college at NYU, and going to the dorm late at night just looking for someone to hook up with. It usually wasn't very hard. I'm not talking sex here, but just playing around. The women I'd hook up with would become part of this routine when I got drunk. I'd scan through my phone and call until someone answered. It was like a roulette wheel, and the first person who answered the phone would be where the ball landed.

As time went on, though, as I hooked up with more and more people, I felt increasingly hollow inside. It seemed like this cycle I had fallen into had no end. I knew people in their thirties and forties in the city who were still drunk dialing the same people they had for years. Sometimes it feels like time stops in the city. Like every person is on this playground with no rules, where accountability doesn't exist. It's so overwhelming and refreshing and invigorating at first. And then it starts to feel really sad. Only occasionally do you get a wake-up call, in the midst of that chaos.

The first one for me happened while I was at a friend's house, after a poetry open mic where I had performed. My friend, who is also a poet, had invited a friend of hers to come to the show. We had some drinks after and flirted a bit. Back at the house, we started hooking up. As we both got naked she asked if I had a condom. I told her I didn't.

"Okay, don't worry about it. I trust you," she said, trying to pull my penis inside of her.

"Whoa," I said, "no, relax. We can just play around."

"It's cool. I'm on the pill," she responded. "What? You don't think I'm clean?"

In my head I was thinking, *HELL NO! Not if you're fucking random guys you just met! AND trying to convince them to have sex without a condom!*

Finally she settled for a hand job. Shortly after I ejaculated, I remember becoming hyperaware of her hands. She didn't seem to want to wash the semen off. Then she started rubbing it over her breasts and moving down her body.

"Whoa, chill. Hold on. Let me help you wash up," I said, trying to playfully coax her toward the bathroom.

"No, it's okay. I love it," she whispered, nibbling on my ear.

"No, seriously. Come with me," I said, helping her up from the bed.

I carefully washed her hands and then moved to her chest to make sure none of it was left on her body. I tried my best to make it seem sensual and playful, whatever it took to not have anything that might get her pregnant anywhere on her body. Brent and I had heard stories from one of our friends about women who'd take the semen from their mouth or hands and try to impregnate themselves with it. Who knows if those rumors had any truth to them, but we both believed them. I didn't know anything about this woman. I just got a feeling that I didn't trust her after we started hooking up. I still hooked up with her, of course (the fool that I am), but then tried to control the cleanup. The next morning I found out she had a nine-year-old son. As far as I know, she was the first mother I ever hooked up with.

New York City scared me straight a second time shortly thereafter. This time was with a former fling who I had just recently reconnected with. We went on a couple of dates and seemed to have a stronger connection than ever. I was even thinking that what we had might even be relationship material. For our third date, we went out for dinner at a nice Greek restaurant near her house in Astoria. After delicious food and plenty of wine, she invited me back to her place.

As soon as we tumbled through her bedroom door, we tore off our clothes and began feverishly kissing and sucking and groping each other. Almost immediately, she started to suck my dick, deep-throating it, and then looked me right in the eyes and said, "I want you to titty fuck me. And then put your dick in my mouth."

That was nothing I was going to argue with. And so I did. Her massive breasts pushed tightly together as my penis slid out from between them and into her mouth.

"Fuck me," she said. "I need your cock in me—NOW."

Her hand pulled my fingers out of her and aggressively grabbed at my penis, trying to hastily drag it toward her vagina.

"Hold on," I said. "Chill, chill. Let's just keep it simple."

"NO. Fuck me. Please, just FUCK ME!" her tone rising into a bratty whine.

"I don't have a condom," I pleaded with her.

"I don't care. I'm on the pill. Get inside of me," she demanded, getting more aggravated by the second.

"No, I'm sorry. It's not happening," I said.

"Fine, just come on my tits then," she quipped back.

I felt like I was on an assembly line. What the fuck was this? Don't get me wrong, a lot of the hook-up was very hot. I liked her take-control attitude. But this final twist had creeped me out a bit. Did she have any clue where I've been? I could have been fucking half of Manhattan for all she knew. After I finally convinced her to let me wipe the semen off her breasts, we sat in bed naked and sipped white wine.

"Let me ask you a question," I asked her. "What would you do if I got you pregnant?"

"Have the ba-by," she said in a singsong baby voice, smiling playfully.

"Seriously?" I said, shocked.

"Yeah," she shot back, very serious now. "I support women's right to an abortion, but I'd never have one."

I started to break into a cold sweat. This is the woman who had my semen covering half of her body, angry that I wouldn't fuck her. What if I had? What if she wasn't on birth control after all? Nothing seemed to make sense anymore.

"I'm sorry, but I have to go," I said, quickly getting up and starting to put my clothes on. "You're amazing and beautiful but this isn't going to work."

I knew that I didn't want to have a relationship with this woman. Nor did I want a baby with this woman. It was time for me to leave. And that's right about the point when it got completely insane.

She walked to her door and locked it and started pulling and clawing at my clothes as I tried to put them on.

"Stop," she pleaded. "Where are you going? Just stay. Please. Come on. Let's play again in a little bit. Please?" she teased, biting her lip. "No, seriously. You're not leaving."

That last part actually scared me a bit as she latched onto

my sweatshirt, tearing the sleeve as she tried to pull me into the bed again.

Over and over, I calmly told her to take her hands off me and please move so I could leave. This only seemed to aggravate her further as she continued to beg for me to stay, vacillating between begging me to not leave and demanding that I fuck her. After about twenty minutes of her screaming and clawing at me, with scratch marks and a torn T-shirt and sweatshirt, and her roommate intervening through her locked door, she finally let me go.

"Fuck you, Carlos!" she screamed. "You're an asshole!"

As I hopped in a gypsy cab back to my apartment in Manhattan I started doing some serious soul-searching. What does this city do to us? Why are human beings so insatiable and desperate and hungry and *insane* while they're here?

To be fair, a lot of alcohol was involved in both of my cautionary tales. I don't think that excuses or explains what happened in either, but it certainly greased the wheels of craziness in both. I don't think either woman was trying to trap me or use me as a sperm donor without my consent or manipulate me in some malicious way. What scared me most, in both cases, was how much the women *trusted* me. Besides being a generally nice guy and relatively sociable, I hadn't given either any real reason to trust me. What had I done to earn their trust? In the first case, I'd read a few poems, drunk a bunch of shots, and gotten naked. In the second case, I'd gone on three dates, had some conversation, and gotten naked. What was there to be trusted in me? Do I just seem like a trustworthy guy?

After college, I worked as a social worker. I did a lot of work as a sexual health educator. One thing we always emphasized was universal precaution. If you treat every instance as though you have a risk of contracting an STD, and protect yourself each and every time, then you've lowered your risk considerably. I live my life by universal precaution. These two women just trusted me. Maybe they looked at me and thought I looked clean, the most dangerous eyeball test in the book. Or maybe they just wanted to be loved or even liked so much that they were willing to risk their health and well-being to get it. I can't believe that any person is ever worth that risk.

Since graduating college, I had been hooking up with multiple people. I had finally indulged myself, like a gluttonous, chauvinistic pig, with the single lifestyle I was so afraid of losing if I was in a relationship. Now I found myself lonely and still aching, deep down, for a meaningful connection with someone. All of the experimentation and single playing around had left me feeling exactly how I had characterized those two women in my stories: lonely, desperate, and hollow.

There was only one woman who had been consistently in my life since I had graduated. Her name was Whitney. I first met her in the lobby of my friend Eric's college dorm. I glanced over and saw this breathtaking woman. Her eyes were pure sunshine, flooding every inch of the space. It wasn't even that she was just gorgeous; everything about her drenched the room with sheer radiance. And every ray of light pouring out of her body connoted goodness.

We hooked up on and off for a couple of years. She'd never had a boyfriend before. She grew up in a small, sleepy New Hampshire town. There was something so pure and real and genuine about her. I realize now that she was the first woman since my breakup and collapse with Melanie that made me believe in the world again. Every word from her mouth was so damn earnest and heartfelt. It made me gasp sometimes. Was this woman for real?

She was. But I guess I wasn't prepared to believe it yet. For two years I continued to stall and tell her I wasn't ready for a relationship. And then, one summer night, I abruptly broke things off. In complete contradiction of everything I had been telling her, I left her to pursue a relationship with someone else. I had broken her heart and it seemed certain that things with us were done. A year later, though, both of us were living our separate lives, and I had the life-altering revelation that she was the woman of my life. I needed to be with her. So I called and emailed and wooed and pursued her. And then finally, after relentless apologies and promises to make things right, she gave me another chance. But it wasn't quite so simple now. Up until recently, she had been dating someone else. My relief at getting a second chance with Whitney quickly morphed into insecurity, as I couldn't erase from my mind the image of them together.

Sex was one of the hardest things to navigate when we got back together. Every single time we were intimate I thought about the guy she had been seeing. I pictured them fucking on a day I was most vulnerable, when I most needed to hear her voice. It was just before we decided to give it another shot, and I had called and called and heard nothing back. When we had finally worked through some of our issues and decided to be together, a few weeks later, I couldn't let it go. That's when I asked the question all men want to ask but should probably shoot themselves in the face before they decide to: "Was he better than me?" I dropped the question out of nowhere.

"What? Why do you ask that?" she played off the question, knowing exactly what I meant.

"It's important to me. I need to know if he was better." The words burned through my skin as I spoke, trying so hard to stay calm.

She stayed silent for a moment.

"Okay. I guess that's a yes," I said finally.

"Okay, fine. He was . . . ," she said.

My whole world felt like it was crashing down. One of my biggest fears had come true. I had found a woman I loved more than anything else and I had finished second place in sexually pleasing her. All of my illusions of sexual supremacy, of the prowess I was so proud of, had evaporated. I was worse than mediocre. I was not as good as someone else.

". . . only better in one area," she finished her statement.

Oh God, I thought. *Now she has to feed me the full spoonful of truth medicine. I mean, I asked for it. There you go, Carlos, you dumb fuckhead. You asked for it, right? Well, now you get it. Maybe, if you're lucky, you can leave this conversation with a small penis complex too . . .*

She shared with me her feelings that I didn't reciprocate or give priority to her sexual needs like he did. Too often it was just about me. The other guy had made it about her, not putting himself on the pedestal like I had myself for so long. And as much as I wanted to yell and scream and disagree with her, I couldn't. She was completely right. I was just a narcissistic kid when it came to sexuality, and she was helping me learn what a real profound connection with an intimate partner should be.

In a weird way, a whole bundle of animosity and resentment and anger and hurt got squashed in that conversation. All I had to do was look into the eyes of the woman I loved, watch the façade of my sexual identity almost collapse, and then recognize that what she was telling me was not only fair but the honest and raw truth. And at the end of it, she was saying, "I want to be with you."

A real sexual connection with someone can never be built around achievement or supremacy or comparison or conquest. It is actually the exact opposite of everything I had learned, as a man, sexuality was supposed to be.

Sex is jazz. It's improvisation, tuned to the most heightened frequency of aliveness. It's the ultimate freestyle in a cipher. It requires the most intensive and single-minded listening your body and soul are capable of. Then it requires you to play, to commune, to call to life all of the senses of your body like a symphony, in a chorus ready to harmonize and counter-harmonize with the rising swells of another human being.

In those two years that Whitney and I hooked up before we stopped talking and then started a committed relationship, our sexual connection was not built on reciprocity. It wasn't built on freedom or exploration or the curiosity of observing and then shattering the boundaries of who we were. It was just fucking. And I was doing it like a selfish little boy. She would take me in with her entire body and spirit, and I would just writhe and throb until I finished—until *I* finished, never mind her.

In many ways, I think that's what men are trained to do. I remember when I was younger having friends who talked about not losing control when they orgasmed. How that was the ulti-mate sign of being a "bitch"—to lose control as you ejaculated. To moan. To call out. To scream or squeal. It was what a woman was supposed to do. I had been treating Whitney like a good friend, one I enjoyed talking to, and then used as a blow-up doll when I got horny. Those two years I was the ultimate stereotype of what I've been socialized to be. To remain in control at all times, never show who I really have hiding underneath my façade . . . to just fuck.

From experience, I can tell you that believing sex is a straight-faced orgasm is barely scratching the surface of what's there. I can tell you that playing the role, sexually, that you may feel inclined to play is often the most limited version of what sex can be. I can say now that I know sex. More than that, though, I finally know lovemaking.

Before anything else, it is giving. That is the ultimate plea-sure. It is the polar opposite of the archetypal male dominator. It is the supreme, primal symbol for what love is—spoiling and pampering and doting on the person you love and honor in that moment. It is absolute freedom and letting go and moaning and screaming. And it is messy and surprising and fierce and gentle and beautiful. There are no winners and losers. There are no medals or trophies. There is no accomplishment or supremacy to be had. There is only the moment both of you might arrive, never more sure that there is a higher power on this earth.

I could have lived the rest of my life and slept with thousands of women (instead of the six I have), gotten my dick sucked a million more times, and known just as much about sex as I did when I was a naïve, cocky teenager. Only after eight years of having sex, only after confronting who I was and what I feared and what I couldn't let go of, did I finally actually learn about sex. And sometimes now we'll lock eyes for a second, in that moment right after Whitney and I have finished making love, as we gasp and grin, having glimpsed the other side and know we have both been given proof: God exists.

Excerpt from solo play MAN UP

Written and performed by Carlos Andrés Gómez
Directed by and developed with Tamilla Woodard

"Julio"

The summer after my junior year in college I worked at a camp for kids with HIV. It was the second time, and with the same group of kids. The first day, as tends to happen, all the kids realize all the stuff they've forgotten to bring. Usually it's something we have like sunscreen or a towel or swim trunks but, this time, one of the kids, Ritchie, forgets his medication at home. Now, it's a sleepaway camp outside the city, so me and another counselor have to go back to his house and get it—obviously, no extra HIV meds hanging around. So we get in the clunky camp van and drive the almost two-hour trip to his mom's house.

By the time we make it there it's already starting to get dark. The sun has already started going down and it's kind of that in-between, twilight time when you can still see fine and it looks like the sun might still be up but it's actually just dipped below the skyline. We pull up to a four-story townhouse. The street is packed alive with little kids playing in a fire hydrant and a group of about four playing stickball and two tiny kids having a water gun fight and some little girls playing jump rope.

As we pull up, Ritchie's mom spots the camp van and slowly trudges over to the window. She flashes a polite smile and I see that her eyes are bloodshot. In Spanish, she jokes about how her little boy is always forgetting his *something*—it was only a matter of time that it would be his meds. How he's forgetful like his father was about things. How her AIDS is making her start to forget things like her husband did when he was around. Then, something cracks in her voice. She says she went to the doctor yesterday and he told her that she doesn't have a lot of time left. And she's afraid that there is no one left to take care of her kids. Her oldest son locked up on a drug charge and her second oldest, Julio, recently paralyzed when he got shot.

> "Julio has been in the car for almost three hours. He won't go upstairs," she said. "I just don't have the strength anymore. He's so stubborn. He won't listen to anybody."

They live on the fourth floor. Four flights of narrow, steep steps that need to be climbed to make it to their apartment. Without an elevator, usually two or three men from the neighborhood help carry him up the stairs. But today, no one is around to help. Just a few moms and kids. And, of course, he doesn't want to call one of his friends to carry him up to his room.

> "He peed on himself, you know. It's not his fault. He can't control it. I tell him that, but he just gets mad and tells me to shut up. He won't let anyone get near him. I told him he can't sit there forever."

I can see his silhouette in the passenger seat. Leaning across toward the driver's-side window yelling out to the kids in the street; whistling and making wise cracks and quips. Playfully clowning the kid up to bat in stickball who must be on his eighth strike and is still batting.

"Carlos, can you please just try to talk to him? Maybe he'll let you convince him to call one of his friends or something," her head pressed against the door, her weight buckling.

So I turn off the van and get out. Start walking toward the worn-down Hyundai, not really having a clue what the fuck I'm going to say.

As I reach the car I look in and see this handsome, proud Puerto Rican kid sitting there. His facial hair all shaped up perfectly. A gold chain around his neck with a cross on it. I know this kid. He must have been that playboy, smooth cat in high school, I just knew it. He must have been that guy who was the best at everything but never really seemed like he was trying. That cat that picked up a tennis racket for the first time and beats a varsity player, or the guy who played guitar and piano and didn't even know how to read sheet music. He was definitely that kid.

I offer my hand out to him, "Wassup, Julio? I'm Carlos. How you feelin', hermano?"

He looks up at me with a kind of vague familiarity, "Yo, Carlos, what's good, kid? So you're Ritchie and Isabel's counselor at the camp, right? Yeah, I seen ya van when you was pulling up."

"Yeah, you know how forgetful Ritchie is. He forgot half his clothes for the trip so I gotta go upstairs and grab the rest of his stuff for him."

"Ritchie won't remember to put on his kicks if I don't put 'em on for him! He's always walkin' around barefoot. I'm like, 'Yo, Ritchie, what happened to those Jordans I bought you?? Why you walking around barefoot?'"

"I hear you. Ritchie is forgetful, for sure. . . . Well, I'm going up anyway—you wanna roll up with me?"

"Naw, man, I'm chillin', dawg. Just playin' with the kids right now—takin' in the sights—you know what I'm sayin'? Plus, I can't really use my legs right now so it's kind of hard, you know what I mean?"

I know what he means. What he really means. But tell him we'll do it real quick. "And your mom seems like she really needs you upstairs. I think she's really stressed out."

"Yo, dawg, that'd be fresh. . . . Well, you sure? Naw, naw, forget it. You sure? I'm sorry, man, I know it's kinda weird and shit. Alright, Carlos."

He slowly opens the rickety car door. I notice his wheelchair folded up in the empty backseat. I see a spotless pair of brand-new Air Jordans on his feet that match the shirt he is wearing.

> "Sorry for the fuckin' piss smell. You know these fuckin' kids at the pool—got me all wet and shit. It's just fuckin' kids, though, you know?"

I reach down, trying to stabilize my feet in between the street and sidewalk curb. Trying to get a strong foundation to pick his 160-pound frame out of the car. Using every ounce of strength I have to do it quickly and smoothly, so as not to make him self-conscious. But it's so much harder than I thought it was going to be. For a second, I think I'm not going to be able to get him out of the seat and I'm about to make a fool of myself. I'm looking for anything to make this happen. Start praying to a God I'd never even tried to talk to. Praying to God to just give me this one blessing. To give Julio this one blessing. *God, please let me carry him up to his apartment. I know we're not really that tight but I'm a good dude.* My arms struggling to not buckle under his weight. Trying so hard to not visibly strain or struggle so Julio can still be "allowed to be a man," even with another man carrying him. Finally, I get him out of the car, trying so hard to casually smile and keep our relaxed rapport going.

> "Yo, man, nice kicks. I been lookin' for those."

We get to the steps in front of the building and I start to count them to take my mind off of his weight. I lift my head to the sky so he can't see my eyes welling up. He sits in my arms, stiffly reclined, like he is in a lowrider or an easy chair, trying to hold onto his dignity, his pride as all the little kids he was just making fun of stop playing and watch. All the moms stop their gossiping and watch me hold another man in my arms as the light is starting to fade. Watch my clumsy feet try so hard not to trip. Watch sweat pour down my face—me trying so hard to play it off.

> "Good lookin' out, dawg," he whispers to me with tension in his jaw.

"Yo, Julio, don't even stress man," I say.

> "I'm sorry, I'm kinda heavy . . . ain't been able to play ball too much lately," he says.

And we finally make it inside the building, beginning to slowly climb the steep and narrow steps. One story and then two. Then, some stumbling up to the third but no catastrophe. Trying so hard to have him believe I almost meant to trip. Trying so hard not to breathe heavy to make him believe his weight is manageable. My feet feeling like two blocks of cement in clown shoes stumbling on every single crack and rivet and nail. Then, halfway up the final set of stairs on the way up to the fourth floor, he rests his head against my chest. Softly lays it up against my collarbone. Two Latino men—trying so hard to both be men—our arms wrapped around each other . . . his head buried in my chest.

I trip and stumble my way to the fourth floor, struggling to get his apartment door open, and finally lay him on his bed. I spot a PlayStation next to the TV. Soaked in sweat and feeling a pinch in my eyes, I'm looking for anything to distract me from my annoying sensitivity. C'mon, Carlos, I say to myself. *C'mon, man—none of that artist shit right now. Suck it up. Stop it. Man up.*

> "Alright, Julio, stay up man. We'll rock some PlayStation next time," I laugh and give him a pound. Then, I look into his eyes filled with tears. I feel a big knot swelling in my throat. His jaw starts to quiver open, no words coming out—as if he can't make them. Then finally:
> "Carlos . . . gracias, hermano." *

CHAPTER 5

Heroes and Villains

As far back as I can remember, my mom had planted this idea in my head: I was a hero. I never really questioned it, especially when I was little—anything my mom said was sacred. So I became obsessed with superheroes—mostly, Superman—wanting so badly to one day emulate any aspect of his heroic life. But think about Superman for a second, this one-dimensional cartoon of a man. He's always swooping in to save some damsel in distress, but he always has to use a superpower, which, by definition, is not human. He uses his superhuman strength or vision or flight or speed. But he never shows emotion. He hardly communicates at all and doesn't seem to break too much of a sweat. He wears what's basically a form-fitted leotard with a cape and looks handsome with his chiseled jawline and broad chest. He is not so different from the caricaturized, fantasy-evoked images so many of us men have of ourselves. And

while my mom did nurture the complex, less masculine charac-
teristics I had, she still always pushed me to be the hero.

She bred this urgent, overpowering sense of justice in me
since birth, which made up the foundation of this heroism.
She'd say, "If someone is being bullied or picked on by someone
else—no matter who it is—it is *your* responsibility to step up
and say something." Or as she put it, "Look that coward in the
eyes and tell him you're not afraid of him—because anyone
who's a bully is a coward. You know that, right?"

"But why do *I* have to, Mommy?" I'd ask.

"Because you're a leader," she'd say.

"I don't want to be a leader," I'd respond.

"It doesn't matter. People don't decide: Some people just are
and others aren't. And you were chosen."

And that was it. She told me about the bravery of her father,
who was a counterspy for the United States during World War
II, posing as a Nazi spy. I would sit on my uncle's lap and look
at old black-and-white photos of my grandfather. He had an old
pistol with a swastika that he used to carry in the war. That
Panzer Luger frightened and inspired me. I wanted to someday
have a fake passport and name and try to undermine the Nazis
like he did. All of his medals from the war were framed on the
wall of his study. He had been awarded every single medal except the Congressional Medal of Honor. My grandfather had
been awarded *four* purple hearts for Chrissake!

My mom was born in Stuttgart, Germany, where her family
lived while her father maintained his cover after the war looking
for Nazis who were in hiding. When they finally came back to
the United States, they were relocated to the tiny forgotten town
of Barnesville, Georgia, where he taught at Gordon Military
College and would drive around with a gun stashed under the
steering wheel of his red-and-white Buick.

My mom would always tell me how honorable my grandfather was, not just in the army, but in everyday life. Once,

when they were driving through town, she made a face as they passed a homeless person. Her father stopped the car immediately and pointed in the direction of the homeless man. "There but for the grace of God go I." His eyes locked angrily on hers. "Do you understand me? With the flip of a coin, that man could have been you. Never forget that."

There's another story about my uncle as a bratty little kid, when they were living on the army base. This was in the 1950s, right around the time of the first *Brown v. Board of Education* decision, but certainly well before neighborhoods were integrated. The army base, however, *was* integrated and my mom's neighbors were black. They were family friends, and my grandfather and the neighbors' father were colleagues. Every week they would have family dinners together.

One day all the kids were playing kickball in the neighbors' yard. The boys from both families started to get more and more competitive as the game wore on. One of the neighbors' boys kicked a towering shot, well out of the yard. He high-stepped his way around the bases, maybe stuck out his tongue or teased my uncle as he crossed home plate for a home run.

"Well, at least I'm not a *nigger*!" my uncle screamed, quickly bolting back to his house. He knew he'd be in big trouble. My grandfather had no tolerance for bigotry, and any hateful language was out of bounds. My uncle hid in his room, crying with a sheet wrapped over his head.

My grandfather didn't arrive home from the base until the evening, when both families would get together for dinner. At dinner that night at the neighbor's home, all the children sat at the table in solemn silence, each of the fathers sitting at opposite ends of the table.

"I heard about the game this afternoon. What was that word you used?" my grandfather interrogated, his eyes fastened to my uncle's. "I want you to tell everyone what you called your friend today."

My uncle leapt up from the table, tears hysterically pouring down his face.

"Sit down!" my grandfather shouted. "You had a lot of guts to use that word. Now show some real guts and use it again. Use it again as a guest in their home. While you eat their food, and they welcome you in their house."

My uncle's hands covered his face in shame, as everyone sat silently at the table. My grandfather made my uncle apologize—first to the son, then to the father and mother. Not once, during the rest of his life, did anyone in the family utter that word again in my grandfather's presence.

That story resonated powerfully with me when I was a little kid. My mother had all these examples of how her father was so brave and meticulous with how he lived. He was superhuman to me. No moment was unimportant. Each glance, comment, and action had to be accounted for and respected as having meaning. Everything carried weight and, accordingly, should have purpose. He passed away when my mother was nine years old, but he remains one of the most influential figures in my life. He lived each day with conviction, humility, and compassion. He was a real-life hero, a living, breathing one, unlike the cartoon superheroes decorating my room. And I wanted to be just like him.

I'd spend hours upon hours sketching soldiers. Hundreds of them poised for battle. The good guys on the left side. The bad guys on the right side. I wanted to be the leader, the hero, the good guy. I wanted to go to war too.

Anything that I associated with heroism was what I wanted to be. First it was being a fireman, which I chose to be (as much as I could, I guess) each year for my first three Halloweens. While living in Brazil as a baby, my parents could barely convince me to put any sort of pants on—ever—but when it came to my fireman's helmet—we were inseparable.

Around first grade I wanted to be a police officer. I pictured them helping old grannies get their stranded kittens out of trees and catching robbers trying to break into a family home. Then my romantic vision came crashing down. I was seven and we had just moved back to the United States. Leaving a free summer concert in Central Park, I heard a woman scream as a homeless man snatched her purse and began to run. I felt a rush as I looked up to see the woman in her silver-hued fur point and squeal as the man made off down the path. Just moments later a bystander stuck his foot out and tripped the purse thief.

My first thought was elation as I realized that real heroes did exist in the world: an unknown, anonymous man willing to step in and make the world safe again. For no reason but to do what was right. To stop a purse thief from terrorizing a sweet woman on a night stroll after a concert.

Then, I glanced down and noticed a cluster of old photographs fanned out all over the ground. The homeless man's belongings had spilled across the pavement like scattered leaves. There were faded pictures with his kids, and a very old photo that looked like it must have been of his parents. There was also a frayed journal with a rubber band holding together worn pages with postcards and other scraps and mementos spilling out of the sides. I wasn't quite sure anymore if tripping this man had been the right thing to do. I stood awestruck by his hurried hands trying to collect the fractured roadmap of his life from the ground.

It wasn't until my father's firm hand pulled at my collar, probably trying to avert my eyes in time, that I realized what was happening—four police officers quickly pounced on the man who was still crouched over and took turns swinging at his head with their nightsticks. They beat him. They continued to pummel and swing at the helpless man in what felt like an endless swarm of violence. There was something vicious and precise about how they worked. My heroes had become monsters. It chilled my bones and sent a shiver down my spine. I will never forget the dull, hollow thump of those nightsticks hitting the man's limp skull, as his unconscious body lay motionless on the pavement.

"Come on, guys. Stop. That's enough," a man close by called out to the police officers.

"You wanna be next, wiseass?" one of the policemen responded.

No response.

"Okay, then mind your fucking business. I *said*—keep walkin', asshole!" they followed up.

That day I stopped wanting to be a cop. Any heroic notions from before were gone. Throughout my childhood, we moved incessantly, staying at no place longer than a year or two. Being the perpetual new kid gave me a strange, unique sense of independence. From peer pressure, social expectations, and other boundaries that often define childhood, especially during adolescence, I felt unbound. It was my way of coping with being left out, my defense mechanism against feeling like I never really fit in.

How did I use this freedom? Well, it quickly turned into a license I gave myself to challenge authority. And, boy, did I ever. But unlike a lot of the other kids who acted out, I was different. I wasn't the archetypal "bad kid," who just mouthed off and raised all hell and didn't do anything he was told. I picked my spots. I always got straight A's. I did my homework on time. I studied for the tests and got the highest score. I did the extra credit work. Many of my teachers were simultaneously perplexed and intimidated by me, like in fourth grade when I felt my teacher was harassing one of my fellow classmates, a shy girl who rarely spoke in class.

"Ms. Harrison, why are you bullying Stephanie?" I blurted out, without raising my hand, and then, "I think you owe her an apology."

That was the kind of kid I was. Of course, she told me to go to the principal's office, which I refused to do. Then the principal came up to the classroom. And my mother got called, and so went the ritual.

It became a role I heartily enjoyed playing. My parents would often plead with me to pick my battles, but nothing seemed to tame the capricious defiance brewing inside of me. I felt like I *was* picking my battles. I got good grades, was generally very polite, and contributed in my classes, but if someone was getting picked on—regardless of the context—forget about it. I was the first to jump in and stand up for someone. I felt I had a birthright, an obligation even, to embody the heroism for which I felt destined.

In retrospect, my mother says she was scared to death, with good reason, that my defiant streak would someday do me in. She spent hours upon hours reading parenting books and meeting with therapists to try to prevent me from becoming destructive and misguided as I got older. As she puts it, "Carlos understood power and was too smart for his own good." A classic example was when I was five years old and got a glorious, shiny red truck with a long ladder that could open up to taller than my height for Christmas. It was all I ever wanted in a single toy and more.

One afternoon, as was often the case after my snack, I was acting out, bouncing off the walls. Maybe I broke something in the living room, who knows. In any event, my mother had had enough and took away my fire truck to try to regain some semblance of control.

"Give it back," I demanded.

"No, Carlitos. I'm taking it away until you start behaving," my mother said.

"But what if I keep being bad?" I shot back.

"Then I'll keep taking away toys until your behavior gets better." And with that my mother scooped up my fire truck and walked away.

I spent the better part of the afternoon dragging every single thing out of my room—a box of crayons, my G.I. Joe soldiers, water guns, and a silver medieval chest plate, even my

Superman sheets from my bed. With all of my things piled high outside of my bedroom door, I proudly marched down to my parents' room.

"Mommy," I declared, pointing toward the massive heap outside my door, "I want my fire truck back. You can have all my toys. I want my fire truck back or I'm going to keep being bad. And I'm giving you all my toys now, so you can't take them away later."

I can't help but look back on that story with simultaneous pride, at how genius my little five-year-old devilish self was, and horror, at what karmic punishment awaits me when *I* have children.

As I entered adolescence, surprisingly, I began to develop some focus. My defiance started to mature. I was in the eighth grade living in Darien, Connecticut—a pretentious, lily-white suburb full of Range Rovers and soccer moms. I was finishing some less than appetizing cooking experiment in my home economics class with a partner. It was the final period of the day, the Thursday before a long weekend.

A hurried student helper passed a handful of bright pink slips to the teacher, who told everyone to sit in their seats and listen for an important announcement as she carefully laid down the slips on each desk. The assistant principal came over the loudspeaker: "Ladies and gentlemen, I have an important announcement to make. Due to the high volume of unanticipated snow days we have had thus far, the superintendent has decided to cancel the Martin Luther King Junior holiday and requires that *all* students be in attendance this Monday."

I felt like I had just been punched in the head. I was lightheaded and faint as I stared down at the pink slip I had just been given, literally, word-for-word reiterating what our assistant principal had just explained.

Martin Luther King Jr. Day canceled? *Canceled?!* Erase the

day honoring Dr. Martin Luther King Jr.—the iconic face of the civil rights movement? Was that even possible? Before I knew what I was doing, tears began streaming down my face as I tore up the piece of paper.

"This is bullshit! This town is the most racist place on earth!" I shouted as I slammed the pieces into the garbage bin one by one, dramatically spitting on the scraps as they fell.

"Go to the office, Mr. Gómez," my teacher responded sharply.

"*No!*" I shot back defiantly, meeting her stern look with a dagger-sharp glare.

Of course, she called the principal, who stood in the doorway after the end-of-school bell rang and asked me to come with him. I held on to my desk with both arms, filled with this wild, convinced sense of righteousness. *This wasn't the homeless guy in Central Park who got tripped,* I thought to myself. *These racist white people are trying to* erase Dr. King. *I know that I'm on the right side. I am not moving. They will have to saw through my arms to make me leave this desk.*

Then, I realized it didn't really make sense to hold on to my desk forever. I had to eat dinner at some point. So I let go and they called my mother. Who, as she often did, defended me in front of my teacher and principal, then pleaded with me on the way home. Rage spewed from my mouth as hot tears stung my face and my throat went hoarse.

"Why don't you *do* something . . . instead of just screaming about it?" she chimed in after a long awkward pause.

"Like what?" I challenged.

"Why don't you write a letter to the superintendent? We can work on it tonight. I'll help you with it. And we can fax it to her and all of the local papers."

It seemed so simple the way she put it. *Okay,* I thought, *we'll see if this* letter *actually does anything.*

So we sat down and began to write what I wanted to be the

most scathing and incendiary letter ever written. I wanted to call out the abusive, authoritarian superintendent for what she was: a racist. And more than that, call out the entire town, even the entire county of Fairfield for being the same. At the end of that school day, what had incensed me more than anything else was the blasé attitude of all of my classmates. No one else seemed upset. I was the only one who seemed to care that they were *canceling* Martin Luther King Jr. Day!

My mom asked me about a section in the letter where I called the superintendent racist. "Are you sure that you want to use *that* word?" my mother asked thoughtfully, the linguist, word-obsessed anthropologist that she is. "Because when you use that word, it is like pouring kerosene on a campfire."

"Yes," I said. "There is no other word that would say it right."

I had been challenged. I had to be brave. I had to take a stand. *Yes*, I thought. *This is what real heroes do.* They don't take the easy way out. They stand behind what they believe in, behind the words that they use.

As soon as we had edited, spell-checked, and revised the hell out of that letter, we printed up a fresh copy and quickly faxed it out. First we sent it to the superintendent and then to all of the local papers. With dreams of marching arm in arm with Dr. King in Selma, I went to sleep.

The next morning we rushed outside to see if anything had made the morning paper. And right there, on the front page it said, 8TH GRADER UPSET WITH SCHOOL SUPERINTENDENT'S DECISION, with the entire text of my letter right there for everyone to read. We hurried down to the convenience store and found that my letter had been published in not just one but *every single paper* we had faxed!

At school that morning, I was like a celebrity with my classmates. To my surprise, everyone seemed to applaud what I had done. Suddenly, everyone seemed as incensed by the decision as I was. My social studies teacher even compared my action in class to those of Henry David Thoreau and Dr. King: "Carlos is taking this material to heart, folks. He spoke out for what was right." Everyone in class stood up and gave me a hearty ovation. At the end of the school day, we received another bright slip, similar to the one received the day before, except this time it was bright yellow.

The superintendent had reversed her decision. There was no mention of my letter anywhere in the note. Instead she cited laws regarding national holidays and a miscommunication between her and her advisers that had led to a "misguided attempt to address the school dismissals for snow." Then, she added that the Tuesday and Wednesday following the holiday would now be filled with activities and events honoring the late Dr. King's legacy.

I had effected change. I had stood for something that was right and won. Even though she hadn't come out and said that it was me who caused the quick about-face, I felt there was nothing else that could explain such a stirring reversal.

For the first time in my life I felt this revelatory sense of what I wanted to be in my life. It was simple: I wanted to be the next Dr. King!

I became obsessed with anyone who spoke out against injustice. I began reading about Gandhi (who Dr. King mentioned frequently) and Henry David Thoreau. As I grew older, I began embracing dissenters who did not believe in nonviolence, like the Black Panthers and Che Guevara.

Looking back, I think of this heroic narrative that I bought into as something I saw as inextricably bound with my identity. To be a man is to be heroic. I aspired to be a man—and not just a man but the *ultimate* man. Much like the spelling quizzes and algebra tests I expected to get a perfect score on, I wanted to get a perfect score on manhood, get a 100 percent on my aptitude in being a man, be the best, like in everything else. I wanted to go down in history as being as heroic as the icons I looked up to.

Over the course of the next year, I would move twice, get

kicked out of a Catholic school, suffer the death of my uncle, watch my parents get divorced, watch my father get remarried, and then, to top it all off, grapple with my father's new bride being pregnant with twins.

Having made it through that harrowing stretch, as I entered high school, I began to feel conflicted about right and wrong. The world seemed too fragmented and complex for the heroes and villains that I had projected onto my every day. I was getting confused as to who was "good" and who was "bad," why seemingly bad people did good things, and good people did bad.

I was pretty much done. Forget being a hero. If that's what a man is supposed to be, then fuck being a man. All of these "heroes" never seemed real anyway—they were certainly not like any of the men I knew. *Or maybe,* I thought, *there's another way I can be a man.* I was a freshman at a public school in Providence, Rhode Island. I remember watching the stars of the basketball team strut the hallways of our school like celebrities, every single girl gushing and swarming around them. *Now* that's *who I want to be,* I thought.

I got a new haircut just like them, a tight fade with a French part near my left temple. I got a new bubble jacket and baggy, Chinatown rip-off Tommy Hilfiger jeans. I changed the way I walked. The way I talked. The way I moved. I wanted to be just like those guys. I wanted to be a star. Who wants to be a hero when you can be a *star*?

I played basketball like it was going to save my life, playing so hard, wanting to win so badly it hurt. But I didn't want so much to win as to look good doing it, to show up the other guy I was playing against, to be the top dog at all costs, the alpha male by any means necessary. Impress all the whispering, huddled girls near the bleachers watching. And just like everything else, I didn't just want to be good—I wanted to be the best. I wanted to embarrass, to humiliate whoever I was playing against. I wanted to be the king.

As an adult, I can look back and see this for what it was: a kid trying to find himself, trying to carve out an identity as best he knew how, trying to cope with his parents breaking up while once again being the new kid in the midst of adolescence.

I remember going back to visit my friends in Connecticut and feeling them treat me differently. Something about the new way that I dressed, walked, and acted seemed to have a new power to it. I had always commanded respect with my outspokenness, but now I seemed to intimidate in a way that I never had. It was definitely a double-edged sword, though. Quickly, I learned how conditional my status (and who I was) had been with a lot of my old friends and mentors.

I was back in town from Providence watching a high school basketball game. I had my new haircut, a bubble jacket, baggy jeans, and a red polo shirt with "POLO" in big blue block letters stamped across my chest. I was dressing the way the kids in Providence did. Walking into that gymnasium, I could feel the stark contrast between myself and everyone else who was there. I could feel the energy repel away from my body, the people in my path parting like the Red Sea. No one else was dressed like me. I noticed all of my old friends and classmates with their khaki slacks and bent-brimmed Princeton lacrosse hats, New Balance shoes, and argyle shirts. Unlike my polo shirt, theirs had a barely noticeable logo over their heart—the sharp contrast between the subtle, bland, affluent style of Darien versus the brazen, loud, working-class dress of Providence that highlighted brand names and logos and celebrated flair and swagger.

I felt completely disconnected from the place I had once called home. People who had known me, been close with me, and said they loved me averted their eyes as I walked into the bleachers. Only after I tapped them on the shoulder or called out their names (sometimes two or three times) did they look up with a frown and then slowly move from confusion to a hesitant smile.

At halftime I grabbed a ball and started shooting free throws, amid a throng of younger kids doing the same. I had found my place of peace and serenity, my respite away from the judgment and alienation.

"Excuse me," a vaguely familiar voice with an unfamiliar tone cut through. "Excuse me. You can't—"

I spun around to see one of my favorite teachers (and people, for that matter) from middle school, Mr. Delfini. Immediately my face broke into a smile. His face had been contorted in a scowl and now looked stuck between confusion and embarrassment. His tone had almost sounded like he was reprimanding me.

"Am I breaking a rule by shooting so badly?" I joked, walking over to give him a hug. He still looked confused. "Mr. Delfini, it's me. Good to see you."

As I opened my arms up, he didn't budge, extending his right hand formally with his left arm tucked across his body.

"You staying out of trouble?" he asked me, concern mixed with accusation. I could see the hurt in his eyes taking me in as though I had been the superstar kid who fell from grace.

Staying out of trouble? I thought to myself. *What the fuck does that mean?* Sure, I got into enough trouble in middle school, but there was something about the *way* he said "trouble" this time that seemed more sinister. I felt like what he was really saying was: *Are you in a gang? Is your family on welfare? Be careful going to an inner-city public school—I hear they have niggers.*

Fuck this white town, I thought. I still had never gotten a B in my life, but because of how I dressed and who I went to school with, the love had been taken away. I had heard whisperings from friends, who'd seen pictures of me with my new pals at Northeast High School—filled with high-achieving Cambodians, Dominicans, Laotians, Puerto Ricans, Nigerians, Russians, black kids, Muslims, Italians, and the big motley mix of working-class folks who I went to school with. It was a magnet public school in Rhode Island for Chrissake! *Rhode Island!*

Everyone in that gym looked at me like I'd just returned from doing a year on Rikers Island.

Fuck these white people, I thought. *Fuck 'em. You want a villain? I'll be a* monster. *Fuck these teachers. The friends that I thought had my back.* The only person who stuck by me was my best friend, Brent. He'd moved about as many times as I had and knew exactly what it was like to be the outcast, to be misunderstood. We both embraced the role of outsider, walking around town and spitting in the face of the yuppified norm that held its nose up in judgment at anything that wasn't white, safe, rich, and boring.

I'd spend a lot of time during those first two years of high school traveling down to New York City to visit my dad. I had lived with him briefly and then moved to Providence to be with my mom, and I yearned for that connection with people I loved, at this point in my life more than ever. As I yearned to be loved, I seemed to be drawn more and more to finding the party. I would hang out with my older cousin, then a student at Columbia, and sneak into bars with him and hit on women in their twenties, do whatever I could to try to drink beer and maybe make out with an older woman. Much to my dismay my cousin would never let me get any further than kissing, one time dragging me out of Cannon's Pub by the collar when a twenty-two-year-old invited me back to her place. I was fifteen. He was saving me from myself.

If only he could have been there a few weekends later when I visited Brent in Connecticut. After a Friday night visit with my father, I decided to head out to the suburbs for a night of partying with my best friend on a Saturday night, a night that Brent had promised would be full of drinking and girls and debauchery. More and more I was beginning to embrace the bad-boy persona that I felt like people expected from me when I would visit my old stomping ground. I could feel people simultaneously threatened and enthralled by it. I could feel girls drawn to me who used to not even give me a second glance. I was suddenly enticing to them now for one reason: I was dangerous.

The way Brent had described the night was like this: We were meeting up with two older girls (juniors while we were freshmen) who had a thirty-pack of beer and wanted to bring us to a party. One of these girls was Brent's on-again off-again ex-girlfriend, who he'd been hooking up with for close to two years.

They had been very much in love initially—Brent in the eighth grade and Erin a tenth grader. Her being in high school immediately lent greater credibility to their relationship. They were inseparable, head over heels. That was, of course, until Brent found out that she was cheating on him with her ex-boyfriend.

Ever since that day and the messy breakups and make-ups that followed, they had developed a strange sort of friendship. Erin realized that she didn't really want to be with her *other* ex-boyfriend and that Brent was who she really loved. But by that point both were at a place in their lives where they weren't looking for a committed relationship. The puppy love romantic notions of youth had given way to the exploration and opportunity of being a single teenager. They remained close and still hooked up occasionally, but were more friends than anything else.

Brent had made sure to have Erin bring a friend for me—a busty brunette with a sharp mouth like mine. He assured me she was "down." As in: "Yes, she's into you. She saw your picture. She wants to hook up."

Erin had a driver's license and could get beer whenever she wanted with a fake ID. We climbed into Erin's Jeep and drove off into the night, with a thirty-pack of Miller Lite tucked in the backseat between me and Erin's friend. We didn't think too much about the risk or consequences involved, just cracked open beers and started drinking, first one, then another. Then, a couple more. I don't remember us ever making it to any party.

Who knows? Maybe we did. I just remember the Jeep stopped with the lights off in a park somewhere. I had my shirt off, as did Erin's friend, and we sloppily made out while Brent and Erin did the same in the front seat.

Somehow we made our way back to Brent's house. Erin's friend passed out on the couch downstairs and I made my way up to Brent's room. Not that there weren't other beds available in the house, but somehow Erin, Brent, and I ended up in the same bed.

Erin laid in the middle of Brent's bed, flanked by two shirtless boys—her ex-boyfriend and his best friend. I remember laying on my back with my eyes closed, feeling a hand begin to rub my stomach. Sensuous circles. Her nails brushing and teasing my lower abdomen as they moved down my body. Before I knew it, her hand was moving down my pants, as her fingers wrapped around the shaft of my penis and began sliding up and down.

Without a second thought (or any at all for that matter) I began mirroring her hand movements on her body—first massaging her stomach and then sliding my fingers into her underwear and inside of her. Only after she started moaning softly did I notice heavy breathing on the opposite side of the bed. Only then did I realize that only her right hand had been moving down my pants and that Brent was breathing heavily like she was.

I suddenly realized what was happening. My first thought: *I am hooking up with my best friend's girl. I am betraying the person I love most in this world. He is still in love with this person and I am treating her like a hand-job whore, like a drunken fling that I'll never have to see again.*

Hastily, I pulled my finger out of her and back toward my side, as if to undo what I had done, as if I could somehow take it all back. My finger, still wet from being inside her, suddenly bumped against something as my hand left her underwear—it was Brent's hand. She had been giving him a hand job at the same time and his hand had instinctively begun to move where mine had just been.

In an instant, I was sober. All the hands stopped. All the moaning ceased. The night rushed in through my eyes like lightning. The air tinged in my nostrils. What had I just done?

The following morning was awkward and quiet. He drove me to the train station. I went home on the train and stared out the window, wondering if I had lost the only person who had remained loyal to me during the hardest years of my life. Brent had been the only stable force, the only constant, the only friend who had never judged me or looked down on me or walked away when I needed him. Now I had betrayed him in a way that no amount of time could ever excuse. How do you ask for forgiveness for something like that?

The worst part was—I had no idea why I had done it. I had just sort of gone with the flow and played this part and not really considered either the consequences or the significance of what I was doing. I just wanted anything to make me feel wanted and loved and sexy. I didn't care how it happened. I didn't care who got in the way of that. In many ways, my new bad-boy persona had encouraged what I had just done. But it wasn't a persona or alcohol or anything else that was at fault—it was me. I was aware enough, and the same person I had always been, and I had done something despicable . . . to my best friend.

I was crushed. I finally started to realize the myth. This hero I had believed myself to be my whole life was nothing but a fraud. It had been nothing but a façade that I had bought into as though it was my birthright. Who was I to call myself a hero? And what is more important in the end—everyone believing you are the hero or actually *being* it?

In Colombian culture (and many cultures, for that matter)

appearances are everything. I think about all of the family secrets and layered ways of communicating in my family. Everything is in code. I remember finding out my uncle had cancer
by overhearing a conversation between my dad and a friend of
his from high school. He had been diagnosed two years earlier.
Another uncle was murdered in Colombia and it was called a
car accident, even to this day, by some family members. All
kinds of whispering and posturing takes place when any of my
cousins are having financial or marital problems.

This was my blueprint for how you communicate in the
world. For how you present yourself—you drop names, you
smile, you dress well, you make sure to be doing something
important at any given point in time . . . or say you are. The
contrast between how I appear and who I really am underneath
has always haunted me. I have always strived to be a good person, a good friend, a good son and sibling, and, ultimately, a
good man. But, by any of my standards (and maybe anyone's,
for that matter), I have always fallen short.

Two years after the incident with Erin, I had transferred to
a private school and seemed to turn over a new leaf in the process. Once again, I had become very politically involved in the
student body and also socially involved in the community. I
tutored kids twice a week; joined the student senate, where I was
elected vice president; and became cocaptain of the varsity basketball team. I was a leader again. I was a model citizen. I was
getting great grades and praise from teachers, and I won a bunch
of awards at the end of my first year. I was no longer the villain
I had become that night in Connecticut by betraying my best
friend. I was a hero again. Over time, things had seemed to return to normal. In typical guy fashion, Brent and I never spoke
about that night in Connecticut. Time passed. We were distant
for a few months. And then one night, after a few drinks with
other friends, we laughed together, he put his arm around me,
and I understood that he had moved on. Not that he had neces-

sarily forgiven me (not that I would expect him to), but we were brothers again.

Last year my best friend got sucker punched in the face at three o'clock in the morning. In the ER, his doctor told me that if he had been by himself and no one had called an ambulance, Brent would have bled to death in twenty minutes on that sidewalk.

Just before it happened, I was annoyed. I was exhausted and wanted to get home. Like always, Brent was daydreaming and lagging behind and texting (probably some random chick) as I walked across the street to the garage where our car was. I was trying to speed up our slow saunter home. Then, as the light turned to yellow and Brent stopped on the curb to look at his phone, a girl looked up and said casually, "Hi, guys, my name's Ashley," with a thick southern drawl. Brent and I, out of impulse, responded, "Hey Ashley," at the same time, right before a cluster of words and an overprotective boyfriend jumped forward to punch my best friend in the face. In that quick breath of a half second, in which I would have given anything to turn twenty-five feet into two feet, I felt time stop as I watched a stranger smash his fist across the vulnerable jaw of my best friend.

For the longest second of my life as he fell, no one moved. I looked the man in the face as shock and paralysis washed over me. Everyone was surprised. It was a one-in-a-million cheap shot, sucker punch, coldcock fist throw of a man trying so hard to prove his worth to a woman clearly more focused on a tall, handsome man texting on the sidewalk curb.

Then everyone broke out running. I ran after the man like he stole my grandmother's purse, while my best friend, head cracked open, lay bleeding out into the street. I looked back briefly and thought, *What am I doing? What about Brent? He's in the street.* And then later, *What would I have done if that guy hadn't run? Would I have fought to the death? Would I have cowered and run away? Would I have gotten my ass beat? Would I have knocked him out and gone to jail? Would both of us have just stood frozen and not moved?*

To this day, based on the "bleeding to death" narrative from Brent's doctor, I'm remembered as a hero for that night. All of the messiness and failures of that exchange carved away with only a single word remaining: hero. And how convenient it would be for it all to be so simple. Because it's too easy to get caught up with wanting to be a hero or a villain. To either define yourself as a "good guy" or a "bad boy." But, there is no such thing as either a hero or a villain. There is only a single act, the one you make in this moment, driven by your impulses, over in the bat of an eye. And sometimes these are actions we regret; sometimes we romanticize them after the fact (as though we had some greater plan), or we look back on them as the right thing to do. Sometimes they feel heroic in the moment, only to be remembered as cowardly in hindsight. Some seem inherently wrong and turn out to be the only choice we could have made. Some never resolve their moral positioning, even decades or generations later. I have met men serving life sentences for double murder who have caused a knot in my throat for their courage and grace, who have taught me about love and forgiveness. When I was a social worker after college, I would meet pimps who both scared me and made me laugh and smile with their big personalities and huge, conflicted hearts, crack dealers and bus drivers who were more polite than my kindergarten teacher ever was. Last week, I sat for an hour and listened to a homeless man play his alto saxophone on the Times Square subway platform like he had finally made it to heaven.

Each day I am alive, I try to give the world the best version of myself and treat each person with humanity and compassion, as I would hope to be treated. A lot of the time I fall short. I think about men trying to prove how tough they are or strong they are or "thug" they are. I think about men who try to prove how pious they are and righteous they are and brave they are.

Men who go to church twice a week or go to war and return with medals fastened over their hearts or men who raise kids like it's their chance to rectify their own childhood. Men trying so hard to prove their worth, constrained by the same hubris, ultimately the machismo, that imprisons us all.

There's a great quote by Germaine Greer that always sticks in my mind: "The tragedy of machismo is that a man is never quite man enough."

I am no hero, nor was I ever. Hopefully, though, I have inspired more waves of good with what I have done than bad. I know now that heroes and villains only exist in cartoons. Dr. King and Gandhi were both men. They were both human. They were both flawed. They were both, at times, crippled and haunted by their uncompromising visions of how this life should be lived. They both certainly fell short, I'm sure, of their own expectations of themselves.

I am no Dr. King or Gandhi. But what is most beautiful, and what has taken me almost fifteen years' hindsight to realize, is that neither were they. They were Martin and Mohandas, a preacher and former lawyer. Two men with extraordinary ideas about this world, and many of the same flaws, struggles, and compulsions with which we all wrestle. And it is okay to struggle—that is human—but it doesn't mean our ideas or actions have to be anything less than extraordinary. That ordinary men are not capable of the most divine examples of heroism.

HONEST/CLEAN

by Carlos Andrés Gómez

"I love it. I love the fight. It's just I don't think we should be fighting in that country. I don't think we should be fighting a war there for any reason whatsoever. But when it actually happens, for those few brief seconds it's—it's honest, it's clean. There's no politics involved when it actually happens."

—Joseph Hatcher, 1st Infantry Division, U.S. Army
(February 2004–March 2005, Iraq)

let me be
   a mold of soft foam
   inside reinforced silicone

let me be
   a soggy piece of plywood
   nailed across another

let me be
   a 50 cm scrap
   of folded cotton fabric

   an inch and a half
   of worn brown leather

   a simple grip of two plates
   of poplar wood or stainless steel

something made to hold
   someone
   or be held
   or worshipped
   and nothing else

encase me in iron
feed me fuel and gunpowder
make me machine sharp
fingerprint me cutting edge
a smart bomb
a docile land mine

not this vicious human need
don't make me this clouded, raw heart
all conflict and contradiction
all horror and beauty

let me be
    a mold of soft foam
    inside reinforced silicone

but not the upper arm
attached to it
not the soldier saluting
above the flag-encased coffin
of his best friend
don't call me prosthesis
as the ghost arm salutes
against his right temple

let me be
    a soggy piece of plywood
    nailed across another

not a cross
fitted with crude nails and screws
not a symbol of religion or belief
not lighter fluid ignited with a blow torch
not the man shouting to a gathered group
not the pale sheet hiding his cleft palate scar
the nightmares of his alcoholic father
the torment of poverty in Neshoba County, Mississippi
not the stutter he found hate to overcome

let me be
    a 50 cm scrap
    of folded cotton fabric

let my color be incidental
neither signifier nor signified
neither red nor blue
neither Athens Park blood
nor Eastside crip
not the symbol of family
a fatherless son finds
not the tears he hides
the hands he once used
for break-dancing and poems

let me be
    an inch and a half
    of worn brown leather

not a belt lashing
a little girl's face
not the father holding it
not those nightmares of his father
holding his little boy hand in scalding hot water
for forgetting his backpack in 4th grade
not the 41-year-old man
that still wets his bed
is still afraid of the dark

let me be
    simple
    a simple grip of two plates
    of poplar wood or stainless steel

attached to a large blade
or a heavy clip of steel tipped rounds
but not the hand
hewing the sugarcane
hacking up a neighbor
the shaking finger about to fire
a woman dressed in a black hijab
in the scope
about to pull a white flag
from her shopping bag
as the 2nd bullet exits
her 4th vertebra

let me be
    absolute

that woman's final breath
a heavy release from the heavens
flood rain like sobbing

a god
that never has to answer
for itself

I want to die an idea
a desperate myth in the sky

as the whole world kneels
not sure
if this is their last day
on earth *

_____

*   Connect Online: **"Honest/Clean"** http://www.cdbaby.com/cd/carlosandresgomez
(audio sample/download)

CHAPTER 6

Going to War

Manhood is proven on the battlefield. Call it right, call it wrong, this is what I was taught. Fight for the woman you love. If your friend gets in a fight, have his back. If someone calls you a bitch or faggot, pummel him. If a stranger physically confronts you, fight to the death. We are brought up to hold might over compassion. My ability to fight has always been more valued by society than my ability to love. It's probably why, for most of my life, I proudly called myself a fighter.

That's what you'd get if you asked me to describe myself in one word. I'd carved out an identity for myself as being the scrappy, tough kid who folks underestimated and then never gave in, gave up, or stood down. I had the toughest resolve, the most guts, grit—and would die over a nickel if I had to.

In basketball games, I was the enforcer. On every team I played on, I was the guy who stepped in after a dirty foul and confronted the perpetrator on the other team. Without even being asked, I'd usually clothesline or flagrantly foul that player on the next play, just to set things right.

In my family, my explosive temper was infamous. I would shout and punch and scream and break things. I'd lose my cool quickly and often. "Uh oh," they'd say, "there goes Carlitos again." Or as the family still refers to that period in my life: the "little Carlitos" era. I had one speed: infinity. And nowhere was a brake pedal to be found.

When I was ten years old I got in an argument with my cousin. We had been climbing a creek in these high mountains in North Carolina, having just reached a massive stone drop-off next to a waterfall. My cousin and I were deep into another debate about the Civil War (yes, this is the shit we argued about). And he had started in on another racist diatribe, letting the word "nigger" slip out a second time, after I'd already warned him. He probably said it mostly to push my buttons. Regardless, I punched him in the face, as hard as I possibly could. And he *almost* went over that forty-foot drop-off, just inches from where we were. My mind rarely processed consequences during that time in my life—before, during, or after anything happened. I just knew I had to enforce a boundary I'd set, so I socked him.

I was obsessed with war when I was a little kid. My mom thinks I was a soldier in my last lifetime because I was so infatuated with anything to do with war. When I was six years old, I won a prize for being a good marksman at a carnival. With just three shots, I hit all three of these tiny balloons floating around in an enclosed cage. No one else that entire weekend, adult or child, had been able to do it. I had to kneel on a stool to shoot because the rifle was almost as tall as I was.

That was the first time I ever fired any sort of gun. I'm sure my parents hadn't anticipated how obsessed I became with them, or how skilled I was. At every carnival from then on, I'd seek out the shooting game. Almost every single time, I'd win. It was inexplicable. Guns felt so natural to me, from the first time one touched my hands. I began to collect toy guns. Soon I had a drawer full of them—the gun drawer.

When I wasn't playing a soldier at war (with the guns from the gun drawer), I would draw these elaborate war sketches. I'd spend hours and hours meticulously sketching hundreds of soldiers facing off for battle. Then I would draw in fighter planes and submarines and warships. One of my most cherished possessions at that time was a book that illustrated the major conflicts in world history—from the conquests of Genghis Khan and Napoleon to World War I and Vietnam. Well before I could read, I pored over those brightly colored pages for hours, captivated by the regal uniforms and elaborate weapons.

I'm sure the stories from my mother's family only piqued my interest, as my uncle talked constantly about being stationed on a submarine during Vietnam and my grandfather being a double agent during World War II. It all sounded so exciting and brave. I wanted an exciting and brave life too. It seemed like everyone in my mom's family, going back multiple generations, both male *and* female, had been in some branch of the armed forces. I wanted to be a part of that legacy. I wanted to be a soldier when I grew up. More than anything else, though, I just wanted to be a part of *something*.

Early on, I learned the power of force—how to use my body as a weapon—and I quickly mastered it with consistency and precision. It's scary when I think about it now. I soon figured out that the easiest way to get whatever I wanted from my older sister was by making her cry. And the easiest way to make her cry was by punching her on top of her head with my middle knuckle. Then the sudden tears would flood down her cheeks and she would submit. I was only about seven years old or so. But I had proudly learned a cheap new trick: being the bully.

I was drunk with my ability to get what I wanted, the same

intoxicating, elusive power with which so many men are enamored. Shortly thereafter, I learned when I studied karate that real power is never having to exert it. To know you have the capability but never exercising it, only in the most dire of circumstances—that's real power. To only ever use it as a last resort—such as to save a life—and always with the utmost restraint. But I wasn't at that place in my life yet. I had finally gotten stronger than my sister, and I wanted to use that advantage to further my own selfish agenda—whatever that may have been: more candy, watching my favorite TV show, playing with a toy.

Only when I started seriously taking martial arts did I finally begin to curb my physical outbursts and aggression. I watched in awe at the control, presence, and strength of my sixth-degree black belt sensei, Master Lee. He was like a superhero to me. He seemed so peaceful and caring when you'd meet him, and then you'd see him break a board with a jumping roundhouse kick or "gently spar" with him—his hands felt like bricks. *This guy is a man,* I thought. *This guy is tough but doesn't need to show and tell everybody about it.* I had started to mature beyond the phase of just hitting and kicking my way to anything I wanted. It probably also had something to do with my mom having a very stern talk with me about how a boy should *never* hit a girl. Not that it's ever all right to hit anyone, but hitting a girl is the most shameful act of aggression. And she completely forbade it.

I had made great strides in my self-control by the end of elementary school, but, as usual, my quick temper occasionally still got the best of me. I stopped being driven to karate when I was nine after I kicked and punched my dad in the hallway one day. He was trying to discipline me for something. I'm sure it was necessary, but I was too young to understand that I needed boundaries. I was confusing thoughtful parenting with him bullying me, so I felt like I needed to fight back. It wasn't until the following summer, at a big family reunion in Colombia, that I finally learned the price and seriousness of my violent phase.

Almost the entire family on my father's side had planned to spend a week together up in the mountains at my Tío (Uncle) Luís Ernesto's ranch. Everybody was there: uncles, aunts, cousins, my grandmother, long-lost people we called family even without any blood relation. Every night was a party. We would have a big celebratory feast full of drunken stories and nostalgic wisecracking. It still remains one of my most precious childhood memories. In the days before we traveled up to the mountains, I played basketball for hours with my two favorite cousins, Mauricio and Natalie.

I had always been the baby. By a long shot. Mauricio was about six years older than me, and Natalie had almost eleven on me. Mauricio was athletic and social, a total ladies' man, with a playful sense of humor and a relaxed, thoughtful disposition. Natalie was the life of the party. Sensitive and opinionated, standing just over six feet tall, and athletic as well—she and I were like long-lost twins. They were both heroes to me. When I grew up, I wanted to be just like both of them.

The first day up in the mountains with the family, we did the usual: ride horses, milk cows, eat a big lunch together. That afternoon we took a walk around the ranch, led around by a couple of the cowboys who worked on the land. They saw my big, naïve eyes and anxious heart leaping from my mouth and immediately knew they had me in the palm of their hand. Those guys were like gods to me: tough, strong, and seemingly unafraid of anything. As the afternoon wore on, the stories they were telling became taller and taller, hamming it up for the gullible little gringo from New York.

That's when one of them said to me, "See that big pig over there?" pointing to a boar that looked the size of a small bear. "Yeah—that one. He ate a little boy last year."

I laughed this time, head back. *How dumb does this guy think I am?*

But nobody else even cracked a smile.

"No, really. It was a small child that was walking down this road to go get water. And that pig dragged him in here and killed him. He was hungry, so he ate him."

I laughed again, this time watching the men's eyes. And nothing. Neither of them even smirked as they gave the Oscar-winning performance of a lifetime, sending a frightening chill down my spine. *Are they telling the truth?* I wondered. I wasn't sure, so I scurried off to go ask my dad.

Of course, they weren't. They were just having fun with me. But I had been totally fooled. On the way to find my dad, I stumbled into my cousin Natalie and told her what I had heard. I was trying so hard to guard the fear in my throat. I didn't want her to know I had been shaken, in case they *had* been joking. But even if it was the truth, I wanted to be tough like those two cowboys. I smiled as though I knew it was a joke, but the earnestness in my voice must have outed me.

Maybe, then, she was convinced for a moment too. As similar as Natalie and I are, both gullible and full of belief in people, it wasn't outlandish for her to have believed a little boy actually got eaten by that pig too. But she was thinking I was trying to pull one over on her now.

"They didn't say that, Carlitos. That's crazy," she said, dismissing the story.

"No, they *did*! I *swear* they did! Go ask them." I was hurt that my favorite cousin didn't take me at my word.

"A pig *ate* a little boy?" she challenged.

"That's what they said! I swear to God," I said.

"Swear to *God*? Wow . . . Wow. I didn't think you would but you did. You just *broke* a 'swear to God' . . . ohhhhh . . . You're going to hell! You're going to he-*elllll*," she singsonged out, holding her index fingers in a cross as though I were possessed by the devil.

"I'm not lying! Natalie! *They said it!*" I screamed.

"Tell that to God because . . ." she began.

And I snapped. All of the rage and hurt and humiliation and insecurity thundered up through my body like a lightning bolt as I swung with my right hand and slapped her as hard as I possibly could across the face.

I can still hear the gasp from my grandmother, two aunts, and father, barely twenty feet away from us, as though all the tires on an eighteen-wheeler had just blown out at the same time on an interstate. I watched, horrified, as Natalie's glasses flew off her face and shattered on the ground. She was stunned. Tears swelled up in her eyes. I knew that it wasn't the hard slap that had caused those tears as much as it was that I had betrayed my favorite cousin. I had hit one of my favorite people in the world. And there was no possible way to take it back.

There is no worse shame than I felt at that moment, as her tender eyes looked down at me with horror and shock.

Before I could say a word, I felt my dad's firm arm grab me by the collar, as he gruffly said, "Carlitos. Let's go."

Most of that hour-long walk we took is a blur. We walked in complete silence for a while. It felt like a few years. Then my dad started in on a diatribe about how unacceptable what I had just done was. He kept saying, "I just can't *believe* . . . ," and I sort of blocked out the rest. I bawled the whole way as we seemed to do endless laps around the outside of the ranch house where we were staying. At the end of the walk, I crawled into one of the empty rooms and tucked myself into the cobwebs and dusty floor beneath one of the beds. I had never wanted to be swallowed into a black hole so much in my entire life.

Around dinnertime, my dad came and found me.

"Come on, it's time for dinner," he said, compassionately

locking eyes and running his fingers through my hair. I was an immature little boy in the midst of trying to figure stuff out. And I had to learn a tough lesson by slapping my favorite cousin. It was awful seeing her at dinner that night looking at me with hurt in her eyes. Her forgiveness inspired me to grow up. Since that day, never have I aggressively laid my hands on a woman. I feel lucky to have encountered that feeling in my chest and learned that life lesson by the time I was ten. Little did I know, though, this was only the beginning of my education on violence, as I quickly learned how permanent its consequences could be.

When I was nineteen and working at a summer camp, one of our cocounselors, Cynthia, didn't show up one day. The next day she didn't appear either. No one had heard anything from her. Concerned about her, we tried calling and emailing her to no avail. Finally, on the third day, we found out why she had been absent.

Her fifteen-year-old cousin had just arrived from Puerto Rico. With very limited English and overwhelmed with culture shock, he sat in the backseat of his uncle's car staring out at the unfamiliar sights of this strange new place he now lived. They were driving down the interstate when a state trooper pulled them over. His uncle immediately slowed down into the breakdown lane, bringing the run-down sedan full of Latinos to a stop. The state trooper drew his firearm, yelling for everyone to show their hands. Maybe Cynthia's cousin wanted to hear what was being muffled by the closed windows. Maybe in Puerto Rico or San Juan you show your hands by holding them out of the window. Regardless, Cynthia's cousin, flustered and scared, tried desperately to roll his window down and the state trooper shot him in the head.

I tell that story not so much to make a point regarding police misconduct or racial profiling but a much more profound and far-reaching one: Men of color live their lives at war. They are hunted and seen as disposable and, often, treated like animals. Ask a room of black men living in a city how many of them have been "spot-checked" and patted down and frisked for no reason. Then, ask them how many times it has happened. I've never been patted down and frisked randomly once in my life. When I was unlawfully arrested in Philadelphia during my junior year of college, it was after my name had been shouted multiple times by housemates as I challenged three police officers who were harassing one of my guests. It remains one of those examples in my life where I could feel, like a button had been pushed, the shift in behavior of the police toward me as they realized I was a light-skinned Latino man.

So how do we value ourselves when everything around us tells us we're worth shit? How do we learn to drop our weapons when every day of our lives is spent at war? Like that moment in Connecticut when I returned to my old stomping ground in high school, feeling the antagonistic stares and fear from my former friends, we're expected to be monsters. And similarly to how I responded to the double-edged sword of that bad-boy tag they bestowed upon me, many of us say, "All right, fuck it. That's all I can ever be? You want a monster? I'll *show* you a fuckin' monster."

One week after my girlfriend and I moved into our apartment in Bed-Stuy we were walking home just before midnight. Her sister and brother-in-law were visiting us for the weekend on a warm, clear summer night. Walking back from the subway, we decided to save some time and cut through Sumner Projects. Suddenly, just a few blocks from home, we heard a loud *pop-pop-pop*. I tumbled onto my girlfriend and ducked behind the closest parked car, grabbing her sister and brother-in-law to get down as well. A few more shots rang out from across the street, some hitting within feet of where we had been walking.

As we crawled on our stomachs behind more parked cars and eventually around the corner, I glanced up and saw what couldn't have been a boy of more than fifteen holding that gun. Who knows why he was shooting? Maybe he thought he saw someone on his turf who shouldn't have been. Maybe that someone was us. Maybe he just wanted to play with his new toy, feel the power of warm steel in his young, still-growing hands. Maybe he'd been called soft or a bitch or a pussy by someone for never pulling its trigger. I remember being shocked at who I saw holding that weapon. It was a kid. And he wasn't scaring anyone without that gun. I certainly wouldn't have taken him seriously otherwise.

Moreover, in a world of such desperate extremes—where the disparity is so appalling it reeks of historic conspiracy—how is a man of color to be heard? How is he to be listened to when everything around him is a reminder of his irrelevance, his invisibility? When the most notable memory of your people's history in your public school textbook is a short blurb on slavery and a photo of a lynched black man hanging from a poplar tree? One morning on my way to work as a social worker in Harlem, I got one of the more vivid, terrifying examples of what I'm talking about, of how often men of color, particularly, are reminded of their place in society.

I was on a packed subway train heading uptown during rush hour. The capacity of the train car had probably been reached about ten people ago and thirty seconds prior. A black gentleman, rather nerdy-looking with wire-rimmed spectacles, a peacoat, and dreadlocks trailing down his back squeezed into what probably should have been the last spot on the train. As the doors began closing, a white man pushed his way in, aggressively shoving his forearm into the chest of the black man.

"Stop pushing," the black man demanded, his intonation rising anxiously.

"I'm not," the white man responded defiantly, extending his forearm closer into the black man's chest.

"I told you to stop." Now the black man's eyes were welling up as he scanned the subway car urgently as though looking for a friend.

The white man locked eyes with him, not saying a word, as

he took a half step forward until he was almost at the black man's chin. People were backing away from the car, that tense moment any city dweller knows all too well when conflict arises. Most people retreat, but a handful move closer. To be honest, I thought this crazy white dude might be on PCP or having a psychotic episode and completely unaware of what he was doing. Or, he had a weapon he was about to pull out and spray this packed subway car with. So I slowly inched closer to the two men, meeting the eyes of a tall, well-built older black man who seemed to have my same idea: If this nutcase tries to turn an Uzi on this throng of people, one of us has to wrestle him to the ground.

Suddenly, before either of us could make our way to the doorway, the doors sprung open and the white man leapt into the black man's chest, wrapping his arms around his torso. Another white man, seemingly out of nowhere, grabbed the black man around the neck. And then *another* white man joined in the fray, dragging the helpless black man onto the Times Square subway platform.

"They're skinheads!" someone yelled, as I stumbled through the people in front of me with a few others trying to get to the men. As one man clamped the black man's arms, the first man took turns punching the black man in the face, his broken glasses on the concrete floor, tears streaming down his face— clumps of his locks strewn all over the ground.

More screams came from the New Yorkers tumbling out of the train, one of the proudest moments I've ever experienced in this city, as everyone flooded out to try to stop what was happening. A handful of uniformed police soon showed up, and we were informed that these three white men were, in fact, all undercover NYPD officers. The one who was punching the black man told the clothed officer he had just been assaulted on the train, and he was taking the man in.

A group of us who witnessed the entire event—me, that

well-built older black man (a Vietnam War vet), a Jamaican nurse, a Mexican day laborer, and a retired Jewish woman— followed the slew of officers, now leading the battered black man away in handcuffs. Each of the NYPD officers covered his badge number while he walked, as if by habit, refusing to reveal his identity. To make a long story short, I ended up being a primary witness in a closed police misconduct trial at police headquarters in Manhattan and also for the civil suit the black gentleman filed against the city and police officers after all charges were dismissed. Rarely have I felt more threatened by men with guns than when I testified at the police trial. It felt like, at any moment, I might get shot "accidentally" for attacking one of the officers there. Which brings me to the questions that continue to haunt me long after that day, in spite of the courageous and assertive response of most of those subway passengers.

If three white men can beat up a black man over a space in a subway car on the Times Square platform during rush hour, where is any man of color safe? I have no idea if any or all of those three white police officers got away with what they did, but, regardless, the mere fact of their entitled action is enough for serious concern. If an overzealous neighborhood "watchman" can gun down a seventeen-year-old boy who is holding nothing but a bag of Skittles and an iced tea, where is *any* male of color, regardless of age, safe? Where does this war end? When does it ever pause and stop? Where is there a safe haven? Or is everywhere a battlefield?

It's necessary to contextualize race when we talk about violence *among* men as well, along with identifiers like class and other criteria that help explain why people are dehumanized, alienated, and disenfranchised by systems and institutions. When the only consistent force in a person's life is violence, how can you expect him to be peaceful? To know how to communicate in a contentious exchange? To know how to defuse a volatile confrontation? And when our government figures act like those police officers did or carry out unjust, ruthless wars, how are we not expected to follow suit?

When I walk in the city with my black girlfriend, occasionally men have said things to us. It has always been black men. It's either a challenge to my masculinity as a non-black man or to her as a "sellout" or a "traitor" for not having a partner of her own race. The hardest thing for me in those moments is to walk away, when I know that I must. And I don't mean that I want to punch any of those guys in the face (maybe occasionally), but usually I just urgently want to talk. I want to unpack all that's happening in that moment. I want the guy to know that my dating my girlfriend is not an indictment of his humanity or self-worth. I am no proof that he is less than a man. But in a world in which everything, from our textbooks to the media messages we absorb to the words we use, tells that black man that he is less than I am, how can the mere sight of my face not emasculate him in some way? With images and tales of black men *literally* being emasculated—and I mean castrated, balls cut off and lit on fire, and this in our not-too-distant past—until we start to really unpack *that*, the pain in this country will continue to rain out in fists and bullets and hurtful words.

It's funny. I get aggravated beyond belief sometimes with how black men respond to me and my girlfriend, yet I react the same way to seeing a preppy hipster white guy with his Latina girlfriend, a guy who probably doesn't look too different from me. I look at them with utter disgust, my body completely unaware of the absurd irony and hypocrisy in my reaction. I remember all the white girls in college saying they like that "all-American look," and then, the Latina girls who graduated from private Quaker schools like mine agreeing with them. Or those same girls saying how they like "soccer players" and "British accents" and "foreign guys" (but never meaning an international student from Nigeria or Cambodia or Bangladesh). And the subtext never needs to be vocalized because it's so thoroughly understood.

White men are at the top of the food chain. Most people who see me, understandably, put me in that group. I look at the Latina woman with her white hipster boyfriend on the L train and I shudder. I have judged both of them, as if I know their entire life stories, as if I have some right to. The fact of the matter, though, is that I know barely anything. And, oftentimes, that moment of disgust has little to do with thought and everything to do with a feeling rising out of my gut and into the back of my throat.

I am empathetic and angered and understanding and frustrated with what I see in some black men's faces when I walk by with my girlfriend. More than anything else, it hurts me. It hits me in my stomach in the most fragile spot. I want to deconstruct that moment. I want to address it together, right then, by talking about it. But men rarely celebrate a shared language anymore. I sometimes wonder if we ever did.

Sometimes I feel like men are whistling at passing women in a desperate attempt to discover a language, any language, as a way to be heard and noticed, to let other men know that they exist, to let anyone know that they are *here*, alive—right now. When my cousin stopped listening to me as we climbed that creek, or my other cousin, Natalie, called me a liar, or my sister, Sara, didn't give me what I wanted, I would punch, slap, or grab. I wanted a language for what was happening inside. I was desperate for a language it would take me years to discover. Sometimes the mere proof of that language can be the most daunting weapon.

Shortly after I'd quit my social worker job, I was out at a nightclub in Manhattan. It was inching past three o'clock in the morning and we'd entered what I like to call the "hour of desperation"—when the night starts to unveil all of your ghosts, when the loneliness and the insecurity start to become unbearable, when the drinks have been too many. The options for a late-night hook-up are getting smaller. And, now, the men are puffing out their chests, toe-to-toe with each other, each trying to prove he matters.

I was making my way to get my coat and leave. I'd noticed that the club was now almost entirely men, black and Latino, all of us seeing the light at the end of the tunnel. The night was almost done. Only a handful of single women remained and they were making their way out. The pressure was high to stake whatever claims we wanted that night, to have made this night count.

My shoulder brushed the chest of another man, a muscular Latino man about my same height and age. I gently put my hand up in apology, as he pushed me hard with his right hand and yelled, "Bitch, you fuckin' crazy? I will *fuck* you up."

Gathering my footing after falling back for a second, I took an assertive step forward. I'm not sure why. I did it instinctively. For some reason, I wasn't intimidated by him. Maybe I should have been, but I knew I didn't want to walk away.

It wasn't so much independent thoughts I remember coursing through my mind as much as a serene, almost time-suspending awareness, as if the universe was about to share with me some life-changing revelation. Our eyes met, his white-hot with rage and fire, mine still catching up to the moment. It felt like time froze, the music turned off, everyone in the room turned toward us and gently watching. And I looked in the men's faces and saw everyone I loved. I saw my dad across the dance floor leaning against the far wall. And my best friend, Iso, from Northeast in the DJ booth. A guy in a wheelchair was my friend's brother. And the bouncer was my friend Eric. And the guy who had just pushed me . . . was me. I had just pushed myself. And now I was going to kill myself, in a desperate, prideful attempt to prove I existed.

Before I knew it, tears were pouring down my face. That's

when time started again. The Latino man's expression now turned into a contorted scowl of confusion and shock. All of his friends' faces soon mirrored his, as the tears streamed down my cheekbones and onto the beer-soaked floor of that nightclub.

"What the *fuck* . . ." The man was now looking at me as though I were Charles Manson or a nuclear warhead. "Yo, fo' real, son. Chill. Just chill out, man," he said, backing up and bumping into one of the chairs behind him as though I had pulled out a grenade.

Before I knew it, all of his friends were backing away from me as though I were a loaded machine gun, as though I had just pulled the pin on the grenade I was holding. In many ways, I had. In looking around that room, full of all of these beautiful men, so ready to die over nothing, I had committed a cardinal sin: I cried. I had done something more outlandish, more "thug," more shocking than anything else I could have done. In a strange way, it might have actually scared the hell out of that Latino guy whose chest I bumped with my shoulder. I had dropped the performance of manhood.

When he said, "Chill," what he was really saying was, "Fuck—are you crazy? Are you about to do something totally insane? Damn, if you're crying like that in a nightclub in New York City, *after* taking a step toward me; who the fuck knows what you'll *do*." That's how foreign our emotions are to us. It's a language so strange and daunting and frightening it carries the power of a bomb. It is an explosive trapped in our chests, waiting to detonate.

As much as I wish I could say that the nightclub crying incident was some planned act of courage or symbolic protest on my part, it wasn't. It was just one of those strange moments, where my body overtook my mind and acted without my permission. Through some deep-rooted wisdom of my bones and flesh and sweat, I did something unimaginable. Only years later have I even begun to understand what it was that took place. This happened in an era when I was still very much a pacifist, for the most part, but certainly not someone who avoided confrontation.

All of that changed in the fall of 2008 when I visited Rwanda. I walked, dumbstruck, through the country's largest memorial to their 1994 genocide in which more than eight hundred thousand people were killed in a little more than three months. The pictures and images and writings on the walls of that place are beyond description. I decided that I had to look at every single artifact and word in that memorial. No matter what it made me feel. This genocide happened because of who I am and how I live my life, the European colonialism that brought me to my mother's womb, the shoes on my feet, the complacency and privilege and entitlement I continue to benefit from in my life. The world turned its head while neighbors hacked each other to pieces and families were quite literally torn apart. I started at the beginning and began scrawling every single word I saw into my journal, each word seeming as if it were from the mouth of God.

You look at this, Carlos. You take a good look. This is Emmett Till's coffin. This is Harvey Milk's body. This is what men do to each other. This is what we are at our worst, with decades of brutality allowing the stakes to raise so high there's no going back. And this blood is on your hands too, I heard in my head, hot, selfish tears pouring down my face, a guilty knot, like an apple core, lodged in my throat. It was all just too much. I was so overwhelmed. I had so many emotions coursing through me that my lips went numb, and I couldn't feel my face. My body, once again, was taking over.

And that's when I looked up and noticed something, something that startled me more than anything else I had seen in that entire memorial: my Superman sheets. There they were.

Hanging from the wall. The same ones I had had on my bed until the summer before high school, except these had dark stains strewn across the faded colors. This could have been me. Those toddler's shoes could have been my little brother Nico's, and that little girl's bracelet could have been Sara's, and that torn corny sweater could have been Papi's. It felt as though I were falling down a well, as though I were drowning. Everything in my body was working on overdrive, but everything was moving in slow motion.

I blinked and stood frozen in the family photos room, staring at tens of thousands of pictures, side by side, floor to ceiling, of people who had been murdered:

A middle-aged mother with her hair done, dressed for a night out.

A daughter doing a silly dance at a family reunion.

A graduation.

A young couple on their wedding day.

A laughing grandmother, all teeth and joy, holding her granddaughter's hand as she took her first steps.

Blowing out candles at a sweet sixteen party.

A cocky teenage playboy proudly flaunting his new vest.

A man bowing his head for communion in church.

A crooked, bucktoothed smiling big brother with his little brother in a headlock.

And finally, this photo:

*A father and son in matching new jogging outfits
about to sprint down a hill.*

I have an almost identical shot with my papi. Both of these people had been hacked to death with a machete. I saw my dad's solid, generous gaze in this Rwandese man's face, his son reminding me of my mischievous, excited swagger.

Why? Why? For what? Such simple and foolish and ignorant and entitled words to throw around, all crashing into my head. I just couldn't understand, as I slowly moved through the children's sanctuary, haunted by these wall-size photos of children, most laughing or with carefree, playful smiles, all killed during the genocide. After the last photo, there is an open doorway leading out into a beautiful field. It looks out on a breathtaking view for maybe a half mile ahead, one of the rare spots of this country without some kind of family settlement or farming plot.

I finally felt like I could breathe. Wow. What mercy after six hours of that memorial to give us this pure vision of hope. To look out on this open field of beautiful grass, bathed in a setting sun, and know that tomorrow will be a new day. As trite as that sounds, in that moment, I drew hope from that. Then I heard echoes of those heavily worn-out words in post-genocide countries rattling through my brain: *Never again, Never again, Never again.*

For the first time in six hours, I released the tension in my chest and took a deep, breathy exhale, taking a step forward toward that gorgeous field to lie down. But I stumbled, feeling my right shoe brush against something hard. I glanced down—spotting an easy-to-miss, austere plaque on the ground that read:

Please, do not step on mass grave. 258,000 people are buried here.

"Today all of the violence in me died." I wrote that in my journal that day. I hope that it's true.

I still puff out my chest sometimes, walk down the sidewalk like I'm a tough guy, feel the combative streak in my pride screaming to punch some drunk asshole in the face. I pray that I never do, that I always remember something someone very close to me recently taught me.

His brother was shot in the back of the head, murdered in cold blood by the eighteen-year-old drug dealer his brother had stolen from. The eighteen-year-old girl, that drug dealer, lived just three blocks away from the young man she killed. They were neighbors. They went to the same school, had mutual friends. Who knows? Maybe they even played on the same playground once when they were toddlers, fighting over a plastic shovel. Or maybe she shared it with him.

In the neighborhood where my friend is from, he is a person of power and stature, a former football star and hero to many. In his neighborhood there is a code and consequence to what took place. As he drove with his wife back to his hometown for his little brother's funeral, he got a phone call.

"We know who did it," the voice on the other end said. "I'm standing outside of her house now. Give me the word. And it's done."

My friend held the phone for a few moments, thinking back to everything he saw growing up as a kid. Brains splattered on the sidewalk curb from a gunshot victim, his siblings hooked on crack cocaine, bored kids wandering the streets—their single moms struggling to make ends meet to week's end—those same kids looking for somewhere to go. So many of them found gangs or drugs or hustling. My friend found football and escaped the fate of his brother.

"Yo, did you hear me? I said give me the word. I'm outside of her house."

Maybe my friend thought back to his brother and him throwing a football in his yard, or to the poverty that ravaged the lives of the beautiful people he called family, whether or not they were kin. Maybe he thought back to all of the things they each had inside of themselves when they weren't strung out or depressed or scared. He knew that what he said on the phone in this moment would alter not just his life forever but set an entire chain reaction into motion that there was no coming back from.

"No. Just call the cops, man," he said finally. "It's over."

He recently told me he was fifty-fifty at first. Then he looked at his beautiful wife and his hands he had now softened to hold things instead of break them. He thought of not just that eighteen-year-old girl but her mother, just a few blocks away from his own. Maybe the girl had an older brother too.

Maybe, one day, I will be half the man my dear friend is. I remember him each and every day I walk out into this world and onto a battlefield. Maybe we might all learn something from him, learn about what it really means to be courageous and tough and show grace, in spite of everything you've known and everyone around you saying otherwise.

To me, he is a true fighter, a real warrior—the kind of fighter I now aspire to become.

SAYING GOODNIGHT

by Carlos Andrés Gómez

I looked for Superman
and he was gone.

Out of the rubble, a sepia-stained photograph
with a small boy laughing, flanked by four sisters,
propped on his father's lap.

The ache in my chest felt familiar, wind knocked out,
and I could barely watch but hardly turn away
as my dad held the phone to his ear like a shell
having just lost its ocean sound.

His mom, my Abuelita, had gone to bed
and he wouldn't be able to see her before
we left.

This is probably the last time we're going to see Abuelita,
he said to us, throwing away the words,
with an eerie matter-of-factness,

the reserve ducts behind his eyes
gently dampening the outskirts of his irises.

I knew then that there would never be enough time
to say *I love you* to the ones I protect myself from.

When it all cuts so deep
you fasten the wounds closed like curtains,
afraid that everything will flood out
if you open them.

I don't want to need an excuse

to place my hand softly over my grandmother's
shaking knuckles while she watches her *telenovelas*

or hug my sister for too long when I remember
how she taught me to taste food with my fingers

or say something I might have put off
until the last possible second I could.

It's hard to see a god lose his grace
and suddenly become more beautiful

when he falters,
the moon like a spotlight
amplifying it all.

We stood in that dimly lit parking lot
below her high rise for far too long, as if
the moment had a long awaited answer
we would have to earn to take with us.

As the time passed, my father's wrinkles deepened
in the shadows, his walk crumpled slightly near the car

and I opened my mouth to tell him something
I'd been building the courage for 12 years to say,
forgetting it suddenly,

when he turned back around.

CHAPTER 7

Weakness:
The Death of Superman

I have a hard time asking for or accepting help. I am aware that it's such a silly "man thing" to see seeking support as some sort of failure, but I still struggle with it. I spend so much of my life encouraging other men to value themselves—acknowledge when they're hurt or tired or depressed and get support—yet I rarely do so myself. Yes, I am the worst kind of hypocrite, I know. And I consider myself lucky that the person closest to me, my girlfriend, constantly reminds me: "Baby, you need to take better care of yourself. You're not Superman."

I had a show in Toronto last year. The theme of the conference was "Behind the Masc"—attempting to "un-mask," so to speak, and challenge many of the traditional notions of masculinity. I was delivering the keynote address, which I did through some of the most excruciating pain of my life. My abdomen felt like it was being ripped in two, a dagger twisting into my gut each time I took a breath or spoke.

A week earlier it had been Thanksgiving. My mother asked me to retrieve a section of an oak dining table from the basement. Despite my protests, my girlfriend had come downstairs with me to assist. Two things:

1. She had suggested I remove the three boxes obstructing the path of the table leaf I was picking up.
2. She had offered to help.

What did I do? Well, I chuckled (as if I would ever need help, right?) and told her, "I got it," and reached over the three boxes to lift up the heavy section of oak wood with the worst possible lifting form. When what I was lifting turned out to be much heavier than I had anticipated, did I stop? Did I put it down and change my form or move the boxes in the way? Of course not. I just exerted more power and force, finally lifting it off the ground and then feeling a pop in my abdomen. As I winced hard and shrieked, my girlfriend scolded me for being such a stubborn man. She was right. Did I go to the doctor after what had happened? No. Did I take anything for the pain? No. Did I clench my teeth and bear it? Yep. Good ol' masculinity.

So, now, suddenly I found myself on the verge of giving an important keynote at a conference in Toronto, without one minute of sleep. Why? Because I had gritted my teeth all night in my hotel room, worrying that I might have an umbilical hernia or appendicitis or some other awful condition I discovered on WebMD.com. One of my best friends is an emergency room doctor. In fact, two of my three best friends are doctors, yet I turned to the Internet to diagnose my condition. Why? I was embarrassed. I was proud. And those feelings were leading me down a road of absurdity.

It wasn't until my dear friend Eric, the ER doctor, diagnosed what was wrong with me (after taking a cab directly to his apartment from the airport upon returning) that I found out I had torn something in my abdominal wall. I spent about ten days lying on my back in bed, taking loads of ibuprofen and alternating ice and heat packs. It took nearly a month for me to fully recover. If I hadn't pushed it, the injury probably would have healed on its own in maybe a week or two, but it ended up taking a month, all because I tried to be Superman. Or thought I was. Well, I'm not. My girlfriend, once again, is right. But, as I've seen with other men close to me, it is only when Superman is so obviously gone ("dead," so to speak) that we acknowledge our limits. It is the only time we admit that we, in fact, are susceptible to that cardinal sin of manhood: vulnerability.

I grew up scared to death of how sensitive I was. I always felt like I had something to prove because of it. I would dread losing control of my emotions and the rare case where I couldn't cover up my real feelings with anger. Anger was my go-to shield. If I was about to cry, if something hurt my feelings, I would fight back with all of the venom and spite and rage in my body. Do everything I could to push the "girly" feelings down. Only little girls cry, right? Everyone knows that.

This is what boys learn early playing sports. "What are you, a little girl? Stop crying." Or later, "What are you, a little bitch? Faggot?" And on it goes. This is how we learn to cope with what we feel—physically and emotionally. Your feelings are hurt? Suck it up. Or punch that motherfucker. You sprained your ankle? Walk it off. Retape it and get back in the game. That's how I learned things go.

Sports—basketball in particular—were the centerpiece of my life until I was seventeen years old. Basketball was, and will always be, my first love. It was where I learned most of the pivotal lessons of manhood. It was where I developed my work ethic and many of the values I still hold dear, such as teamwork and honor and poise. And most important: being tough. You play no matter what. I had the flu and played. I tore ligaments in both of my thumbs, dislocating them at different points, and played. I broke my right wrist at basketball camp when I was twelve and played. I broke my toe and played.

My hero was Michael Jordan. I had watched him play in the NBA finals against the Utah Jazz and drop thirty-eight with a 103-degree fever. I remember Larry Bird banging his head hard in a playoff game and going back in. Or Isaiah Thomas severely spraining his ankle and getting back in there to score sixteen points in a few short minutes of a key fourth quarter. Those guys were who I wanted to be. You'd have to handcuff me to the bench to prevent me from playing. And that was true for practice as well—rain, snow, sleet—I would be out there playing, healthy or not. The greats were out there doing drills and shooting free throws, so I would be as well.

There were a few points in my life when I wasn't able to play through the pain, when, symbolically, I couldn't keep playing and I had to admit I couldn't do it alone. These instances were necessary to me accepting that I was not infallible. There are times, much more so now than ever, when I must seek out the support of someone to get me through a hard time. And I don't just mean physically; I'm also talking about emotionally. Most of the times I do seek help now, in fact, are related to some emotional or psychological hurdle I'm struggling to overcome. But in those formative years when I habitually pushed through the pain in basketball and other sports, there was no way I would ever admit to anyone that I couldn't cope with an emotional or psychological obstacle by myself. It would be an admission that I had fallen short of everything I was expected to be. A powerful example of this happened in sixth grade.

Middle school isn't easy. I was downright scared going in. I had to be independent and responsible, and try to make my way in a strange new place with kids who dressed different and spoke in a hip way. Everything seemed more sophisticated than elementary school. It's a time to grow up and start to hold your own. But along with the fear came a solid dose of excitement as well. Most of that excitement came from one thing: girls.

Oh yes. I was excited. I was barely stumbling my way into puberty, but I was fascinated by girls who were starting to develop and look like women. I was smitten with practically every girl I met. I wanted a girlfriend just like those older eighth grade boys who seemed like grown men to me.

In one of my classes was a girl named Bianca, who was my lab partner. She had been held back twice and was nearly fourteen years old. She was pretty, but something about her gave me the chills. She barely spoke, and when she did it was in a high-pitched whisper. She seemed completely uninterested in anything to do with school, her eyes eerily trained on me throughout the period. For all of those forty-eight minutes she would just stare at me, occasionally adding a comment here and there.

Everyone at school talked about how she was crazy. They said awful things about her, as middle schoolers often do, making fun of her fully developed breasts, being tall and lanky and clumsy, of living on the wrong side of town, and also for being adopted; her mother looked like she was in her seventies and always seemed so harsh and severe. It bothered me how the rest of the kids treated her, so I was nice to her. We weren't really friends, but we were cool with each other.

One day at home, while I was eating my Cap'n Crunch cereal and watching *Full House*, I got a phone call. It was Bianca. She wanted to ask me a question. Her friend Erica liked me, and she wanted to know if I liked her too. You know how it goes. Typical sixth grade stuff. I wasn't really into Erica but felt flattered and excited by the attention. A girl *likes* me? Like *that*? It made my skin tingle. I thought about all of the stuff people do in middle school when they "like" each other—going to the movies, holding hands, *kissing*. Wow. This is a new world. I stayed on the phone for a while, enchanted by the idea of someone being infatuated with me. It was the first time since moving to the United States that a girl had "liked" me. It was a high like nothing I had encountered.

Finally, I told Bianca (and a giggling girl in the background, probably Erica) that I had to go. I hung up and went back to my cereal and television. I daydreamed about other girls liking me—the ones that I had a crush on. *How amazing that must be when two people have a crush on each other at the same time,* I thought to myself. *Wow.* Middle school was a whole new ball game. I couldn't wait for what was to come.

The next day at school Bianca passed me a note. I opened it and found one of the classic surveys of adolescent infatuation: "Do you like me?" with the provided options of "Yes," "No," or "Maybe." I didn't like Bianca, not like that, but I felt bad and couldn't bring myself to check "No." Who would do that to this girl? Why add that rejection to what she deals with already? But that didn't mean I was going to check "Yes." And "Maybe" just seemed like a mind-fuck, so I just shoved the note in my pocket and decided to figure it out later.

The entire day I walked around with that note in my pocket, overwhelmed by the predicament I was in. I hated this shit. Why did she have to like me? With Erica, I didn't feel bad saying I didn't like her, but it was different with Bianca. And now I felt like there was no way for me not to come off as the bad guy *and* not hurt her feelings. How do I win? How does anyone?

So I decided not to respond at all. I hadn't *caused* this. Had I? What—by being nice to her? I was just going to keep being cordial with her and move on with my life. Eventually, she'd get the message and we could all move on. I had made peace with the circumstances and felt proud of myself for reaching what I thought was a mature resolution.

The next day Bianca was quiet and withdrawn. She didn't

make eye contact with me and seemed angry. As little as she spoke before, she said even less now. The few words she did say were pointed and cutting. It was pretty obvious that she was hurt I hadn't responded to the note. I felt bad but relieved that, at least, the message had been communicated. Now it'll be done. We can all move on.

After school that day I was once again eating a bowl of Cap'n Crunch cereal and watching *Full House* when the telephone rang. I picked up and heard peculiar, high-pitched music and heavy breathing rumbling through the phone.

"Hello?" I asked. "Hello?"

Must be a wrong number, I told myself as I hung up quickly. Then it rang again.

"Who is this?" I was getting angry now. Actually, I was more scared than anything, but I was trying to regain some control. Once again, I heard the sinister music, as if in another room from the caller, with deep breathing into the receiver. Once again, I hung up. And the phone rang again. And then again. And again. And again. Thirty-six times in a row.

I was by myself and couldn't have been more freaked out. I felt suffocated and violated and encroached upon. Finally, I left the phone off the hook, but that started to scare me even more when the haunting phone-off-the-hook beeping sound kicked in. It had to be Bianca. I didn't want to believe it but something told me it was her. Who else would be calling me like this? Who else had a reason to?

The next day in class, Bianca and I didn't say a word to each other. She smirked at me and looked satisfied with herself. I guess she could tell, by the look on my face, that she had gotten to me. I might not like her, but she was in control. And she knew it.

That night the phone calls started again. This time, though, I heard a baby talking on the other end. It was just endless babble from this toddler and the heavy breathing again. I felt trapped. I hadn't told anyone about the phone calls the first night because I was embarrassed. I wasn't supposed to be bullied by a girl. I wasn't supposed to lose power. I *definitely* didn't tell anyone at school. I would never hear the end of it, especially if someone got wind of how scared I was.

I decided to just listen and not hang up anymore. I wanted to try to recapture some control on my own and that's when I finally heard Bianca's voice. But she wasn't talking to me. She was talking to the toddler in a baby voice. As I strained to listen, I realized that she was talking to the baby as if it was our child. Talking about me as though I were the absent father. That's when I hung up for good and, again, left the phone off the hook.

I couldn't take it anymore. I didn't know what to do. I was scared and overwhelmed and needed help. I was at the end of my rope. I finally told my mom what had been happening. She immediately looked up Bianca's number and called her house. No one answered. Finally, a few days later she got Bianca's mom on the phone. Despite Bianca's mom's defensive pleas, my mom told her to cut it out. If her daughter called back again, we'd call the police and show them the phone records of what had been happening. At last, the calls stopped.

Only months later did I tell my friends. It wasn't too long after that when someone saw her at a fair with three little kids and they waved hello. She greeted them politely and then said, "These are me and Carlos's kids." So, of course, when my sixth grade classmate is telling everyone we have three children, I have to give some kind of response. "She's a stalker. She's nuts," I'd tell everyone. I felt bad for Bianca—even now I still do. Who knows what kind of abuse or trauma or whatever she was going through? Only after working as a counselor with people with severe mental health issues and abuse did I start to understand some of the reasons why she may have acted like she did. I have no idea what happened to that girl. I hope that she is okay.

The rest of that year, Bianca and I pretty much ceased contact with each other. Shortly thereafter, she moved away. Everything, ultimately, turned out okay for me—all thanks to my mom's assertive, take-no-shit demeanor, which had saved me, but only after I had been humbled enough to feel like I *had* to ask for help. My mom, as she has been through so much of my life, had been my savior. It wasn't until the end of middle school when I asked for her help again. And, this time, it was to make it through the most humbling challenge of my life.

Fourteen is hard enough. Add to that my parents' messy divorce, and my father and his new wife expecting twins, two moves, three schools, and a transition to high school. Then I broke up with my first serious girlfriend. Then my uncle in Colombia was murdered. I was emotionally breaking down. I spent nights in my room sobbing and literally tasting the bile flooding up from my stomach. Some days I felt like I was dying. Some days I wished I did.

Not surprisingly, with all of my emotional and psychological struggles I hadn't noticed that things weren't right with my physical health. I had bouts of stomach and abdominal pains so severe I thought I had appendicitis. But, as with most of the pain during this time, I gritted my teeth and fought through it. I wanted to be more powerful than all the things around me trying to defeat me. That's how I felt. The world is trying to break me. But it won't. I am too strong. And I will do it on my own. They'll see—the world will see.

The abdominal pain continued to get worse. My digestive tract was totally off. I couldn't go to the bathroom. Then all I could do was go. I could feel my intestines swelling up to the surface. This can't be normal, right? I was worried something was very wrong. I would also have heartburn so extreme I could barely swallow. Then I started getting migraines. My bones felt weak. Some mornings I felt so tired I would try to get out of bed and my body would refuse to do what my mind was telling it.

Am I dying? Have I finally reached the bounds of what the human body can take? I noticed my pants getting baggier and baggier. Acne exploded all over my face like a rash. I remember visiting my family in Miami during my spring vacation and my cousin saying to me, "Carlitos, why are you so skinny? You look like a skeleton. What, do you have AIDS or something?"

Who knows, maybe I do, I thought. I had gotten bad amoebic dysentery while in Colombia the summer before. In the hospital, they had taken blood samples from me with a reusable needle. *Have I contracted HIV? Did I get some other disease from that needle?* My mind was spinning out of control with possibilities. *Maybe I have cancer?* All of the stress had finally taken hold of my body. Now it would kill me slowly.

I entered high school with a body teetering on collapse. I was wasting away, day by day, and my mom was doing everything she could to try to keep her composure. She put me on a strict regimen to put weight back on. I'd eat pounds and pounds of pasta, bread, any starchy food that could give me calories for my system. But I felt even worse. She suggested I cut back on how much I played basketball. But I wasn't playing any more than I had before.

My mother went into panic mode when we realized that first year of high school that I had lost forty-eight pounds in less than five months. Something was seriously wrong, maybe even terminally. I went to doctor after doctor. Nine in all. So much time was spent at appointments it became difficult to keep up with my schoolwork. And the things the doctors were telling me made it hard to concentrate.

A psychiatrist diagnosed me as clinically depressed and told me I was possibly bipolar. When I told her that I was happier than I had been in the past two years, she said I was in denial. Another doctor thought I had an eating disorder. She stared hard into my eyes, unconvinced, as I told her I didn't have any issues with my body. A gastroenterologist believed I might have stomach cancer. Others feared I had AIDS, leukemia, diabetes, a thyroid imbalance, lupus, or some yet-to-be-discovered terminal illness.

Strangely, I was more happy and at peace during this period than I had been the previous year. Closure with my parents' divorce and where I would be living had given me a peace I hadn't had in a long time. Even the seemingly pending terminal diagnosis of whatever I was suffering from didn't bother me a whole lot. Okay, I was dying. For some strange reason, I was at peace with it. There are much worse ways to go. I've had an incredible life thus far—gotten to see the world, have a girlfriend, play basketball. What else do you want?

I had more things ingested, stuck, poked, and jammed into my body than any human being should ever experience. They put cameras into every orifice of my body. I tried every diet you can imagine. Maybe it's the food? Maybe my body can't absorb the nutrients in something I'm eating. Maybe it's that simple. One doctor suggested I eat rare game meats and obscure root crops for six months. No salt. No seasonings. Just room temperature water to drink with boiled ostrich meat and some bland starch that tasted like cardboard. He was supposedly a noted nutritional expert.

"No patient I've ever had has been able to do this diet for four or five months but that's what it would take," he told me. "Do it for two and you'll be a million times better than you are now. Your body is in shock from something. It needs to recover and regenerate. If a person stuck to this for six months, they would be cured of anything. Do it for that long and you'd be cured of whatever it is you have—one hundred percent."

Anything? One hundred percent? Big words. But I like anyone who says anything that outlandish. Maybe he's telling the truth. I'll give it a shot.

The next six months and two days were some of the toughest of my life. I didn't need a psychiatrist to tell me—I was depressed as hell. I *love* food. To me, eating is one of the most joyous, central experiences of being human. There is nothing I enjoy more than sitting around a table of delicious food with people I love. Now I was eating these prescribed portions of completely tasteless food. I was grumpy and negative. I was frustrated and down. My mom was cooking her ass off for me for this diet and I couldn't be less appreciative. She empathized with me. But we both knew this had to be done.

Two days after the six month mark, we went back to that doctor. He couldn't believe I'd actually pulled it off. "You didn't cheat at *all*? Even *once*?" he asked me, as though it were the most incredible thing he'd ever heard. He laughed and told one of his assistants bustling about. His face lit up with awe, as he paced back and forth and shook his head in disbelief.

"It was really hard. But I just wanted to be better," I confessed.

"Well, you did it! You're cured. Go out and eat a piece of double chocolate cake," he exclaimed with a big, confident smile.

"Shouldn't he ease into it? Or maybe slowly rotate those foods in?" my mom asked, her brow furrowing.

"Nope. If he'd done it for five or six weeks, that'd probably be a good idea. But six *months*? Forget it. It's like he has a new body now," he said as he walked us to reception. "I'd say enjoy your cake. And, unless anything else comes up, I'll just see you for a follow-up in one year."

Excited, I bolted out to the car. It was the first time my mom had seen a smile like that on my face in six months. She smiled weakly, afraid to get my hopes up, only to be let down again. He was the ninth doctor we'd visited. We'd gone to traditional doctors, homeopaths, Reiki therapy, alternative practitioners, tried everything you can possibly imagine. About the only thing we didn't try was getting my mom's friend Davi Yanomami, who is a shaman in the Amazon, to heal me. *Well, hopefully, ninth time's the charm*, I thought.

I will never forget sitting at a table in that Italian bakery, a heaping slice of double fudge cake right there in front of me. My mouth was foaming, I was salivating so much. I was about to eat the most glorious piece of food I had ever experienced. My heart pounded with fear, anticipation, and excitement as I slowly put a heaping bite into my mouth. And then another. And another. Oh goodness, if I could have just died and gone to heaven then, I would have been at peace. I had reached nirvana and heaven at the same time. I was more in love with food than I had ever been.

Suddenly I felt a sharp pain rising in my gut. It was dull at first, and then expanded into sharp thunderbolts throughout my body. It felt like a knife had been lodged into my abdomen, now being turned and bent at whim. My stomach felt like a pin cushion, the needles pressing in deeper with each inhale, releasing slightly with each exhale. I was having the same symptoms as before. Nothing had been cured. I had done six months for nothing. I was back to square one.

We angrily drove back to the arrogant doctor—"number nine," as I like to think of him. This time he promised me that I was "probably better than before" and that "nothing is one hundred percent certain in life." Now this motherfucker was a *philosopher*? We quickly stormed out after a heated debate among the three of us. Exhausted and defeated when we arrived home, my mom and I sat at our kitchen table and cried.

For one of the first times in my life, I felt completely helpless. What do we do now? My body was breaking down and there was nothing I could do to make it better. No one had any clue what to do. And we'd seen *everyone*. I was afraid to eat anything. I had trouble concentrating and staying awake in my classes. I was too tired to work out and do what I love: play basketball. Now I *was* starting to feel insecure about my body—I looked like a skeleton. I felt like a sack of bones about to shatter into pieces at any moment.

My whole life I had prided myself on being unbreakable and I now found myself undeniably weak. Sitting in my basement, I had the humbling realization: I cannot just tough my way through this one. I needed to be humble to what my body was teaching me. I needed to accept that I was not well right now. That something was wrong. And trying to push harder against what my body was telling me would only make things worse.

My body continued to break down, as my bones and joints started to fail me. Tendonitis in my right wrist became so bad that it required surgery. Shortly after that, I snapped one of the main ligaments, my talofibular, in my left ankle. Barely two months after fully recovering from that, I broke the main bone, my calcaneus, in my right foot playing basketball. The two most important years of my athletic life, my junior and senior seasons, had been completely sabotaged by injuries. After years of being an iron man who prided himself on playing through anything, I had to admit that I couldn't go on.

Spending all those months on crutches or in a walking boot or in a cast, I was finally forced to figure out who I really was. As silly as it sounds, I probably only ever became an artist and a writer because I could no longer cling to my jock identity. For the first time, I felt frail and humbled. I no longer felt like the superhero who could will his way through anything. I couldn't ride my cool kid, varsity athlete label through the tough times. I had to take a good hard look at myself. For the first time in a long while, I had to reflect on who I was and start to get real.

By the time I had made peace with a life of frailty, we finally figured out what had been the source of my body's collapse: my diet. What an irony that all of those starchy foods my mom had been feeding me to fatten me up had, in fact, been making me more sick. I was allergic to a wide variety of ingredients found in everything I loved: wheat gluten, sugar, yeast, soy, peanuts, plantains, bananas, and mushrooms.

It was amazing how quickly I felt better after removing the bad foods from my diet. Not that it was easy to do, with this all taking place before gluten-free diets became common, but I immediately felt better than I had in years. The stomach pains became less and less frequent. It wasn't until they finally went away that I realized I had been having excruciating abdominal pains almost continuously for the past two and a half years. It's funny how the human body can become accustomed to suffering—and you only notice it in its absence. Even the acne I had struggled with began to disappear. My energy increased, but I was still rail thin and not at full strength.

This period was particularly frustrating for me because I could see the light at the end of the tunnel. My mind was so much happier and healthier than my body was. I struggled with being patient. But I had to. My body had a long way to go before it was recovered from the poison I had been putting in it. I wanted the healing to happen faster than was reasonable. Let's be real: I wanted all of that shit to happen *right then, right there*. Again, though, I had to embrace humility—my body frequently refusing to cooperate with what I demanded.

My energy would just drop out sometimes. If I pushed myself too hard, which I often did, it would take me days to recuperate. Even worse, I started to see sexual side effects. (Yeah, my dick didn't even do what he usually did.) Of course, my high school sweetheart, Vanessa, was supportive and understanding, but it frustrated me to no end. I couldn't get my penis hard, then I'd ejaculate before I was hard. I didn't even know that shit was possible! Then I'd feel exhausted. I started to rethink myself. *I'm a failure. I can't do shit. I hate this,* I thought.

I wanted to die when Viagra commercials would come on TV. I would see these old retired guys and think, *Fuck. I've got the body of a sixty-year-old.* Vanessa was the best, though. She'd have such a grace and sense of humor about it. She understood what was happening. Or maybe she just pretended to. My body was not better—it still was not well—and only with time would I have back my seventeen-year-old body.

By the spring of my senior year, I was back. Never had I felt better. My penis was back to being that of an overexcited teen, my energy was through the roof, and I was ready for the transition to college. I had made it through the toughest period in my life, health-wise, which came right on the heels of the toughest year for me emotionally, and I was still standing. I was proud of myself. Despite all of my vulnerabilities and struggles and sadness and pain and sickness, I had survived. Only with the humility and self-awareness I was forced to embrace in admitting that my body was in fact weak had I made it through. No longer could I power my way through life when I was vulnerable. I had been forced to finally open up those tight fists I fought every battle with and accept what obstacles the universe had placed in my path, be more Buddhist monk and less soldier. And, of course, I had not done it alone. More than anyone else, I had my mother to thank for making it through. And how fitting, right? My mom, the ultimate survivor, held me up through the toughest times.

Not until my final year of college was I forced to face the limits of my body again. This time, though, it was the emotional bounds of my mental health. It all started with a phone call from my mom: "Hey Carlos. Can you talk? Yeah, nothing to worry about but . . ."

My mom never talks like that. I practically blacked out everything she said. She mentioned that the doctor needed to do some more tests on her heart, which was acting "a little funky." Yep. That's how my mom describes *congestive heart failure.* I could hear in her voice that she was scared. She was about to spend a long weekend by herself, so I hopped on a train from

Philadelphia (where I was at college) and headed to Providence, Rhode Island, to see her. She cried when I called her from the train station. I knew something bigger was on the horizon.

The follow-up tests confirmed our deepest fears: Her mitral valve wasn't working correctly. Blood was flooding into her heart. She needed to have open-heart surgery immediately or she could die. She scheduled to have it done at the Cleveland Clinic the next week. The next month was a total blur. I pulled out of my classes and traveled to Ohio to be there with her for her surgery and the week and a half recovery. God bless those incredible people we both have in our lives. My mother's boyfriend flew in from Holland. My best friend, Brent, pulled out of classes at his college in Maine and came to be with us. My sister, Sara, also flew out to be there. Even my mom's older brother drove up from Florida with his wife to be by her side.

As comforted as I was by everyone coming, though, it scared me that so many folks were traveling to see her. *Is she treading a lot closer to death than I want to admit? What if her body can't take the surgery? What if she never wakes up from the anesthesia?* The questions flooded my head, like the blood pouring back into her heart through her faulty mitral valve. As always, with life-and-death situations, my mom was poised as ever—jovial, playful, and lighthearted. I watched her grace as her body deteriorated into the weakest it had ever been and learned about a new kind of strength.

Then in recovery, her kidneys started to fail. I watched the panic in the nurses' eyes and knew that she was in trouble. Her other organs were weakening with the trauma of the past few days. I remember sneaking out of my hotel room one night and going to her bedside to see her. She was lying there, peacefully, and I clasped my fingers around hers and sat there for hours. I just sobbed and clung to her hand. I was not ready to lose my mom. It was not time. I was squeezing her hand as though I could keep her here, remind her body to regenerate and allow her to stay.

Those nights after her surgery in Cleveland were endless. I dreaded the sun going down. It felt like the darkness would never subside, as if the silence was suffocating me. I imagined the walls crawling into my eyelids while I slept, boxing me in and transforming my hotel bed into a coffin. Nowhere did I feel safe or at peace. I felt paradoxically trapped and rootless, as if I was simultaneously locked in a small cage and drifting, directionless, on a piece of ship wreckage in the ocean. I thought those weeks after my mom's surgery would never end. I was so afraid to lose my mom.

Slowly she came back around, though. Her kidneys started working again and her body revived. The recovery process was slow and challenging, but she did it. Going to physical therapy for almost two years, she rehabilitated her body into the best shape she'd ever been in. Today, all that lingers from her mitral valve repair is a faint four-inch scar on her chest. She wears it like a medal. It is undeniable proof that she is a survivor, that, as she puts it, she is in "bonus time."

You can't beat what makes you weak. You have to respect it and make peace with it. You can't kill it or run from it. You can't punch your way out of a corner, especially when the enemy is inside of your own chest. Only when you accept it can you survive. That's what I learned when my body started to break down. Even with a plethora of ominous prognoses, I only recovered when I made peace with my body. I only learned that fully by watching my mom cope with her congestive heart failure. She accepted what was happening, knew she needed help, sought it out, made a plan, and then gave her trust to the universe.

I worry about my dad when it comes to health. He's more of that old school "don't ask, don't worry" mentality: Tough it out, keep it moving, and hope that you die of old age, one day, in your sleep. Like I still struggle to not be. Like most men, my dad and I are not good about advocating for our own health. It is a plague among our tribe. It is spread by the false idea that admitting you need support is somehow a sign of weakness. I have two things to say on this:

1. Strong people are the ones who stay alive. If you never ask for help, that won't be you.
2. We *are* all weak. Every one of us. Not always, but sometimes—and it's all right. Yes, I said it. I also admit that I am as bad as anyone about admitting it when I am.

And when it comes to seeking out support, I'm not referring to just physical weakness. Even more so with men, I'm talking about mental health. Never was I forced to confront my own emotional and mental health more than when I was a social worker in Harlem and the Bronx. I spent every single day talking with people who felt like they had no reason left to live. Who told me that no one would care if they died *today*. I looked them in the eyes and said, "Yes, you do. *I* want you to live."

I wanted them to know that they weren't alone. I wanted to be their support system. I knew they wouldn't be attending a recovery support group or counseling session if they didn't want to live. They *were* reaching out for help. In the most dire moment of their life. And as I looked them in the eyes and tried to persuade them to stay alive, I realized something scathingly hypocritical in myself: If I were them, I'm not sure that I would have the humility to seek help. Would I have the courage to say, "I cannot do this alone"?

I hope that I would. When I walked away from my life as a social worker, it was because I needed a break—more than I ever cared to admit. I had asked every wise person in my life for guidance before I did: my mom, my dad, Sarita, Leila, Eric,

Brent. I felt like walking away from my job was quitting on the clients I saw every day, giving up on all those brave people. How dare I say I can't keep doing this? What kind of failure does that make me? But everyone said the same thing: "Please, Carlos, stop. This environment will only burn you out or, worse, break you. There is no sustainability on this path."

At first, those words felt like a dare, like a direct challenge to my manhood. *I will prove them wrong,* I thought. Then came the week when I lost two of my dearest clients forever: one murdered; the other sentenced to life for killing someone. No, I realized, I cannot keep doing this. I finally admitted to myself, *I need to heal emotionally from what this last year has been, or possibly risk descending to a place I won't be able to recover from.* And it wasn't about quitting or not being strong, it was about self-preservation. It was about me acknowledging that my sanity and happiness and heart needed to be healthy. It was me going against my guilt and obligation and saying, "I am an artist. I need to write and perform—that is why I am alive."

When we, as men, lock away our pain and vulnerability, it slowly kills us. It casts a dark shadow over our gifts and our heart. It slowly eats away at the sacred, fractured pieces of ourselves that will, ultimately, make us whole. We all collude in this silent game. And in those moments when I catch a glimpse of men battling against the imprecise, unscripted magic of their bodies, I think of this saying that's a takeoff on a quote from Henry David Thoreau:

> *"Most men lead lives of quiet desperation and go to the grave with the song still in them."*

PART III

MAN ENOUGH

Photograph by Jonathan Solarte

WHAT'S GENOCIDE?

by Carlos Andrés Gómez

Their high school principal told me
I couldn't teach poetry with profanity
so I asked my students,
Raise your hand if you've heard of the Holocaust.

In unison, their arms rose up like poisonous gas
then straightened out like an SS infantry,
Okay. Please put your hands down.
Now raise your hand if you've heard of the Rwandan genocide.

Blank stares, mixed with curious ignorance.
A quivering hand out of the crowd halfway raised,
like a lone survivor struggling to stand up in Kigali,
Luz, are you sure about that?
        No.
That's what I thought.

        Carlos—what's genocide?

They won't let you hear the truth at school
if a person says *fuck.*
Can't even talk about *fuck* even though
a third of your senior class is pregnant.

I can't teach an 18-year-old girl in a public school
how to use a condom that will save her life
and that of the orphan she will be forced
to give to the foster care system—

        Carlos, how many 13-year-olds do you know that are HIV-positive?

Honestly, none. But I do visit a shelter every Monday and talk with
six 12-year-old girls with diagnosed AIDS
while 4th graders three blocks away give little boys blow jobs during recess.
I met an 11-year-old gang member in the south Bronx who carries
a semi-automatic weapon to study hall so he can make it home.
And you want me to censor my language?

        Carlos, what's genocide?

Your books leave out Emmett Till and Medgar Evers.
Call themselves *World History* and don't mention
King Leopold or diamond mines. Call themselves
Politics in the Modern World and don't mention Apartheid.

Carlos, what's genocide?

You wonder why children hide in adult bodies. Lie
under light-color-eyed contact lenses. Learn to fetishize
the size of their ass and simultaneously hate their lips.
My students thought Che Guevara was a rapper
from East Harlem; still think my Mumia t-shirt
is of Bob Marley; how can literacy not include Phillis Wheatley?
Schools were built in the shadows of ghosts. Filtered
through incest and grinding teeth, molded under veils
of extravagant ritual.

   Carlos, what's genocide?

Roselyn, how old was she? ¿Cuántos años tuvo tu madre cuando se murió?

   My mother had 32 years when she died. Ella era bellísima.

. . . what's genocide?

They've moved on from sterilizing Boriqua women.
Injecting indigenous sisters with Hepatitis B—now they just kill
mothers with silent poison, stain their loyalty and love into veins
and suffocate them.

. . . what's genocide?

Ridwan's father hung himself in the box
because he thought his son was ashamed of him.

. . . what's genocide?

Maureen's mother gave her skin lightening cream
the day before she started the 6th grade.

. . . what's genocide?

She carves straight lines into her beautiful brown thighs
so she can remember what it feels like to heal.

. . . what's genocide?
. . . what's genocide?

   Carlos, what's genocide?

Luz, this . . .
this right here . . .

is genocide.˙

---

*   Connect Online: **"What's Genocide"** http://www.youtube.com/watch?v=Qnl_zG
2KwR0

CHAPTER 8

Finding My Voice in a Poem

E very human being on this earth deserves to find his or her voice. And I don't mean the physical voice that rises out of one's body, but the vessel for the urgent, primal need to speak and be heard that bellows from one's soul. For my girlfriend it is through crafting—making dazzling collages and intricately decorated mementos to celebrate the meaningful moments of her life. For my sister it is through sculpting and painting and drawing. For my mom it is through gardening. For my best friend it is through music. For me it is through poetry.

Poetry became a launching pad for who I would become. It completely transformed me—who I was and how I moved through the world, even the way I listened and spoke. It gave me a permission to ask questions and take risks. It opened me up to an entirely new way to live and be a man. It acted as a gateway to my other artistic obsessions: acting, music, prose.

Before I stumbled upon my love for poetry, I was just moving out of the darkest, most difficult period of my young life. For the first time in my entire adolescence, I felt like I finally had some room to breathe. I was finally ready to move on to the next stage of my life—one that was truly my own.

It was the summer before my senior year in high school, and I was seventeen years old. To be exact, it was the evening of August 8, 1999. On a whim I had rented an independent film called *Slam*, which told the story of a "young MC" who goes to jail and finds freedom through his words. The young writer's poems become his way of escaping the drugs and gangs and violence surrounding him. Straight up, the movie was like a Bible passage for me. It tore into me like the word of God, like something I had been waiting an entire lifetime to hear. Never had I been so mesmerized by a piece of art. The entire movie just opened me up like a gutted fish. Every scene felt so raw and truthful, and the words that exploded off the screen were unlike any I had ever heard. The main character, played by Saul Williams, was doing poetry but in a way that was totally different from anything I had ever seen. And as I watched and rewatched the film that night—probably five or six times—I could feel inside of my body a shift, a turn. I knew my world would never be the same. I had written only one poem on my own at that point. Sure, I'd scribbled trite little things for an English homework assignment, but I had never sat down to write a poem by choice . . . except for one.

I was fourteen years old and it was the night before I moved to Providence, just after having the painful talk with my dad on the steps outside of our apartment. I wrote a poem called "Blue" through sobbing heaves as I sat next to my bedroom window. Never had I felt so alone. That poem was the friend I needed that night. It was about relating to the East River, onto which our apartment looked out, how the dark water reminded me of my life. When I felt most powerless, my journal and pen gave me a redemptive rush I needed to believe in. On one of the darkest nights of my childhood, poetry saved my life. It saved my life before I had even really discovered its power.

To be real, the poem I wrote that night was pretty bad. I don't want to make it out to seem better than it actually was—it was corny as hell! But I did mean every single word of it with every atom in my body. "Blue" was significant because it was the first time in my life that a poem screamed its way out of me. I furiously scribbled out the words, afraid I might lose one. I didn't know why I felt compelled to write it but I just did. For myself. It wasn't until almost three years later that I picked up a pen again with the same kind of urgency.

Thinking about who my friends were in high school, it makes sense that I finally got the writing bug. Throughout those years, my world had been saturated in hip-hop. I'd spend most weekends going to watch hip-hop battles between emcees and b-boys. One of my closest friends was an emcee. Almost every weekend I'd stand on the sidelines, in awe of the courage these guys had to step into the fray and showcase their gifts in front of a room of rowdy onlookers. I never jumped in, though; I always stood with a stupefied smile on my face, cheering my friends on. But it was that influence of hip-hop culture and those weekends in Providence at the Strand and Lupo's that led me to that movie on August 8, 1999.

I rented *Slam* that night because a part of me dreamed to have the courage to get up and battle someone. I wanted to be brave enough to get up and read something *I* had written, have a room moved by something I had inside of *me*. Beyond that, I was so moved by the power of art to bring people together in a constructive way, where you'd see all of these black and Latino men in a room, going toe-to-toe with everything they had, but never letting it break down into something negative—into violence or conflict. This movie sounded like it took it to the next level. I wanted to see how a lyricist could use his words to escape hell, how this man could use the power of his writing to transcend the prison walls enclosing him—to break the cycles of violence in his housing project. It was the kind of hope I needed at that point in my life. I had never considered myself an artist or even, for that matter, a creative person. Everyone knew me as very expressive—I was opinionated, outspoken, and even contentious. But never had I picked up a pen to write or a paintbrush or danced my feelings out of me. For so long, whatever I felt had simply spewed out of my mouth when I couldn't hold it in any longer. Poetry finally gave me the vessel I didn't realize I had been searching for my entire life.

I was in my own prison until I found poetry. My mind and heart haunted me with the grieving I had never properly done. Nightmares strangled my sleep and I was emotionally numb. I read the movie synopsis and imagined myself as the main character, except the prison I was trapped in was my past—and I wanted a way out of my own hell. I wanted to find an escape from the things that had trapped me for years. Watching that film was like inhaling a parable from my own body.

The night I rented *Slam*, I became a poet for the first time. I sat down after watching the film all those times, and wrote a poem called "America the Beautiful." With a superclichéd A-A-B-B rhyme scheme, I scribbled out a passionate piece condemning the hypocritical rhetoric of the United States. Then I wrote another poem slamming globalization. And another about misogyny. I didn't sleep. I sat, hurriedly eating breakfast, and started furiously writing out lines on napkins for another poem. When I ran out of napkins, I started to use grocery store receipts and even my forearm when I ran out of those. It was like seventeen years of poetry was spilling out of me all at once. The dam had broken. The water, desperate to be released, drenched my brain with stanzas I didn't know existed.

My writing was like an unending flood. The poems continued to flow. No amount of time could be enough to get them all down. It felt like I would sit down for a few minutes to write, then I'd glance up and it would be three hours later. I spent the days eager to get time by myself again so that I could sit down and write poems. During class I'd daydream about writing poems, start scribbling new ones in my journal instead of taking notes. It was the strangest thing. I had never been this guy. Why now? Why at nearly eighteen years old—about to finish high school—was I discovering that I was a writer?

It makes perfect sense, looking back, but at the time it seemed utterly perplexing. I was cocaptain of the varsity basketball team. I had been a track and field athlete, played soccer and volleyball. I was vice president of the student body. I was also a top student who was involved in different clubs and organizations at my school. I was the scholar-athlete-citizen guy. I volunteered twice a week to help second graders with their math homework. I was going to be a public defender someday and, hopefully, a member of the Supreme Court (that was my plan!). And here I was, wasting all of my free time, now, *writing poems.*

While my time used to be to spent chasing girls or doing push-ups and sit-ups or playing basketball with friends, now all I wanted to do was sit in my basement and write. My sister had always been the artist. I was the athlete. She was the shy creative one. I was the outspoken sports guy. That's how it was. Why would things suddenly change now?

I still joke with my parents that they misled my sister and me during childhood, identity-wise, because of sexist, presupposed gender roles. My sister is a brilliant artist but she's actually an incredible athlete as well. She has a natural sense of coordination and physical awareness of her body. She also has power and toughness in her petite frame. Whether it's throwing a baseball or kicking a soccer ball, she does it *hard* and with precision. Even with basketball, which was my sport, she's fantastic. Never having practiced more than a few minutes in her life, she can pick up a ball and start hitting free throws with pretty solid form—no formal training whatsoever.

She liked to draw and sketch when she was little, so I guess my parents assumed she didn't like sports. I liked to draw and sketch too! What little kid doesn't? But I didn't get pigeonholed with the "artist" label. Sometimes I think back and regret that I wasn't. Where would my writing be today if my artistic impulses had been encouraged as much as my athletic ones? I played sports so much as a kid, it's understandable that I'd have some level of aptitude by the time I was seventeen. It was a self-fulfilling prophecy. It's the confirmation bias that comes along with boys expected to play sports and then being assumed to be better athletes than girls. In actuality, though, it has nothing to do with innate ability at all. Those gendered myths are just that—myths. It's complete bullshit. It's gendered role-playing that sets things into motion and confirms the assumption.

Today I spend my life as an artist. Hours each day are spent writing and rehearsing and working on scenes and tinkering with poems. Whereas my sister spends hours each day practicing martial arts—one called aikido—being flipped and thrown on mats that feel as hard as concrete to me. When I visited her last year, I jumped into one of the beginner classes. *I mean, how tough could it be,* I thought. Well, let's just say I got my ass kicked.

That first year, every poem I wrote was a political manifesto. There was clever rhyming and historical references and a lot of preaching. I had been very politically and socially involved, and my poems almost exclusively reflected that. It wasn't until I had written about a hundred of those trite, angry, and platitudinal political poems that I turned the mirror on myself. And, even then, there were only brief glimpses of anything specific to me or my life.

It's ironic. When I started writing poetry, I believed that art needed to serve a purpose so much greater than myself. I thought of my own life as something too insignificantly small to ever warrant a poem. I even believed it narcissistic to ever write about my own life. Little did I realize then that by writing so generally about the world around me, and never my own experiences, I was, in fact, being the ultimate narcissist. I was narcissistic in the most egregious of ways—looking cool reading poems in which I had nothing personally at stake. I was basically putting things down on paper that screamed out for recognition and acknowledgment without ever really showing who I was, without ever revealing *why* I needed to scream out these poems and be heard. Only *years* later did I realize that sharing your own story is at the core of the artistic process. And it is not about being narcissistic. It can be if the process is only about romanticizing your role in something as a hero or something similar, but if the exploration is about digging for the deepest truth, however ugly, fragmented, contradictory, and frightening it might be, then it serves the greatest purpose.

When I started studying acting at twenty-three it was a turning point, and I realized how impersonal all of my poems had been. Why was I so passionate and loud in my delivery of all of them? Sure, I was angry and upset about what was unfair in the world. But was that really at the root of my urgency in those poems? Was I just yelling out against poverty and racism and exploitation? Or was it something else?

And one day it clicked: All of those poems were really about my father. I had been getting up on stage for years yelling out to my father. Those poems had been a vehicle to heal from the hurt I felt from our relationship. From the broken promises and the move and changing schools and the family being split apart. I was screaming with such intensity, making my throat go hoarse, because I wanted to be acknowledged. More than anything else, I just wanted to be heard.

During our last session of family therapy when I was in middle school, right before it became obvious that my parents were not getting back together, I had written my father a letter. In it I told him how much I loved him and asked for him to hear what I was feeling, to take in why I was hurt. Toward the end of the session, I stood up and read the letter aloud to my father. I was humbling myself and gently asking for him to come back. I was asking for our relationship back—all the good times we had shared together that defined most of my childhood. I cried as I read that letter. And my father walked out of the room.

I have no idea what he did after he left. While we all sat in the room together he showed no emotion. Up to that point in my life, I had never seen my father cry. I had never seen him lose control. I had never seen him humbled by something greater than himself. He was the most powerful human being I knew. And I wanted to see him be vulnerable for once. I needed to see a chink in his armor that afternoon. Knowing what I do now, he probably left the room and cried. Maybe he didn't but wanted to. But in that moment, as I felt ignored and pushed away, I wanted to stand on top of a building and scream until the world turned around. I wanted to scream until my throat gave out and the traffic stopped in the streets below and everyone waited to hear what I needed to say.

From seventeen years old until probably twenty-two, all I did was stand on top of buildings and yell. Although it didn't move me any closer to healing, the acknowledgment and recognition I received calmed something in me that had been restless for years. It showed me a power I had inside of myself that no one had told me about. I *was* powerful. I *did* have a voice that people would listen to. And, however briefly, on that stage as a poet—I was God for three minutes. I was the maestro of a room full of people's heartstrings and thoughts.

If I hadn't found poetry, who knows where I would be today? I probably would have acted out a lot less as a kid if I had had a creative outlet. Even later, when I was basically screaming my way through poems in my late teens, I was releasing years' worth of toxic and pain-filled energy from my body. I guess, in that sense, those old poems did serve a purpose in curing some of the festering wounds I had clung to. And, moreover, five years of those angry poems enabled the healing pieces I would later write.

I watch men walk around, their emotions clenched tight in their chests, and I wonder, how many great poems are trapped inside of them? How many brilliant paintings and choreographed dance pieces? How many guys in my neighborhood in Brooklyn would have their lives saved by allowing themselves to sing? To sculpt something with their own two hands and rediscover what the greatest power in their palms might be?

One fall morning at an assembly during my senior year of high school, my poetic aspirations became solidified. The visitor that day was a man named Martín Espada, an astounding Puerto Rican poet from New York who read from his book *Imagine the Angels of Bread*. For months I had kept hidden the poems I had been writing. No one had heard any of these pieces besides my girlfriend and best friend. And, even in front of them, I was insecure about what these poems meant. Who did they make me into? Was I allowed to be this person?

With tears in my eyes, Mr. Espada gave me the final permission I needed to embrace the poet inside of me. At the end of his performance, I walked up and bought a copy of his book, which I still keep close by on my bookshelf to this day. I told him how proud I was to hear a Latino poet read. His was the first Latino poetry I had encountered and I had been blown away. He looked in my eyes, a hint of mischief in his own, and said, "You're a poet yourself . . ." A broad smile overtook his face.

Was he asking a question? Was it a statement? To this day, I'm not really sure. I didn't confirm or deny what he said, just handed him the book I had just bought without a word along with a pen.

"Poeta del futuro."

That's what he wrote in my book. In Spanish, it means "Poet of the future." He anointed the path I was on. He let me know that I could be who I was and not feel afraid to share it. I never forget that now when I perform and meet a younger person with that same look in his or her eyes. The same look, craving permission and acceptance, that I had in mine.

I went from fighter to athlete to artist. I think back to teachers who thought I would never go to college, who pointed to my reading comprehension scores on standardized tests and thought I'd never read or write at a high level. What a strange, unexpected ride it has been to becoming an artist. In many ways, my journey to finding art has defined this journey to becoming a man, a different kind of man, a man who lives and moves and acts outside of the predetermined boundaries of masculinity. A man who asks questions about what defines that label, who seeks to push the boundaries and, hopefully, each day erases those lines and walls that continue to constrain who we are.

WAIT

by Jeanann Verlee and Carlos Andrés Gómez

You told him he was a good man,

      I want to point you out
      in a crowded room say,
      That's my wife, but

his mouth is full of splinters.

      I associate marriage with death.
      Last night, I couldn't sleep.
      Heard wedding bells in the street.

His name is a clock you hang
above the stove.

      You wait.

He wants to be your husband.

      You wait.

He wants to run.
You wait.

      You wait.
      It is a quiet elephant I drag everywhere
      I go.
      Attached at the neck by an invisible
      leash.

Babies reach for your breasts from
passing strollers. Your hips are an
invitation. Your face, a love letter.
You wait.

      I want to watch the years build altars
      of your face.

He is beautiful in the morning—
nestles into your chest
as if you are something worth needing.
His eyes are a treason:

      Nestles into your chest
      as if you are something worth needing.

      I want to fuck half of Manhattan,
      forget their names and call myself
      complex.

pairs of pearl-glossed lips,
chestnut braids. He feeds you his smile
like a string of candied gemstones.

      You told me I was a good man.
      But I am mere *man*, flesh and cheap
      whiskey.

His promises are gospel.
His skin,
flintspark.

      Flintspark.
      I want to raise a defiant daughter. A
      curious, sensitive boy with my mouth
      and your hair.

The kitchen in your future is full of living.
Children and toy cars, rainbows crayoned
into counters. You wait.

      I am a simple, easy-way-out kind of fool.

His voice is the sound of gears
rotating in the hollow of a bell tower.
All you want is a pretty lovebird
to sing you to sleep.

I never want to lose who I am.
Something must be surrendered.
Could not forgive myself
if I ever had to walk out.
I imagine my mother
abandoned in a marriage,
her face flood-ravaged. I see her now—
Proud. Lonely. Free.
Single plate at a table for six.

Could not forgive yourself
if you ever had to walk out.

Proud. Lonely. Free.

When did your lips become echo?
Why couldn't you stop him?

I want to be a better man.
More than this circus show of impulse
and ache.

Or did he just go?
Pack a satchel and run?
Where is he running?

Where am I running?
I'm scared of coming home
to an empty house.

Why are the dead the only ones
you can love?

I will be there.
I wait.

Don't you want to cut it out of you?
That incessant
thrumming?

Thrumming.

This life is a hard dying.
A sick everlasting.
You call yourself fool.
Say these good hearts.
You give. God you give.

This life is a hard dying.
A sick everlasting.
I call myself fool.
Say these good hearts.

I am neither hero nor monster.
You gave me permission for what I am.

He is a man bound and bellowing.
Coated in sugar.

You dream someone is always
reaching for your hand
Kissing your sturdy neck.
You want to die in his arms—

trapped between maybe *and* should.

I dream someone is always
reaching for my hand
Kissing my sturdy neck.
I want to die in your arms.
I'm just
trapped between maybe *and* should.
Childhood nightmares and fatherhood
dreams.

How long before you just leap?
Say yes.
Say love.
Slowly the song crawls out your throat.
Your fingers are a nest of tangled thorns.

How long before I just leap?
Say love.
Say yes.
Slowly the song crawls out my throat.
My fingers are a nest of tangled thorns.

You want to be a better woman—but
you wait.

I want to be a better man—but
I wait.

* Connect Online: **"Wait" (with Jeanann Verlee)** http://www.youtube.com/
watch?v=5qH1ck-MjpI

CHAPTER 9

A Knight in Tarnished Armor

No matter how despair-riddled the state of men in the United States becomes, one popular myth persists: the knight in shining armor. It is as American as apple pie—a fantasy I have heard from the mouths of female friends in their late twenties and thirties, still holding out hope for their perfect man. And who can blame them? I only moved back to this country when I was almost eight and I know the story well—the little girl plays house, dreaming of her fairy-tale wedding, while the little boy plays war, ready to protect his castle. It cements the gender binaries from childhood. And then, in a perfect world, the two grow up and get married—a now beautiful, dainty, and soft-spoken princess, straight out of a Disney movie, with her ravishing knight in shining armor by her side—and they live happily ever after.

In college, I attended multiple talks at Du Bois College House (UPenn's historically black dorm) in which women of color lamented the meager number of men of color at school and even smaller number of single, eligible, "good men." Oftentimes, I was the only man in the room. Women looked at me admiringly. At the end of one such talk, a friend said to me, "Your girlfriend is so lucky. I'm still waiting for my knight in shining armor."

It's so obvious on paper, I can't help but parade myself as though I actually am one—I have an Ivy League degree, I'm well built and able-bodied, I say the right things, I have light skin and green eyes, I do work in the community, I speak out for what is right, and most people think I'm a nice guy. All I need is a bright white horse and to be drawn into the next Disney fairy tale. But I am neither cartoon nor knight in shining armor.

If anything, I am a pimp, one who conveniently co-opted this narrative throughout his life, on frequent occasion, and exploited the act of honesty to get what he wanted. So deeply was I inundated in my own self-deception that for much of that time, I had no conscious recognition of what I was doing, as obvious as it should have been to me at times. Examining my relationships with women, whether shallow or meaningful, proves my point.

For example, let's take hooking up. Over and over again, I would put the women I was intimate with on trial. Actually, sentencing would probably be a better analogy than trial. And I would justify it under the pretext of me being moral and responsible, but really I was carefully building my case for an escape route for whenever I might need it. And that's how I did things. It was my way of methodically doing the dirtiest and sleaziest shit and walking out the other end clean.

First, I'd ask the woman if she'd been tested for STDs. Then I'd ask how she felt about abortion. Next, if she was willing to be unattached and keep hooking up. And then I'd tell her I only *receive* oral sex outside of a relationship. And, finally, after I'd gotten whatever I wanted, I'd discard her. I'd kick her to the curb, after ravenously feasting on her body and heart and spirit. And as she sobbed on my shoulder, or, oftentimes, over the phone, I'd sit there with my partly genuine, mostly strategic empathy and, ultimately, remind her, "I told you this before— I'm not ready for a relationship."

I would know when women were getting attached. And I would continue to hook up and placate them, justifying my actions through communication and straightforwardness and— my favorite—honesty. I did it relentlessly, using the act of honesty to get myself off the hook while keeping intact the narrative of me as a "good guy." I was the king of using my convenient moral high ground as a vehicle to justify and act out the ugliest parts of myself. With so many women, I'd abstain from sex, as if it was some grand sacrifice or monumental offering to female empowerment, and instead let them suck my dick or titty fuck them and then come on their face. Each time, I would first say with words: "I respect you too much to just have sex with you," then communicate with my actions: "So I'll just use you like a blow-up doll instead."

As I finally grappled with that ugly past and to get honest and break this cycle, I realized that I have been prostituting my honesty since adolescence. As a freshman in high school, I watched in awe as the senior guys blatantly lied and cheated and did whatever it took to get what they wanted from girls. In the locker room and in basketball practice and hanging out at parties, we applauded and congratulated each other for what we could get away with doing. At fourteen years old, all I ever wanted to be was one of those guys, smirking and bragging about my latest exploit.

By the end of my sophomore year of high school, though, I no longer wanted to be that guy. I was ready to be the kind of person my mom and sister might be proud of. Or so I thought.

Leaving my public school as I entered my junior year, I had

convinced my close friend Vanessa to come with me. Both of us had been accepted to one of the best private schools in the state. And we had each other for support as we made the big transition.

I had been painfully infatuated with Vanessa while we were at Northeast. Statuesque in her build, with caramel-toned skin and long black hair cascading down her spine, she was breathtakingly gorgeous. She didn't seem quite so smitten with me, but we'd developed a strange sort of friendship in the process of switching schools. She was a complete nerd like me. She had been student body president at Northeast. She was curious about the world and many of the same social and political issues that I was.

Transferring schools immediately intensified our connection. Providence Friends, our new school, was nothing like our public school. I got a B-minus on a *quiz* in one of my classes after I first transferred, and the guidance counselor called my mom in for a meeting. Wow. Now this school was hands-*on*.

There was nowhere to hide at that place. Some days I felt like I was having flashbacks to my days in Connecticut, with all the wealthy white classmates I had around me in the halls again. Vanessa and I began spending more and more time together. We were each other's support system. She confided in me that she'd never had a boyfriend, never been on a date, never even kissed anyone. She even told me that she didn't want a boyfriend until she got older, wanting to focus on her studies and laying the groundwork for her future.

Of course now I look back and realize that she was protecting herself from getting hurt. Similar to the way I pushed people away as I moved from place to place so that I wouldn't be hurt by them, Vanessa was protecting herself from being hurt by a boy. And little did I know that that boy was *me*.

For much of my junior year I had a crush on a girl named Alexis at the new school. She was this striking Nigerian-Italian girl with a presence and a smile that would captivate a room. The minute I met her and looked into her sensuous eyes, I was smitten. There was this undeniable spark between us. The only problem: She had a boyfriend. The even bigger problem: He was in the Marines. He was older and supposedly possessive and supposedly *crazy*. Aren't they always? For some reason, though, I couldn't get over her. For months we'd "study" together, which really meant hanging and talking for hours about anything.

It wasn't until about one week before he was coming home that she and I kissed for the first time. Shortly thereafter, he came home, she told me we couldn't see each other anymore, and that was it.

I was completely devastated and, as usual, my best bud in Providence came to the rescue: Vanessa. I remember crying with my head in her lap and her fingers running through my hair. Now, we didn't have a very physical relationship by any stretch of the imagination, so this was a pretty big deal. It was the first time either of us had ever held each other. It was the first time she'd really seen me vulnerable. I could see this layered, loaded hurt in her eyes as she consoled me. It seemed like there was anger in there as well.

That summer I was going on a trip to Thailand for seven weeks with an exchange program. The night before I was leaving, Vanessa and I hung out. Something about her was off. She was distant in a way she had never been with me.

"Why are you acting so weird?" I asked her with a playful smile.

"I'm not acting weird. You're acting weird," she said, dismissively.

"All right, whatever," and I left it at that.

She seemed to get more and more quiet as the night wore on. *What is wrong with Vanessa?* I thought. She was my best friend in Providence. She was my anchor at this new school. And now, suddenly, she seemed like she was mad at me or didn't want to be my friend anymore. And the night before I'm leaving to go to Southeast Asia for almost two months? Seriously!?!

Around midnight I drove her home and then, as I always did, walked her up to her door.

"All right, Vanessa. I'll try to make it back alive. Hope we're still friends when I get back," I said jokingly.

Abruptly she collapsed into me, sobbing into my chest, hysterical and holding me like she would never let go. *What is going on?* I was thinking. For almost thirty minutes she just sobbed, as I ran my hands through her hair and told her it was all right.

Then, out of nowhere, our lips seemed to stumble onto each other's. Our mouths were like the crests of two waves crashing at the center of a massive storm—the most passionate, sloppy, beautiful kissing one could ever imagine.

"I love you, Carlos," she said.

"I love you, Vanessa," I responded.

That would be the starting point of my yearlong relationship with my high school sweetheart, the woman I would go on to lose my virginity to, really explore my sexuality with for the first time, and learn about love and loss on a scale that I could never have previously imagined. More than anything else, though, beyond being a girlfriend or a lover, Vanessa was my best friend. My safe haven in this new place, Providence, which for those four brief high school years I would call home.

At school everyone thought of us as the perfect couple. She was a high-achieving student and leader, involved in photography and activism, and I was the student-athlete, vice president, cocaptain of the basketball team. We would walk through the halls like we owned them. Everyone knew she was my girlfriend and that I was her boyfriend. And no one would ever dare cross the line with either of us. Everyone would tell us how lucky we were to have each other.

But there was a secret—a rotting, dirty secret that, even to this day, she has never known about. Something that only heightened the tension between the apparent knight in shining armor I was to everyone publicly and the shameful, pathetic boy I felt like inside. It is probably one of the main reasons I broke up with her just before we went off to the same college. I got to a point where I couldn't live with the duplicity underlying what we had, and, paradoxically, she (like most of the women in my life) was the one forced to pay the price for it.

The summer we started dating, Vanessa and I were together almost every moment. We would go to the movies and the beach and out to dinner. It was like we were connected to the same body. When she moved, I moved, and vice versa. After my being away in Thailand for so long, we wanted to spend as much time with each other as we possibly could. And that was pretty much every single waking moment.

The last weekend of the summer, Brent had invited me down to visit. By this point, his family had moved again (much like mine) and he was now living on the Jersey shore. He was going to a concert with his friends and thought I should come down for the weekend to hang out before school started. So I hopped on the train and headed down.

In the parking lot before the concert, we opened up a case of beers that had been stashed in the trunk of his friend's car. Thousands of young people were tailgating in the parking lot like us, so we joined them in the drunken fray. Similar to the other time with Brent, one beer became two, two became too many, and before I knew it I was waltzing through the impulsive haze of drunken debauchery.

"Let's play a game," his friend proclaimed. "See who can hook up with the most girls before the last song."

Without even acknowledging whether anyone had a girlfriend or not, we all went our separate ways. I know at least one of Brent's friends was definitely *not* single because at one point in the night his girlfriend (who was *at the concert*) confronted him—while he was making out with some random girl—and broke up with him in a very dramatic display that was punctuated with her telling anyone who would listen that his dick was "smaller than [her] pinky!"

I felt this intense guilt as we walked our separate ways, as though I had already cheated on Vanessa, as if I didn't really have a choice to decide to not partake in this game of male bonding. My identity was on the line here. Forget the fact that it was with three guys I'd never met and would probably never see again—I had to prove my worth. It was a foregone conclusion that I would "be one of the guys" and just do what we do. My stomach felt hollow, as though I had already hooked up with one of the drunken teens who, like me, were looking for themselves in the desperate, sweaty throngs of people.

"You know you don't have to do this," Brent whispered to me, as though it were the most obvious thing in the world.

"Shut the fuck up. I'm not a bitch," I responded and walked off, more resolved than ever to find someone with a tongue to suck.

I didn't do too well in the game by anyone's standards. I got a peck on the lips from one girl and made out with another. The girl I made out with pushed me off after I tried to put my hand down her pants. Why was I doing that? I still don't know what my plan was. We were in the middle of a well-lit grassy patch, watching a concert with about twenty thousand other people. Maybe I just needed to let her know that I was one of the guys.

On the way home I felt like my heart was dying. It felt like there was a big hollow grave in my chest. *Why did I do that? WHY?!?* I kept asking myself. I had violated the sacred trust of the girl I loved. Right when I had finally seemed to mature and turn over a new leaf, I had thrown it all away. Why would I do that? For what? For a drunken, awkward make-out session at a concert? To be able to say I was one of the guys? Why not just *tell them* I made out with someone if it was so important? Who would ever know? It's not like I enjoyed it at any point. The whole night my body moved as if compelled by some other-worldly inertia dictating its course. That is not to say I don't think I was responsible for my actions because I clearly was. But it almost felt like what I've heard addicts describe as the "itch" or the "fiending" when they need their drug.

Is that what the stamp of manhood is for me? Is it that drug? The force that compels men to catcall at women on sub-way platforms as if they're dogs? The impulse in men to grab women as though they're pets? The burning need in little boys to grow up to be philanderers and deadbeat dads like the men they never knew?

The pattern continued into college—like so much of my growth in life—one step forward, two steps back. By my final year, I was struggling with my recent breakup from my college sweetheart, Melanie. As she flew out multiple times to visit me during that time, trying desperately to reconnect, I wavered and hesitated to recommit. And then when she finally decided to move on, I was crushed.

But when I returned to school for my final semester of college I was resolved to get over Melanie. Okay, Carlos, time to move on. But as much as I tried to heal and move forward, there was now this dark edge to my spirit. I tried to cover it up, projecting this righteous indignation about how I had been wronged by her. In multiple phone conversations after the incident, I viciously berated her—once, calling her "the most deceitful person I'd ever met." I started to sadistically relish those moments—yelling at the top of my lungs atop the proud soapbox I'd constructed for myself—angry at the world for how I had been done dirty. For hours I'd sit in my room, lovesick and defeated, pitying myself to no end.

That spring semester, I was asked to perform with Melanie's

former dance troupe for their big show on campus. Her best friend in the group, Asha, had approached me about performing two poems. The theme of the show was love, with my second poem asked to be about love and betrayal.

As I walked out onto the stage for the show, a sold-out crowd of more than four hundred people packed tight in the venue, I immediately spotted Melanie sitting in the second row, right in front of me. A smile crept over her face as her misty eyes swelled up and I dove into a passionate performance of the love poem I had written for her. As I walked off, many of the onlookers knowing what had just happened with us, everyone stood up and clapped. Melanie beamed, a dumbstruck look on her face as she soaked in this enormous ovation for a poem she had inspired. Maybe in that moment she even believed we were meant to be together after all.

Then came the final poem. It was a brand-new piece I had written about her night in Vegas with the guy she was seeing. The night I had felt she betrayed me and forgot to call me on my birthday. The poem was raw and ruthless, unceasing in its anger and viciousness. You could hear an audible gasp from the audience as I hit the turn. The room fell completely silent toward the end, except for the sobs of Melanie, her shaking head buried in her folded arms.

In my gut it just didn't feel right as I tore her down with that poem in front of all of those people, but in my mind I rationalized it. *Carlos, she did you dirty. Fuck her,* I told myself. *She got what she deserved.*

The rationalizations continued as I used Melanie's one example of "wronging me" (although we weren't in a committed relationship) as my pretext to do almost anything. And it even continued into the next few *years*. I did things that, looking back now, make me sick to my stomach, none more than what happened with one of her best friends.

I had always been attracted to Asha. Working on the show

with her and the rest of the group helped Asha and me develop a special bond. She'd invite me along to rehearse for the show, even though I had just a small role, and we'd often end up at her apartment talking for hours. There was kinetic energy there—a spark. Both of us knew it and were probably equally frightened and enthralled by it. We knew we were absolutely off-limits to each other. It just couldn't happen. No matter what story I told myself about how Melanie had done me wrong or betrayed my trust, nothing could justify Asha and me dating.

And then one night we hooked up, our bodies finally acting out those long-suppressed forbidden impulses. As we held each other afterward, a stunned silence seemed to swallow up her entire bedroom. It felt so wrong, but I didn't want to deny my attraction or impulse for Asha. I was still so bitter and angry at Melanie. I wanted to have a relationship with Asha. Even worse, I wanted to try to get Melanie's blessing.

"Are you fucking kidding me?" Melanie said in utter disbelief at what I'd just told her. "You want to date my best friend?"

I had explained to her that it wasn't planned and had "just happened." I understood that the situation was awkward but I wanted to be "open and honest with [her]. Not hide anything." More than that, I wanted her to be okay with it. What it really was: I wanted to get my final "fuck you" jab in on Melanie and also get my rocks off in the process and, of course, come out clean on the other end. Ride off into the sunset on my white horse.

As one might imagine, things with Melanie were irreparably broken after that. Asha and I stopped seeing each other shortly thereafter. I graduated and moved to New York, ready to start a new adult life. And despite the fiasco with Asha, I still clung tightly to my righteous "good guy" banner, like I was the last of a dying breed, one of the few knights in shining armor left. As I leapt headlong into the single dating scene of New York City, quickly realizing its inevitable hollowness, I was so diluted in that game of playing the field and being a single guy, I nearly missed out on the woman of my life: Whitney.

When we first started to hook up I was still hurting from Melanie. I was cynical and jaded. Everything about the world was conniving and broken. Only in retrospect do I realize that Whitney was the one who thanklessly pieced my shattered heart back together. And what did I do after she got me back on my feet? I abandoned her.

It was the summer before my twenty-fifth birthday, and I had just met this pretty Dominican woman at a show. I was immediately infatuated with her. Little by little I had begun to heal from Melanie and finally felt ready for a relationship again. The single dating scene in New York had become so tiresome and unfulfilling, I was ready for something new. And why wouldn't I have started dating the woman who healed me from all that hurt? Why wouldn't I start dating Whitney at this point? God knows. I had this foolish impulse that this new person I had just met was the one.

I will never forget lying next to Whitney, before my first date with the new girl, and telling her I had met someone. Her body stiffened as she hastily turned away from me, her sobbing the only thing I remember hearing for the rest of that night. Whitney had given me everything. She had waited for me. She had consoled me. She had understood when I didn't want to talk about it. She had plucked her hopeful, generous heart from her body and handed it to me. What had I done? Trampled it the minute I realized I was finally healed.

What's even worse—in the stream of consciousness that came pouring out of my mouth that night—as I scrambled to do anything I could to stop her relentless crying, I actually told her, for the first time, that I loved her. I literally told her, "I love you."

Who does that? Who has a heart in his body and actually

does that? Is there no humanity, no mercy in my bones? I mean, *seriously*, Carlos.

And what was worse than me actually saying it? I meant it. And only as the words carelessly careened out of my lips did I realize that those words were the most honest ones I had ever said to Whitney. I did love her—with all of my heart. And I was about to start dating someone else.

My relationship with the new girl lasted only six months. I quickly realized that we weren't the right match and didn't connect in the way that I had initially thought, and I couldn't stop thinking about and missing Whitney. *What a foolish mess I have put myself in*, I thought to myself. *Who hooks up with someone for two years, breaks it off with her, tells her they love her (and means it), and then starts dating someone else? I'm a maniac. I'm totally nuts. I'm crazier than any of the people in my stories.*

Finding myself single again, with spring arriving after a long winter, my thoughts turned back to Whitney. In fact, it wasn't so much that I turned my thoughts to her as that she kept popping into my head everywhere I went.

I had undertaken an intense artistic endeavor. I was beginning to write my solo play *Man Up*. As I delved into my past relationships and loves and my story as a man, I came to a conclusion: Whitney is the woman of my life. She is the missing piece in my chest. She is the final word of my book. She is the love of my life, the one I have always been searching for and believed I had never found.

Suddenly I felt panicked—I hadn't talked to Whitney in months. What if she had a boyfriend? What if she was over me? What if she was done with my crazy bullshit?!

Slowly we got back in contact with each other. As I had feared, she was seeing someone else. She even admitted to me that she had started to date, for the first time in her life, to try to get over me. She told me that she couldn't sit around forever waiting for something that might never come. What did I expect? And she was completely right.

We met up one night after a mutual friend's birthday party, and I told her that I wanted to be with her. That I didn't care if she was with someone else. That I had been wrong to take her for granted. I didn't care what it took.

She was hesitant, understandably so. What reason would she have to trust me, after she'd generously given me everything for two years and I'd given her nothing in return?

Finally she agreed to give it a shot. Both of us were trying so hard, but we both knew things weren't the same as before. If we did it this time, we had to jump in with both feet. There was no turning back. There was no halfway. This was high stakes, all-or-nothing. We would either have a serious relationship or probably never talk again.

Before we got to the point of both of us committing to each other, though, we had to see if we still had the same connection. We had a lot of mistrust and hurt to work through before we could both dive in. Both of us had to agree to let go of a lot of things in the past. That was the only way to build something new.

I felt hurt one day because I had needed her when I was really down and she never called me back. This was while we were still in the in-between stage and just starting to get back in contact with each other. The next time I saw her was at her apartment, as I walked into her room and watched her hurriedly tear the sheets off of her bed. I could taste the sex from the guy she was seeing. We had planned to have lunch to try to figure things out. And as we took the short walk to the local Korean spot she loved, a heavy silence hung in the air. The tension so thick I could almost taste it in my mouth.

"You were with him on Tuesday when I called you, huh?" I asked her, as if it were any of my business.

She hesitated and then (in her earnestness) said, "Yes. Yes, I was."

I pictured them fucking the whole afternoon while I kept leaving messages on her turned-off phone. *What a lying, deceitful . . . no, wait, we weren't together,* I thought. *What does she owe me? But I thought she cares about me?* Then I remembered how much I had hurt her, how deep her wounds from me may still be.

Whitney had put herself out there like no woman I had ever met. She had given me everything in her being without me ever asking. All she wanted was to be loved back, to be given the same care and respect. What had I done to reciprocate? Nothing. I had told her that there was someone else, and I had dumped her and told her we should stop seeing each other.

She tried to make small talk as the waitress brought out our *bento* boxes. Similar to the righteous martyrdom I clung to after Melanie tried to move on herself, I was in a rage that day. I was out for blood from the moment I arrived. Nothing Whitney could have said or done would have tamed the brewing storm in my body. I felt that she had done me wrong, and I wanted her to pay the maximum penalty for it, after years of countless manipulations on my part, after I'd used her for sex, then thrown her away, and then, just as abruptly, shown up and demanded she be back in my life. I was a nightmare. I was a plague to her life. I was a cancer that couldn't be cured.

"Are you completely done with this guy?" I finally asked, breaking the epic tension.

How could she trust me? As inexplicably and unpredictably as I had left her, I was now back. And I was asking her for promises and commitments with no evidence of anything on my part. More than that, I was *demanding* that she give it all to me—right now. Before we could sort through years' worth of baggage. Before she could have some certainty of whether or not my intentions were genuine. Before I had proven myself to be as good as my word. I looked her right in the eyes, a judge ready to sentence an innocent defendant, regardless of the evidence presented.

She couldn't look at me. She started to stutter and then stopped, and then fumbling with the words again, as though they couldn't get past her teeth. Finally, the tears started to well up in her big, gorgeous eyes, and she fell silent.

"Cool. Have a nice life," I said, tossing a twenty-dollar bill on the table and walking out.

I don't know how long she sat there, stunned and alone at that table. I walked to the closest subway, turned off my phone, and headed back to my apartment downtown. When I walked into my apartment, Brent met me at the door.

"Dude, you gotta call Whitney. She's really upset. She's been calling me. She's coming over," he said. He saw the look in my eyes and pleaded with me to have mercy. He knows that look. I was done.

For six hours, in the pouring rain, she sat on the stoop of my apartment in her favorite white summer dress. First calling me and then ringing the doorbell of my apartment. Message after message on my phone, until my mailbox was full, of her sobbing and pleading and asking to see me. But like a lot of guys do in life, both figuratively and literally, I just locked the door to my room and turned my music up to drown out the world.

A few days later, we reconciled and started the long, difficult process of healing and rebuilding from not just that night but our complicated past together, a past defined, overwhelmingly, by *my* missteps and disrespect and selfishness. I had milked her one transgression, which wasn't even a transgression, for all it was worth, as though I could somehow wipe clean all of my fuckups over the past three years all because she didn't call me back *once*. With so many women in my life, whether it was

Whitney or a one-night fling, they have been the benefactors forced to pay my ego's hefty tariff—all a means to me returning to my moral high ground and feeding the inflated fantasy I had of myself.

Now in my late twenties, I've challenged myself to stop acting out this same stale patriarchal performance, really pushed myself to end the selfish cycle and actually grow up. Coincidentally, the same project that brought me back to Whitney, working on my solo play *Man Up*, also helped me become a better man, one more committed to cutting through that fantasy I loved for so long and getting real, finally. It's only fitting, then, that my artistic process has paralleled my journey as a man as I now try to strip away more of my armor. I played the contrived role for years, another man of a million masks, treating women like shit to feed my ego. A great acting teacher once told me, "Being an actor is not about putting masks on but about taking them off." And each day since, I have been trying to peel away all of this wreckage I once foolishly mistook for armor.

Because that's what it is—wreckage. And men love devastation, the way an addict fiends for a pipe or a needle. It is a yearning for our own destruction, embodying the darkest parts of our despair and hopelessness, mistaking it for our ascension to power. And we confuse the seeking of power for meaning and relevance when it's only destruction. And then we build up flimsy walls around ourselves out of the rubble from our journey, pretend we've escaped the pain and guilt and agony of the stories attached to each artifact. But that's a lie.

I am at a point in my life where I need to remove the clutter and debris, where I need to realize that there is no armor, much less shining shields held by square-jawed knights. It is time to put down our steel. What is outside of us, fastened to our bodies, can never protect us. We are only saved by what is within.

And that is the only way to truly connect and find love—

without the masks and armor to hide behind. Like many men, I spent so long guarding what I had inside I nearly missed out on fully connecting with the woman of my life. And I easily could have gone an entire lifetime like that and then died alone in a graveyard of my own making, buried by the debris of my insecurity, defensiveness, and pride. For years, I told myself the armor was there to keep me safe, but, in truth, it was preventing me from fully living. Because there is no aliveness like that shared with a loving partner, both of you stripped bare—as naked, unapologetic, and revealed as the day you were born.

HALLELUJAH

by Carlos Andrés Gómez

Eight months shy of a hundred. And still
filled with the wonderment of a child. My grandmother
is a revelation tumbling in on itself. Songs
and secrets snaked into the creases of her smile.
Her 63-year-old hunch is washing dishes in the sink.
Her knees in 2nd grade tear through the living room like a derailed train car.
Prayer-swollen hips from her wedding photos call up to a rosary, ask for life. And I
am molded clay from the hands with which she now holds my chubby face. I am small
and curious.

¡Hay, mi hijito! (Oh, my dear son!) She squeals, *¡Tan bello!* (So beautiful!)

These are the words she uses to anchor each day, and I am jealous of how she does.
Coursing through her bones, the abandon with which she soaks it all up.

Her face is a yawning earthquake of tremor and pulse, her hands the tectonic plates
of her body's fierce hope. Her head stuttering out music as it tries to focus on just
one thing.

Now she takes in my sister, awkward middle school face of pock-marked acne in her
hands,
¡Hay, mi hijita! (Oh, my dear daughter!) *¡Tan bella!* (So beautiful!)

My sister smiles. She is beautiful for the first time in her life. Wears a sash
of blushing cheeks.
Mi hijito—my dear child. *Tan bello*—so beautiful.

In a world of envy-fueled violence, where hate explodes out of our scars like weeds.
The lessened versions of ourselves spreading like wildfire. My grandmother is a
revelation tumbling in on itself. A repeating gospel on loop. Where each person she
meets is a child. Returns the miracle and amazement we left in our Velcro shoes,
awakens our bodies with the suddenness of her eyes. Everything is beautiful. Keloid
and awkward is beautiful. Adolescent girls are beautiful. Men, for the first time, can
be called beautiful. Her hands reach for the sun as though it were food, a cloud as we
walk. She shakes, awed by the emerald hue of fresh grass hugging her apartment
building like jealous, thirsty arms.

My grandmother is the ripest hallelujah. Where everyone is a child. Is a dear
daughter. A dear son. Has a story and roots and branches twisting embrace
through the sterile bars of a subway car. Picking it up. Where every object,
moment, everything in this sparkling gasp of an earth is not just beautiful.
It is more than beautiful. It is too beautiful. It is *so* beautiful.*

---

*   Connect Online: **"Hallelujah"** http://www.cdbaby.com/cd/carlosandresgomezl
(audio sample/download)

CHAPTER 10

Love

I t's a strange, seemingly paradoxical thing, love. It is rooted in giving without expectation or condition, while knowing you are worthy of receiving the most divine examples of it. In other words, the more love I give out to people because it's just the right thing to do (not as a means to an end), the more I find it coming back to me. It's something I'm reminded of each instance I am surrounded by those who embody the grace and giving that love connotes.

When I was a little kid, I knew my dad loved me because he'd sneak me peanut M&M's, even though my mom would scold him if she found out. I knew my mom loved me because she'd get out of bed at all hours of the night to get me a glass of water or massage my aching flat feet that would cramp up while I tried to sleep. I knew my sister, Sarita, loved me because she'd play with me in the backyard for hours whichever one of the myriad of absurd games we were forced to invent to pass the endless summer months (in that era before PlayStation and the Internet when kids had to make it up as they went along).

For most of my life, I didn't believe I deserved love. With all the painful things that had been happening in my life, I had become cynical and closed to love. I lost faith in its power and purpose. I thought of it as a mirage chased by fools. It's a trend all too familiar among men. We take on these identities and ideas of who we are (or think we are supposed to be) and often forget to include love in the equation. Or we blame love, as a villain, for the hardships of our lives.

The first time my best friend told me he loved me, we had both been struggling through really difficult health issues and we had been doing our best to support each other through them. We were talking on the phone one night, after a particularly emotional conversation, and before we hung up he said to me, "Carlos, I love you."

I felt this abrupt and sharp defensive clench in my chest, like a shield thrown up too late as a spear tore into my body. I remember the heavy pause that followed. My brain trying to unpack, in the dragging seconds that followed, why I would react so strongly to what Brent had just said to me. I could feel my body literally repelling away from the phone receiver as he said those words. It was instinctual.

Probably to diffuse the tension in my throat and end the call, I quickly responded, "Of course, man. I love you too, dude."

It's a habit among men. It's difficult for us to say things outright, so we hedge. It's how we give each other permission to use words we're not supposed to. "Love" is one of those words like "beautiful." We learn early on that those words come with a price. Men say the word "love" quickly, only in reciprocation, and to a close family member, preferably a woman. The word "beautiful" is never to be used with regard to a man, under any circumstances. It is a feminine word, a word we use to win the affections of a woman (often as a means to try to fuck her).

I make sure to use the word "beautiful" as much as I can these days. To refer to men as "beautiful" during my performances and remind the women in the room that men need to hear that word, especially black and Latino men, whose banners of identity are littered with dehumanizing and monstrous slurs that couldn't be further from the truth. When the words "beautiful" and "I love you" become like land mines in your life—things to be avoided at all costs—what do we become? How do we not begin to devalue what we have to share with the world?

I made it a big point a few years ago to stop using those extraneous words when I tell someone I love them, especially with other men. I practice doing it with my best friends, Brent and Eric, and my girlfriend's brothers-in-law (who I consider my brothers), Darnell and Maurice. At first it was hard. I would have to literally plot my way through what I was saying. Slow down my speech and almost catch my mouth at the end from tagging on a "brother" or "man" or "dude." But with practice it became easier.

"Eric, I love you."

"Brent, I love you."

When Darnell's mother passed away, I called him to let him know I was thinking about him and his family. I ended my message with, "Darnell, you know I love you and I'm there for you." It was less scary to say it in a voice mail, but the words came out more easily than I had anticipated. And I was glad. You think someone may probably know how you feel about him or her, but it's always something else to actually give voice to it.

It's similar to how my dad communicates sensitive stuff. It's almost always the same, without fail. He'll say to me, "Carlitos, you know . . ." and then say something that will alter the rest of my life, like:

'". . . I love you, right?"

". . . I'm moving to Germany in a month, right?"

". . . your friend Elias died in a car accident a few months ago, right?"

". . . she's pregnant with twins, right?"

It gives just enough space, a buffer, to say almost anything. We use devices like that all the time, as men, to say the things that we must. We'll say something in passing, what we've been waiting to say for an entire lifetime, as though it was just an afterthought. Or we'll say it like my dad does, adding "right?" as though it was a given, something everyone inherently knew, the words now only serving as an affirmation or reinforcement of what was already shared knowledge.

And then there are times when the buffer and walls come down, like in an experience I shared with Eric. Like Brent, he's someone who has become a brother to me, one of a handful of friends in my life whom I cherish and love as though they are my own blood. He was struggling through a very difficult point in his own life. His engagement had fallen into shambles, and I had been his primary support system. One day, after a particularly vulnerable talk as he dropped me off at the bus station, he told me he loved me and kissed me on the cheek.

I felt my body retreat again, just like with Brent. It's funny. I had done so much work in my life to believe I had reached some more evolved state of maleness, that I had become this groundbreaking new type of man—one who had tamed the homophobia trained into my flesh. And yet I tensed up a bit as his lips touched my cheek. It was a mere kiss shared between brothers but I almost pulled away from it, out of impulse. I didn't quite recoil like I did with Brent telling me he loved me for the first time, but my body reacted differently than my heart wanted. I felt honored and loved and understood by that kiss. I felt cared for and known and acknowledged. Eric is my brother. I had already known that, but by him taking that risk to kiss me on the cheek, as he would his little brother Scott, he taught me something.

I recognized that day one of the harshest tariffs that comes along with this masculinity I had struggled against: fear of love. Fear of being held and kissed and knowing someone attributes that word to us. We keep our distance because it comes with responsibility and expectation and commitment. There are so many kinds of love, but one thing they all have in common is giving. And there are certain kinds of giving more acceptable to my masculine socialization than others.

For example, when my twin little brother and sister were born, I actually wanted to hate them. I had planned to have as little to do with them as possible. I was angry and feeling like my dad was trying to replace my older sister and me. I didn't want to have any responsibility to these two new little people in our lives. I didn't want to babysit them or change their diapers or anything else. I wanted them to just disappear.

And then I saw those two little pink nuggets in the nursery of Mount Sinai and everything changed. They were each so small and helpless and damn . . . adorable. How can I hate these two little munchkins? I wanted so badly to be able to justify the ugly feelings I had been harboring during my stepmother's pregnancy, but they were swept away in that first second I met Maya and Nicolas at three days old. I was completely in love. And it made no sense, as love frequently doesn't. But it was perfectly acceptable for me to tell people I loved my little brother and sister. They're my blood, my family. That is considered in bounds. It's okay for me to feel protective of them and take care of them. It is the duty that comes along with love.

Over time, fourteen years later, it's amazing for me to see how the two of them, my little sister and brother, have learned about love and also taught me. I've always made it a point to be very vocal about my love to both of them and make sure that I show it to them each and every single time I see them. I've always been an affectionate person, but with them I feel the biggest responsibility. And it's amazing to see the people they are each becoming. Maya is the vocal one, extroverted and social, continually telling my older sister and me how much she cares about us. She always says, "I love you, Carlitos," before we hang up the phone. Nicolas is more shy but no less expressive, often holding my hand when we walk down the street and giving me a hug and kiss every night before he goes to bed. He isn't as vocal with saying "I love you," but he shows it in every moment we're together.

Even I was never as physically expressive as Nicolas is, especially at fourteen years old. It's a huge testament to the kind of parents my papi and Karin have been—showing him that it is okay to be a teenage boy and *show* someone that you love them. I hope that never changes. It inspires me to be the kind of man who never runs when he feels someone expressing something that is tender or vulnerable or filled with love. I wonder, if I was the kind of fourteen-year-old boy that Nicolas is, would I have recoiled at Brent telling me he loved me or tensed up when Eric kissed my cheek?

Growing up, especially being around a divorce and moving constantly, it's easy to lose faith in love. A big part of that can also be the cynicism and viciousness that build up inside when you think love is something with time limits and conditions and, ultimately, temporary—quick to be taken away without warning. Moving every couple of years or so, I struggled with holding out hope for love, as I lost touch with friends, made new ones, got close, and then moved away again. The cycle continued, as I desperately searched for a person outside of my family that I knew would be there for the rest of my life.

With my childhood as the source material, the constant moving and changing schools every couple of years or so, I developed what I call the two-year rule. Here's what it is: It takes two years to develop a meaningful bond with someone and two years to finally lose touch with a good friend. As fate would have it, I moved just about every two years growing up, so as I would be losing touch with my former best friends, I would be solidifying bonds with new people—only to leave them for another place. This was during the era of letter writing, too, so it was much more difficult to stay in touch than it is now with Facebook and the Internet and everything else with social media. I remember running to the mailbox every day hoping for a letter from a friend. More often than not, though, it was me spending my summer sending out letters and postcards to old friends, only to get a rare message or two back. And this is not to say that they were bad friends or people; let's keep it real—who wants to be writing letters in the middle of summer?

But I took it to mean that I wasn't loved, that I had been forgotten, and now, in a new strange place, at a different school, the cycle started again. And that's when it's easy to confuse other things for love, especially during adolescence and beyond, when we're in need of love but feel as though we're not allowed to have it. When sex replaces love, or being in a gang or on a basketball team or part of a crew of friends or whatever replaces love. I spent years desperately wanting to be loved and numbing my pain by hooking up with girls. I wasn't always having sex with them, but I was using them, however briefly, to feel wanted and cared for and acknowledged. It has only been through experiencing the overpowering contrast, feeling the most profound examples of love, that I have seen so much of my past fooling around for what it was: a pathetic addiction. Those hook-ups were a needle or a pipe that temporarily fulfilled my desperate need to be touched and loved.

No one has taught me more about love, in the romantic way and more, than my girlfriend, Whitney. She has been the antidote to the man I was—who sabotaged every meaningful commitment, craved being single, and told every woman I was "not ready for a relationship." I first recognized who she actually was to me when it seemed too late.

I have now been with her for more than four years. We've lived together for three, and I am damn near certain that she is who I want to spend the rest of my life with. I know marriage is important to her, but I have not yet proposed to her. Strangely, it's not even the lifelong commitment that seems to scare me quite as much as the institution of marriage. Maybe that's a cop-out. I don't even know anymore. Marriage feels forever tainted to me, corrupted by organizations and churches and people not responsible enough for what it requires.

Friends of mine give it to me from both sides. Some say, "Fuck everyone else, make marriage whatever you want it to be. Do it on your own terms." And others say, "Yeah, I never really saw you as the type to get married like everyone else. Marriage is cursed." All the while, I can feel my girlfriend's simultaneous unflinching faith and growing fear: *Is all of this for nothing? Will he ever come around and commit?*

Of course, for me being in a relationship and calling someone my partner or girlfriend *is* that commitment. As I've moved further along into adulthood, I've realized that most women do not buy that story. And it's strange because I love the idea of a ceremony dedicated solely to love, especially one that brings together two families who may have never crossed paths otherwise, but still I hesitate. It is as though I can press Pause while I'm where I am and somehow prevent a tragically fated fatherhood in the interim. I feel like I'm hastily trying to solve the problem before everything blows up.

I have noticed things shifting in me, though, over the past two years as my father and I repair and heal from some of the lingering wounds from those divorce years. And my girlfriend and I talk openly about what fears I continue to have, and she encourages me to communicate and try to solve the one riddle that still haunts me. More than that, though, watching the closeness and the blessing and grace and healthiness of her family gives me courage and inspiration.

Her parents are married. She is close with her sisters. The family gets together during the holidays and for a yearly luau every July Fourth. The big birthdays are all family reunions. I look into her father's face and see the pride of a husband and grandfather who knows what he has given to this world. His is a legacy more meaningful than any accolade or grade or accomplishment at any job. He has raised four amazing daughters and helped to raise three incredible grandchildren. He has a marriage with a wife he loves, who he has been with for more than forty years. And when I watch a smile creep over his face as the family sits down for dinner and he looks around that room, I know that I want that for my life. I want to know what that moment feels like inside my chest. And I know Whitney can sense it, knows I want the same life she does. Maybe that's why she has stuck by me.

She has had more patience and backbone and belief and maturity and blind faith than any person I have ever known. During our relationship, she has been poised and strong. She was the one who suggested we move in together, then told me, without flinching, that she wants to have a family together, wants to be my wife. She's the most hopeful and refreshing foil to everything this world seems to offer up when it comes to love. She listens and pushes me and understands and disagrees and then listens some more.

Whitney embodies love for me. More than anything else, it's because she never takes the easy way out. When everything around her is screaming, "*Run!*"—she stays. She fights the easy impulse and stays. Watching her example has forced me to demand much more out of myself than I thought I had, like when I wanted to be the little boy and move out, or when I got tired of the work it took to keep a relationship going. Human beings are work. Real love takes a committed team to keep it in motion. Before Whitney, I only knew love as infatuation and lust and honeymoon. She has taught me more about intimacy and trust and commitment than anyone else on this earth.

Most importantly, though, Whitney has helped me break many of the unhealthy, self-destructive cycles that defined who I was for much of my adult life. I always say that in a great relationship, each person makes the other the best version of who he or she might be. I know that being with Whitney makes me, undoubtedly, the best version of myself.

She lets me know, each and every single day, that I am deserving of love. She champions my unique gifts and sensibilities and, also, the quirks I might be insecure about. She pushes me to be more—not because what I am right now is not enough, but because of her belief that I can be even better, brighter, smarter, healthier, more patient, more communicative, more everything than I already am. She lets me know I am enough while knowing I am better than I ever give myself credit for. And she won't give up on me when I want her to. In that way, she reminds me of two other central people in my life.

Watching my mom and dad stick it out with me during my restless, misbehavior-laden childhood taught me about the kind of commitment and love required of two great parents. I have no idea where they found the resolve and patience to put up with the shit I put them through. And both of them today, with a gentle smile, euphemistically remember me as "a passionate, energetic kid." That's the kind of parental love I hope to have for my kids. To feel their love through all those trying times inspires me to try to one day fill their shoes.

I've been so lucky in my life. I could have easily responded to the heartache and pain of moving, divorce, death, and everything else by spiting the world. I could have lost all faith in love and allowed my passion to turn vicious and full of malice. There were people who stood by me, though, when things were at their most tense. I was lucky to have two parents growing up (as complicated as it got at times), as well as an older sister, a best friend (or three), and Whitney, who demanded I live up to a higher bar for myself.

When a man is told his entire life that he is a monster and is worthless, he internalizes those expectations. They often become a self-fulfilling prophecy, a symptom of his society-shaped lack of self-worth. I've been through periods in my life where I've felt vilified, worthless, and depressed. I've wanted to lash out at the world and project my hurt onto everyone around me. By chance, I've been lucky enough to have people who loved me through those hard times, who didn't give up on me when I wanted to give up on myself. If only more men on this planet could have even one person in their corner when things turned dark, when the pain is greatest and the self-doubt is most daunting.

When I was little, my mom says she remembers thinking, *Wow. This kid is a handful. I better be careful with how I raise him because I might be the difference between him becoming Hitler or Gandhi.*

Some days I walk through Brooklyn feeling other men's energy rake against my shoulder as they pass, locking eyes occasionally. "What the fuck you lookin' at?" a guy said to me last week.

He lives three doors down from me. That's the only time either of us has spoken to each other in almost two years. Being a New Yorker, that's unfortunately not strange to me. I know people who live in their buildings for years in this city who never exchange two words with anyone. And it makes me sad. I don't believe any person actually wants that. Some days I yearn to break through that wall and smile and wave at my neighbors. Occasionally, I greet the old man five doors down who sits on his stoop and watches people. I remember how surprised he was the first time I said hello, his face immediately lighting up as though he were recognizing his grandson. Such a simple act of reaching out can immediately bring sunlight and joy into a moment neither person had previously shared with each other.

"What the fuck you lookin' at?" the guy from three doors down said, flinging the words like a pathetic, defensive punch. It was as though my curious glance his way could only be an introduction to combat, as though a gentle grin and soft head nod in his direction were only patronizing or manipulative or part of a *conspiracy*. That's what men of color learn of love—conspiracy. It is what we are taught. Anything tender, gentle, affectionate, with arms open is a mirage, a Siren that does not exist, only there to crash our ship on the rocks. It is only there to fool us. I have passed my neighbor hundreds of times and never even looked his way. But that day I couldn't pass one more time without acknowledging him. Something ached, cried out in my body—*I know it's been almost two years, but I cannot do this for one more day.*

I wanted to tell him, "I am looking at you. You are here. You are important. Both of us are. Let's keep it that way. We are each irreplaceable. I don't want to die today. Do you?"

And then maybe reach out my palm like I did that afternoon at Rikers. Who knows what he would have done? Maybe punch me in the face. Or laugh and walk away. Or break down and cry, wrap his shaking arms around me. Or maybe just freeze, the accumulated learning of his maleness unable to process such a gesture—like Brent saying "I love you" or Eric's kiss on the cheek.

I have been that guy for most of my life, that's what hurt most that day. My jaw has been clenched and my fists have been balled ready to fight the world—doubting and enraged by anything kind or caring. So many times, I did the same "What the fuck you lookin' at?" as I stepped up and puffed out my chest, ready to die to prove I wasn't a sucker. And then I realized the only conspiracy that existed was in my own perception, in the way I self-sabotaged my own joy and fulfillment by never allowing love in, refusing to accept that any love could be made just for me, that I was meaningful enough for a stranger to notice me on my front stoop and say, "Hello."

Written and performed by Carlos Andrés Gómez
Directed by and developed with Tamilla Woodard

"Rottweiler"

Papi—we each needed time
to grow up and make sense of things.

I love you.
You are forgiven.

For what it is you still hold
in your throat.

I'm too old for this bite
that paralyzes my hands
when I write.

It is not yours;
not your fault.

Sometimes it takes 9 years
to realize you're not angry anymore
and you forgive.
And you love someone
more than ever.

I am no longer that untamed
rottweiler let loose from
a page.

Not like I was.

Now the fire is all righteous
spark and earned rage, ink soaked
with stains of those moments
everyone needs to yell about:

unjust wages
and bruised cheekbones

prostitution
and flooded out 9th Wards

my middle name being constantly
mispronounced and misspelled

    You are forgiven.

          I want to be a father too.
        Throw a ball in a backyard
              with a son
         who has a short temper
              like mine.
          Drive to Anaheim
           in a Mustang

        as an untamed wind
        wrestles with our hair.

CHAPTER 11

Forgiveness:
When There's Nothing Left

The day I forgave my father, I became a man. I was twenty-three years old. For nine years I had held on to the hurt and anger of the night I decided to move out of his apartment and go live with my mom. I had spent almost a decade fueled by the venom of those words my father had said to me on those steps overlooking the East River. And I was tired. I was tired of proving my worth to my father and to anyone who would listen or pay attention. I was tired of wrestling my way through a seemingly antagonistic world full of doubters and naysayers. I was tired of carrying the cross I had fastened to my back since that night. I was tired of being a reaction to something in my past and not a purpose in my own right. More than anything else, though, I was tired of needing to prove my worth to myself. Over the course of a year and a half, I learned many of my most poignant lessons about manhood, finally letting go and discovering true forgiveness for the first time. Class was in session during the countless hours I spent with an eclectic mix of daily teachers, most of whom, by anyone's standards, were considered some of the most despicable men in our society: pimps, rapists, drug dealers, felons, addicts, and abusive fathers.

Little did I realize, when I accepted a job as a fresh-faced, just-out-of-college twenty-two-year-old social worker, that I was about to receive the most important and humbling education of my life. When there is nothing left, no one in your life, and humility and desperation take over, you realize what actually matters. Suddenly the pride and arrogance of youth give way to empathy. The anger and righteousness and martyrdom give way to needing to stay alive, that innate impulse of the body to preserve itself against all odds. When there are things undeniably more powerful than anything you have ever known, humility sets in.

Each Friday at eleven o'clock in the morning, I would sit in a room in a modest health center on 127th Street in Harlem and talk for one hour with a group of seven or eight men. Most were older than me by decades. It was called the weekly Men's Group, a gathering, in most cases court-mandated, for recovering heroin and crack cocaine addicts. It was a place for them to check in about their sobriety, share their goals and dreams and struggles, and build some routine into their fragile world. Most of the men in the room had few friends, if any, besides those sitting in our circle of chairs. All had prison records; most were on parole or probation. Most had served at least one tour of active duty at war. Half had serious mental health conditions: paranoid schizophrenia, bipolar disorder, and clinical depression. A couple had attempted suicide. All had survived abuse of some sort. Almost all stayed in homeless shelters in the neighborhood and had multiple children or other surviving family they yearned to reconnect with. Most had burned bridges so many times, they had resigned themselves to merely dreaming of the loved ones they once knew. I looked into each man's eyes in that circle the first day, and I, surprisingly, saw a good man. I saw a piece of myself.

We went from everyone's head down, not saying a word, at the first session, to confiding in each other and sharing stories about our biggest dreams and fears through tears and hugs and knotted throats. There wasn't one monster I saw in that room and, to be honest, it kind of haunted me. What did I expect? That only monsters do monstrous things? Am I so much better? I saw myself in the proud heart, gregariousness, and swagger of Duane, a twenty-nine-year-old former heroin dealer who bragged about killing men as a teenager.

I saw myself in the weary eyes of Marcus, a sixty-three-year-old war vet who, one day, shared his biggest regret with the group: gang-raping a little girl with a slew of men during the Vietnam War. He told me he hadn't wanted to, but he was afraid what the other men might say. So he did it. He cried when he told the story, broke down for the first time. He said he cried that night all those years ago too. Then he talked about his daughter. Then he talked about the music he loved so much, what he would play for hours on the handed-down Casio keyboard he carefully held in his proud fingers as though it were his only remaining child. In many ways, it was.

I saw myself in that awkward younger version of him at war. I saw a room full of men with big hearts and fragile self-esteem and too many ghosts and not enough champions by their side. I saw a group of guys with the odds stacked so unfairly against them, it was a miracle they were each still breathing. I saw a room full of men at war with the imperfect science and magic of their bodies—ashamed of what they had been told was wrong. It was a war I knew all too well, the war I had waged against my own overbearing sensitivity and my need to be touched and held. The war against my shame at getting choked up when I started to speak as an adolescent because I cared so much, my embarrassment at being afraid sometimes or stupid or just generally inadequate. I could have easily, with the flip of a coin (as my grandfather said to my mom that time), been any one of these men. In fact, in so many ways, I was.

Where is hope? Where is God right now? I asked myself. *Who the fuck am I to be running this session?* That was another question that constantly came up. With the high turnover rate of substance abuse counselors, I had been asked to fill in for one session—"just this week." "Just this week" eventually became one year.

During the beginning of that first session, I asked one of my clients how long he had been clean of crack cocaine and, without hesitation, he turned to me and said, "Eighteen years, three months, seven days, four hours, thirty-one minutes, and fifty-one . . . fifty-two . . . fifty-three seconds," his eyes homing in on the clock behind me. "And not a moment, a breath, a breakfast goes by that I don't dream of that pipe. Crack is more powerful than family and love and money. Fuck what you heard—crack is more powerful than God. Crack would kick God's ass in a fight. And that's cuz crack fights dirty—dirtier than anything you could ever imagine. I've been clean for that long and every single moment is a fight. I lost everyone I loved because of that shit and I still want it. I lost my dream job—driving my own eighteen-wheeler. The future I'd worked so hard for. You tell me—for somebody in that hell—why shouldn't I have picked up that pipe again?" His eyes cut through me like a hot chainsaw through butter.

I had no idea. My mouth froze, jaw hanging slack into a dumb question mark. Thoughts flooded my brain in a jumbled knot, all of the words in the English language drained from my mouth. *Who am I to deny him something more powerful than God?* I thought. *Damn is that shit scary. Just ten bucks to buy something more powerful than God? How or even why should I*

convince him otherwise? I was at war with myself. I was conflicted and confused and in *way* over my head. The addict had
persuaded the "counselor," if that's what the hell I was now. This
man had been clean for almost two *decades* and he knew to the
second the last time his lips touched a crack pipe. That remains,
etched in my memory, as one of the most frightening things I
have ever heard.

"That's how I lost her, though. That last one over eighteen
years ago was what did it. My baby girl. My family. I lost them
all that day," he finally said.

"What happened?" I asked.

"I pawned off my baby girl's first communion cross to get
some rock," he said, his head hanging from his neck, as though
it had just happened. "I've never loved anything like my daughter. But, that day, I loved my pipe more. I would have probably
sold her I wanted it so bad."

"Does any of your family know how long you've been
clean?" I asked.

"Yeah. I actually talk to my daughter from time to time. My
ex-wife still won't let me in the house. I can't say I blame her. But
I get to see my daughter now and again. She's my heart. She's all
grown up now, though. Of course . . . ," and he chuckled into
thought, as if caught in a brief snapshot of an eighteen-year
dream. "After I got kicked out of the house for pawning off her
necklace, my daughter was the one who saved my life. She gave
me a reason to get clean and get my life together. She was the
first one who ever forgave me. That forgiveness is the reason I'm
alive." His watery eyes glistened above a crooked smile.

"So I guess you answered your own question then. You're
proof of why not to pick up that pipe," I encouraged, reaching
hard for some footing.

"Absolutely. I'm not a truck driver anymore but I have a new
life. I want to see my grandbabies grow up. I want to earn back
my family's trust. I want to help others who made my mistakes."

He continued, "I was abused by my uncle as a child. I felt so ashamed of myself for so long because of that. Only after I started going to the drug treatment did I first hear someone say to me, 'Hey man, that stuff ain't your fault. You don't need to run from that anymore. It's okay.' "

The cycle ended here. If when I die that is the caption summarizing what I did, I could live with that. That day, talking with my client Carl, I learned that forgiveness is something we not only grant each other, it is something we must, ultimately, give to ourselves. As I rode the 3 train back to my apartment in Brooklyn that evening, I started to become more aware than ever of all of the ugly baggage I had piling up in my chest.

My father never abused me. I never had an uncle who made me get naked with him in the basement and then suck his dick while he watched the Mets game. But that talk on the steps of the East River, in which my dad had tried to tear down my self-esteem in his futile, paradoxical last attempt to hold on to me, had been something I couldn't let go of.

We are all damaged and imprisoned by the pain we hold on to. My resentment toward another person hurts both of us. My animosity and anger fuel my energy and thoughts and being, dimming the light in all of those who are implicated. Carl's daughter saved his life by forgiving him. His daughter helped him survive during a time in his life when he was seeking out death. Carl then moved from surviving to living when he finally forgave himself. In recognizing the cycle in which he had been trapped, he was able to build the life for himself that he wanted—free of the shame he once hid, with crack cocaine as his lone therapist.

I was taught to wipe my tears and steady my expression as a kid. Don't talk about what's rumbling inside of your chest. Stay stoic and quiet. It's part of the unspoken male code. "Toughen up, son," "suck it up," "man up"—this is how we learn to process emotion. This is the cause of our emotional illiteracy. No wonder so many men bury their wounds and insecurities in alcohol and drugs and violence. That day with Carl I realized I could never become a man without finally letting go of so many parts of my past, holding myself accountable for some missteps I'd rather forget, granting forgiveness for other things, making a conscious choice to stop beating myself up and forgiving myself in others, and accepting the fractured and delicate details that mark me as human.

Every week those men and I would have these amazing talks in our cramped little room, a motley brotherhood trying to venture together through the complex wreckage of our pasts. One of the guys in our group, Fernando, had never learned how to read. He was forty-eight years old. He had gone to tremendous lengths to try to hide his illiteracy. One day, when I shared with the group that I had a hard time with reading myself (not learning until I was almost nine years old), he finally shared his secret.

He had grown up in a family of addicts, everyone hooked on heroin. He had been shooting up since he was thirteen years old. He never finished middle school and spent most of his life in and out of homeless shelters and prisons. Only now, finally clean, albeit briefly, he wanted to confront the biggest fear of his life, so I helped him enroll in a literacy program to address his problems with reading for the first time.

When I had explained that I no longer felt embarrassed about my troubles with reading—having so many languages to juggle and constantly moving, when could I have learned?—he said he no longer felt alone. When could he have learned to read when he was younger, coming home to a house of IV drug users, his mother working as a prostitute, and his abusive father in and out of his life? It took forgiveness, at forty-eight years old, for him to finally admit he had never learned how to read. It wasn't his fault. And that forgiveness came from himself.

During my time as a social worker, I'd spend many of my days doing outreach work, which is basically trying to find the most marginalized folks and getting them connected with the resources they need: housing, a winter jacket, food pantry access, HIV testing, counseling, and whatever else. And to find the most marginalized of people, you can't just set up a pretty booth on 125th Street, next to the Starbucks, and hope new clients will swing by. No. I had to go *find* them. So I went to crack houses, strolls where prostitutes worked, shooting galleries where people would shoot up heroin and cocaine, homeless shelters, and motels where you pay for a room by the hour.

Let's be real—I was scared to death, scared of how I would react to the men I was about to encounter. For example: *How the fuck am I supposed to work with a pimp? I mean this guy literally sells women for a living. Damn. How do I turn that cheek? I sure as hell ain't Jesus, and I'm not trying to be, either. What if he gets aggressive with one of the women? Do I just stand there and do nothing? I doubt it. But what if I do? And what if I don't? And then what if he kicks my ass?*

Let's just say what happened in real life became a lot less complicated than it was in my mind. On a tip from a client who suggested that I stop by to give out condoms and brochures for our program, I started to visit a motel in Harlem that was infamous for prostitution. The first moment I walked in (as was typically the case), everyone stopped and turned as though the police had just walked in. People thinking I'm an undercover cop has saved my life and put it at risk more times than I could ever keep track of.

As I would typically do, coming into a new locale and trying to establish trust, I slowly unzipped my jacket (to show I wasn't carrying anything or wearing a vest, which NYPD undercover officers do) and walked in with a warm, friendly, but still professional smile. I told a gentleman near the madam at the reception that I had been referred here by my client, whose name I gave. Suddenly the door to the reception area swung open and out walked a colossal, towering mountain of a man. Rock solid, broad, and intense, "intimidating" doesn't even come close to describing him. I mean this Puerto Rican dude was easily six foot eight with a shiny gold left front tooth. Without blinking, he briskly and very matter-of-factly asked me in Spanish, "What the fuck do you want?"

For a second, I forgot every single word in my Spanish vocabulary. Then, after a breath, I stumblingly explained, rather pathetically, why I was there. That was probably when he realized I wasn't much of a threat. After I presented my business card and offered up a handful of condoms and brochures, he snatched them out of my hand and laid them down next to the reception window. Now mind you, this window was about two inches of thick bulletproof glass with a small area for money to be pushed through to the madam. But I had done what I came to do. The condoms and brochures were laid out for anyone coming to that window.

"Cada miércoles. A las once," he said gruffly in his slurred Spanish.

Okay, I thought, *I guess I'll be coming every Wednesday at eleven. Hope he's convinced I'm not a cop and doesn't decide to kill me next time.* And that was how it went. Each Wednesday at eleven in the morning, I'd walk up the narrow flight of steps, unzip my jacket for the video camera, do a twirl with a casual smile, and then drop off my brochures and condoms. Occasionally, I'd see very scantily dressed women hovering around the lobby, but, generally, no one was in sight. A couple of times I saw the main pimp (I assume—yes, the big Puerto Rican guy) grabbing a woman by the hair, or aggressively holding her arms and yelling in a stifled whisper, and I would just calmly go about my business as though I were sweeping the floor.

You're not here to change the world, Carlos. Or end misogyny today. Or even save anyone's life, I told myself. *You're just a silly little social worker trying to maybe give one of these women an exit strategy someday. What good would it do if you stepped in? You don't think that Puerto Rican dude would maul the shit out of you? And then what? I can see the headline:* SOCIAL WORKER KILLED IN HARLEM MOTEL. *Awesome. A lot of good that would do.*

That's not to say I didn't have a lot of conflicted feelings about what I was seeing. But I knew enough to know that I was most effective by simply doing what I had been hired to do: Drop off condoms. Drop off brochures. Calmly leave. Then one day at my weekly motel visit, I got a lesson on forgiveness like nothing I had ever experienced.

As usual, I walked up the narrow stairwell, opened my jacket, smiled, and did a slow turn, removed my condoms and brochures and approached the reception window, ready for my usual ninety-second visit and drop-off as I had been doing weekly for the past two months.

I rarely saw men in the lobby who weren't one of the pimps. I sometimes heard moaning and rhythmic thumping sounds, always mixed with this haunting cheap incense smell, but I saw a customer only once every blue moon—probably only twice during all of my visits.

This time was different. As I walked in, I noticed two black men hunched over at the reception window, frustratingly trying to communicate with the madam (her very limited English and their very limited Spanish made it quite hard to make any progress). Should I translate? Should I help? *Naw,* I thought. *I'm not here to be a translator. I'm here to be a social worker. Keep it simple, Carlos. Don't need to have someone think I'm one of those guys' friends or have some other intent or purpose here.*

The man was upset. He claimed he had paid her the forty

dollars she had asked for and had not received his receipt. A receipt? Why does a brothel write out receipts? Who knows? Maybe to make sure the madam isn't skimming off the top or so johns can write it off as a business expense—who the fuck knows? But, yes, they did give out receipts, as asinine as it sounds.

The woman had been watching her *telenovela* and chatting on the phone in Spanish, and she either had forgotten she'd taken his money, or was trying to hustle an extra forty dollars from him. As everyone's anger and volume started to amplify, the big Puerto Rican pimp suddenly appeared. *Oh shit,* I thought. He leaned into the thick glass and started pointing at the black dude and cursing him out in Spanish. The black dude started threatening the big Puerto Rican dude, who didn't waste much time bursting out from the reception room and into the lobby where the two black men now stood.

I could see their eyes get a little big when they realized how enormous and imposing this guy actually was. They had that look in their eyes of, *Oh fuck. Definitely didn't think dude would come out that quick. Damn . . . yeah, he's BIG.* In contrast, the black men were not very imposing at all. The gentleman who had been arguing was not more than five foot eight or so and had a rather average build, and his friend couldn't have been more than five foot six and was skinny.

As is the case in many arguments across racial and ethnic lines, especially when the cursing out isn't having the right impact (because of a language impasse), the Puerto Rican pimp finally reached for a universal word that *everyone* understood: *Nigger.*

He dropped the word like a hand grenade, spit spewing from his mouth and down his chin, as he punctuated it by pushing his open palm into the black man's face, sort of slap-punching, or "mushing" as I like to call it, him backward. Before my brain could catch up to anything that had just happened in the past minute or so (this entire thing, from the door opening forward, couldn't have lasted longer than that), I glanced over and noticed the black man wrestling his arm out of the backpack he had had slung over his left shoulder.

It was a split second, literally *tenths* of a second, and I caught the briefest of glimpses at a glint of black metal. Before I had any clue what my body was doing (very much without my permission, I might add), I was leaping out of my seat and wrapping my arms around the man as he tried to bring a gun up to his chest.

People always ask me, "What the hell were you *thinking*?" The truth? Nothing. Not a damn thing. I don't even remember deciding to tackle this dude. It just happened. It was like I was sitting, blacked out, and then wrestling a guy holding a gun. My body had committed mutiny—it was acting without my input or permission. Barely realizing it was a gun, I tackled this guy— holding on with all of my strength and yelling, at the top of my lungs, over and over again, "I'm not restraining you! I'm *not* restraining you!"

It's kind of hilarious when I think about it now. *Of course* I was restraining him. Why did I keep yelling that? I guess I wanted him to know that I wasn't trying to hurt or embarrass him and I couldn't think of anything else to say.

The Puerto Rican dude didn't seem daunted at all by the prospect of a gun. It probably helped that I was now the primary target if this dude *did* decide to shoot anybody. So the pimp just kept yelling more shit in Spanish as the black dude's skinny friend jumped on my back and started to wrestle with me as I heard the gun's safety click off and we all held on for dear life. The three of us, this strange wrestling mosh pit we had become, stumbled our way into the stairwell somehow and started down the first few steps.

"Listen! Listen! I'm *not* restraining you! You don't need to kill anybody and get life upstate. Please, listen!" I was begging, pleading, my voice cracking, doing anything I could to try to have this man hear me.

I had suddenly had my first thought in more than three minutes. And this is what it was: *I cannot hold on to this man forever.*

My plan was flawed. Oh yeah, that's right—*I never had a plan.* Fuck. Unless I was planning to become Jean-Claude Van Damme or Jet Li and tear a (most probably) illegal handgun from a guy's fingers and kick both guys' asses, I had to let go at some point. I had to be humble and apologetic in this most impossible of circumstances. I had to use the only three weapons I had left: humility, compassion, and communication.

"Listen, I'm letting go . . . if you want to, you can shoot me," I said finally. (Looking back, I'm like, *What the fuck kind of a last statement is that, Carlos? Shit. "Shoot me"?! For real?!? That's what you came up with?!*)

What else could I say, though? I was starting to lose my grip anyway, so why not take the initiative and hope he understands? Beg for mercy. Be humble. Hope that somehow there is a God, or some angel or something ready to help me.

Both men, surprisingly, stopped wrestling with me almost immediately. There was a tense but palpable moment of relief but definitely not resolution. The man with the gun paused, rather thoughtfully, with his head down for a brief moment. Then, as unexpectedly as they'd both let go of me, he tucked the gun into his belt behind his back, smiled, softly chuckled to himself, and said, "Yo, dog. That would have been some *stupid* shit! Fo' real—good lookin' out, son." And he laughed with his head thrown back, giving me a quick pound and a man hug, just before he and his boy trickled down the stairs and out of my life forever.

In retrospect, I have no idea what I *should* have done. What was the right move in that situation? It's not like I can pretend that I had any life-altering revelations during that exchange, especially since I had no thoughts at all that I can recollect. But looking back, there was so much in this incident that, maybe paradoxically, taught me one of the more profoundly beautiful lessons on humanity and forgiveness.

Here's what I mean: If the black dude had shot the pimp, I probably would have been next. What else could he have done, spared the main eyewitness standing two feet away from a murder? So, as I look back, I suppose my body calculated that math quicker than I did and that's why I instinctively tackled the guy with the gun.

How does a situation like that end well? The way it turned out was better than probably anyone on earth could ever imagine, but what *was* that? And what was it that I learned about both humanity and forgiveness that day?

Sometimes forgiveness is granted with a "thank you." It's an acceptance and acknowledgment. Losing your temper or getting scared and owning up to it. Walking dangerously close to crossing that line (where there's no turning back) and surprising yourself and stepping back. No one wanted to die that day. The man with the gun wasn't carrying a gun because he wanted to kill someone; he was carrying it because he was scared. He was undersize and maybe picked on as a kid, being followed around by a friend who was even less imposing than he was. The pimp knew he had to make a point so that others who frequented the motel didn't think they could get one over on the operation. Maybe the madam was defensive because she was distracted and unsure of what she had gotten from the gentleman. All of us were just trying not to look like a fool while staying alive in the process.

Embarrassment and fear: Those were the driving forces of the entire incident. When the man with the gun realized I was probably more scared than he was (even as I wrestled him and his friend into a stairwell), he forgave me. He not only granted me forgiveness, ultimately saving my life, he actually thanked me for protecting *him*. "Good lookin' out, son," he said to me. He had heard what I said about doing a life sentence upstate. Who knows? Maybe he's been to prison. Maybe he's afraid to ever go. Maybe he heard all of my crazy yelling and realized I was just a scared kid looking to make it to lunchtime.

When I think back to that day, and all those negotiations that took place between the four of us men, it gives me hope about the world. Men don't join gangs to hurt people (even if they say they do); they join them to have a family—to not be alone or invisible. Men don't carry guns to kill people; they're just scared to be without one. I didn't throw a tantrum and punch cracks into my bedroom door as a kid to be a brat or just break things for no reason; I was afraid of everyone seeing me cry. Again.

When men are able to forgive themselves for their emotions and vulnerabilities and their desires for family and love and safety, that's when we will live in a less violent world. To fill the void of family, there are gangs. To fill the void of insecurity, there are guns and knives and weapons and wars that presidents fight on behalf of their fathers. To fill the void of love, there are women we use like bus stops, like accessories, like junk food. Shortly after I stopped working as a social worker, at twenty-three years old and stuck in Los Angeles, I finally learned to forgive myself.

In a whirlwind shift from my previous life, I had gotten a role in a Spike Lee movie called *Inside Man*, quit my job as a social worker, and was diving headlong into the full-time life of being an "artist." I had never studied acting and wanted to discover more about that magical world, of which I had only gotten a brief taste. So I headed out to Los Angeles, rented a beat-up car from Rent-A-Wreck, and got a cheap sublet in K-Town. As exciting a time as it was for me, this was one of the lowest points in my life. I have never known despair and loneliness like I did during those months. And if that wasn't enough, I began working with an acting teacher who forced me to confront for the first time in my life what I had been hiding inside, forced me to dig into the basement of demons lodged in my chest.

I was working on the final monologue from Robert Anderson's play *I Never Sang for My Father*. The process became the toughest and most pivotal artistic undertaking of my life. The mere sight of the *words* of that monologue, even just sitting on the page, resonated so strongly with me that I couldn't say them aloud without breaking down, without crumbling into heaving sobs. It was that bad. I had to finally face what I had been standing in the shadow of for more than nine years.

In the monologue, the main character is saying good-bye to his recently departed father, saying all of the things he had wanted to but never had the courage to share. It was the most devastatingly heartbreaking thing I could ever imagine: losing someone I loved so much, like my papi, without telling him what he meant to me. My pent-up anger and resentment over the years at my dad had been holding me back as a person. My pain had been the driving force of my life, dictating who I was and what I did. I needed to have my whole self back. Finally granting my father a reprieve was the only way to do it.

More than that, though, it was about understanding and empathizing with *why* my dad had said those things to me the night before I left for Providence, why he had made promises to me he couldn't keep, why he had not met us at the airport in Cyprus, why he and my mom had split up. And finally it clicked: He was scared. He was proud and ambitious, like me. He wanted to be like his Superman, his papi, just like I did with him when I was younger. He wanted to make sense of a world that no longer made any. He was lonely and watching his world fall apart. And that night on the steps of the East River, when we had the talk, he was feeling like a father who had failed. It wasn't what I was doing or why I was leaving, which had much more to do with the horrible Catholic school I had just been kicked out of, but he may have felt like I was picking my mom over him. However you want to interpret the circumstances that made me leave, for him it might have felt like someone telling him that he wasn't good enough. And this is a child to a parent, saying, "You're not a good father. You failed."

I imagined what I would have done in his predicament. I imagined my greatest fear: failing as a father. I recognized, in my more honest moments, that I probably might have said *much* harsher things than he said to me. I have a temper. And I get. emotional and proud. I use words sometimes to hurt, whether or not they're true, because I know just how powerful every word can be. I'm a poet. I inspire with my words. I punch with my words. I love and even have tried to kill with them.

Who am I to hold on to this grudge against my dad? Who am I to think I am above what he did? What about all of the awful things I did growing up? My father didn't hold it against me. Even after I slapped my favorite cousin, Natalie, at our family reunion when I was ten. Or after I got sent to the principal's office countless times and got report cards back that would say "Needs Improvement—Accepting Constructive Criticism." Or when I cut the strings on my sister's rare Somali guitar for no reason. Or when I would steal coins from his bedroom floor and hide them in a box in our front yard in Switzerland. Or any of the days I got angry or passionate and yelled and screamed and broke things and raised high hell all over the house. My father was there for me. He loved me, without condition, without reservation. And it was time for me to do the same with him.

My papi was and is an amazing father. Sure, there were hiccups along the way. There were better times than others. But, lord knows, parenting is not a perfect science. He might have found a better balance between family and job. He might have been a better communicator about some things . . . okay, *most* things. But, on the whole, God bless the job he did with my sister and me. I can only hope to one day live up to much of what he did as a parent. Which brings me to another lesson in forgiveness that I only truly embraced on the day I finally let go of all of the remaining animosity I had held toward my father.

It was Christmas day just after my twenty-fifth birthday. I sat in the living room with my twin little brother and sister, my papi, his wife, and my older sister. We had opened all of the presents but one. And the final gift was my dad's to open. I will never forget David Gray's "Life in Slow Motion" coming on through the speakers and that last splendid gift from my older sister lying in his lap like a final wish. Like a merciful prayer.

I knew what the present was. She had given a similar gift to me and our mom. Each of us received a beautiful, thoughtfully decorated photo album filled with pictures from different points in our lives, all the most joyful and celebratory moments of our journey together, the ones everyone wants to hold on to forever. When my parents got divorced, childhood photographs became a huge sore spot as things became final. In the messiness of it all, my father kept my mom's grandfather's pocket watch and my mom hung on to all of the childhood pictures of my sister and me. Each year my dad would ask us for pictures for Christmas. For some reason, I'd never really paid much attention to his request. I'm not sure why. Maybe I didn't realize just how much the photographs really meant to him. My sister, on the other hand, spent hours scouring through boxes and carefully picking out the most poignant candids of her, Papi, and me.

And as David Gray began to tear, full-throated, into the vulnerable chorus of that breathtaking song, I watched as my dad started to pull the gift wrap off of his photo album. I could feel the whole room in my chest. It was like all the insects and dust mites were holding their breath. Something was about to happen. We could all feel it.

Unveiling the album, he glanced at the cover with a slightly dumbstruck smirk on his face. He opened the book, then abruptly slammed it shut, as if he had just changed his mind.

His breathing became heavy and strained, as he hunched over, his left hand manically rubbing his forehead. Then, he stretched out his torso, leaning back and breathing in and out heavily again. And then back to his original stooped posture, a strained smile/scowl overtaking his face.

He was trying. He was trying so damn hard to hold it together, to be the strong father, the immovable, stoic Colombian rock of a patriarch we had always known, to retain a control that no man, or any human being for that matter, could ever hope to hold on to in this moment. And that's when it finally happened.

Release.

Tears. Like nothing I have ever seen or might ever see in my life. He finally let go. And, God, was it beautiful. More than beautiful—if only there was a bigger word. It was the most transcendent thing I have ever experienced in my life, as I watched my father break down for the first time.

It came in a rising wave of sobbing as he kept saying over and over and over again, "I'm sorry. I'm so sorry. I'm sorry . . ."

"Papi, it's okay," I said. "You don't have to say sorry."

And I meant every word. In that cathartic moment I let go of every last bit of anger and resentment and hurt that I had been storing away in my chest. I looked up at the people around me and realized how blessed I was to have this life and have these five other people to share it with. And that's when the tears started coming down all of our faces, in this joyous, revelatory moment where we realized what really mattered, when everything is stripped away, when there's nothing left: forgiveness, acceptance, freedom.

I remember my little sister at the time looking up at me and asking, "Carlitos, why is Papi crying?"

And before I could try to come up with a response, my wise little brother stepped in and responded with a huge, knowing smile, "Because he's happy."

Only a nine-year-old could distill that moment so perfectly in three words: "Because he's *happy*."

That is my definition of joy—the moment when a person finally lets go, finally forgives him- or herself, finally drops the performance and the posturing and acknowledges how similar all of us are who navigate this world, with all of our shared fear and self-consciousness and embarrassment and laziness and courage and beauty and pride and coping . . . and everything in between.

Watching my dad cry for the first time, I looked across the room to his wife, Karin, who I'd loathed and resented and held animosity toward for so long. I had shown her malice as though it were my obligation, my *duty* as a stepchild. From the first moment I met her, as my dad's coworker when I was fourteen, and took in her short skirt, heels, and too much makeup, I had made it a point to not give her a chance.

For so long I had settled for civility, which I thought was enough. I had conceded this civility to her with the birth of my little brother and sister. And in that room, as my father cried with that photo album perched on his lap, I watched the humility and compassion in his wife's eyes and realized it was long overdue: forgiving Karin for being my stepmom. Ultimately, that's what I had always held against her, right? The one thing that couldn't have been her fault. I had still not made peace, completely, with the fact that my dad had chosen to start a new family with her. And beyond granting that much-delayed forgiveness, I needed to seek her forgiveness as well after years of unjustified hostility I'd directed her way.

The summer after that Christmas, my father and the family moved to Germany, so I had very little time to continue on this journey toward forgiveness of my stepmom. It wasn't until the following Christmas, just before we all met up with relatives in Miami, that I was able to really take the next step in the process of healing.

"A poem," Karin had told me.

"What do you mean?" I asked.

"I have enough things. I want a poem," she stated.

She had given me the opportunity, without ever knowing I was looking for one. I wanted to get her something for Christmas and she had told me she wanted a poem from me in which she wasn't just "the stepmother" or "the wife," as she said with a chuckle. But the heavy hurt underneath was palpable. Yes, it was time.

And so I sat down and wrote what I still consider to be one of the most heartfelt, corny, and important poems I have ever written. Sure, it wasn't Yusef Komunyakaa or Mary Oliver, but my heart was in every word of that piece. I remember carefully editing and revising and rewriting that thing to death, and then finally just saying "fuck it," copying and pasting it into an email, closing my eyes, and clicking Send.

I waited. I checked my email the whole night . . . and nothing. *Oh fuck. Was this poem too much? Did she hate it? Feel uncomfortable because of it? Damn you, Carlos! Why do you do this? You go too far, dude. It's what you do. Why, man? Why?!*

Then I realized she was in Europe. Oh. Okay. Yep, it was six hours later there and she probably wouldn't read it until the next day. And that's when I got her response.

One of the most raw, open, generous, and beautiful emails of my life. She said she was so moved by my poem, she had been crying—tears of joy and relief—as she shared it with my dad. She told me how much she loved me and cared about me. How long she had been waiting and hoping for this moment.

For the first time in my life, I considered what it must have been like for her when we first met. She, sixteen years younger than my father, shortly after a divorce, trying her hardest to make a connection and find common ground with two disenchanted teens out for blood. How is any of this her fault? She and my dad fell in love. His marriage was done. We don't choose when we fall in love; it just happens.

On top of that, she and I are different. Some of her interests and experiences are not my own. We communicate differently. We process the world differently. We are two *different* human beings. But, at the end of the day, she's a good person. She has a good heart. She believes in many of the same things I do. She loves many of the same people that I do. I love my dad's wife, Karin. And she really loves me. In spite of all the animosity and resentment she must have felt coming from me, she continued to make an effort, for far longer than I would have.

Even to this day, she emails me things she thinks I might be interested in. She forwards something to my Facebook wall or relays a link to a podcast. And what I realized that day, reading her email, is what I'd always known: Each of those moments of her reaching out had nothing to do with the content. Who cares what she's sending me? It was about trying to *connect*. It was about saying, "I respect you. I love you. I thought of you today."

Who isn't moved by that? Who can't see the humanity in that intention? Apparently me—for about nine years. And as I finally forgave my dad's wife, my stepmom, whatever you want to call her, it was like I felt a huge weight lifted off of not just me but the entire family.

Three days after Christmas, with the whole family in Miami, I gave my father something I had wanted to for years. It was sort of a poem, mostly a list, kind of a letter. It was a sheet filled with "I love you because . . ." filling up an entire page. I had made it a point that year to give one to everyone in my family and all of my close friends. I didn't want to end up like the protagonist in *I Never Sang for My Father*, wishing I had said the things I felt for those I loved while I still could. I watched the dynamic in our family shift drastically that holiday. Nothing has been the same since.

Now when we have dinners together or go on an outing as a family, you can feel a lightness and ease among all of us that was never there before. And all the heaviness that would weigh us down in the past—it wasn't just negative and depressing, it was a lot of *work*. It really takes energy and work to hold on to negativity. That's another thing I've learned about forgiveness.

Maybe the guy cutting in line to get on the bus just got fired from his temp job or is having a bad hair day or is just in general an asshole. Okay? So what? Forgive him. Smile, let him go first. Move on. I know now that if I do hold on to something negative in that situation, the person I will be punishing most is myself. I spent *years* punishing myself for the myriad energies and egos surrounding me. After forgiving my father and then his wife and continuing to learn to forgive myself, I began to stop punishing myself for other people's baggage. Let go. Forgive. Whatever emotional clutter is obscuring this moment, it's not representative of anyone who is here, now. It's just energy. Forgive.

When I was a sophomore in high school, a friend of mine's cousin, Malik, got shot in the parking lot of a nightclub. He had broken up a fight earlier, and one of the men may have felt embarrassed. Maybe he felt emasculated or small. So he murdered Malik, ending his life after a short seventeen years. In a series of drive-by shootings that followed, more people were hurt, killed, or paralyzed as the cycle of violence continued. When does it stop? What are we fighting for? When have we finally had enough?

One of my biggest fears is projecting my own shit onto my kids. Another one is projecting my life's pain onto someone else. In the times I've felt worst about myself—when I've felt unimportant and ugly and stupid—that's when I have been most ready to fight. That's when I wanted to just fuck some random girl, have her suck my dick, and tell her to get out when we're done. Those moments when I've been most down and out, that's when I cut in line to get on the bus and have less patience and don't look people in the eye. That's not how everyone copes. That's generally what I've observed in myself.

I used to work at a camp for kids with HIV. They had contracted it from their mothers at birth. I'd meet these miraculous, vibrant little kids, who on some of the tougher days would talk to me about the shame they felt. How they felt dirty and tainted for being HIV-positive. How their parents (many dying as a result of AIDS) and family members (mostly because of ignorance and fear) had abandoned them. How they couldn't ever think of themselves as beautiful. Because of something that could never have been their fault, something that took place before they had their first cry.

The world is stacked against us. It's a conspiracy how we are made to feel inadequate. So we buy things to temporarily quell that self-loathing. We try to cover it up or downplay it or distract people's attention to something else—an expensive handbag, new shoes, or a nice car. We try to numb the pain, however briefly. And sometimes we do it with a needle or a fist or between the legs of a twelve-year-old orphan.

In the year I worked as a social worker, I visited a shelter in Harlem each Monday for sexually exploited girls—which is basically a nice way of saying it was a safe haven for orphaned adolescent prostitutes. As the only man walking into that space, I remember feeling the daunting burden of responsibility on my shoulders. *What if I say the wrong thing? What if I'm the worst man to model a positive male relationship for these girls? What if I'm not enough?*

And then I came back to what I realized with the gun incident at the motel—we are *always* enough. Whatever those histories were—the atrocities and violence and everything else so many of these young girls had survived—none of us was that different. I was playful and awkward and genuine and well-intentioned. Sometimes I got embarrassed and scared and excited and inspired. And so did they. Some of them were

HIV-positive. All had survived severe abuse. None of them had a safe place to call "home" besides this shelter. How could that be a twelve-year-old's fault? How could we blame a child for encountering all of that before becoming a teenager?

They would tell me stories about reconnecting with estranged family members and siblings and guardians and even parents. These girls taught me about forgiving years of endured horror beyond my wildest nightmares so that they could reconnect, so that they might be able to move forward and build a new life, so that they might be able to finally heal and be happy and be whole.

A few months after I quit my job as a social worker, the girls from the shelter had their graduation. The small ceremony symbolized their transition out of their former life and into a new one in which they would be youth mentors to their peers. As the gathering came to a close, one of the girls stepped out in front of the audience. I vaguely recognized her petite frame and introverted gait, then realized she was the girl who spoke least in our weekly sessions—never more than two or three words and barely above a whisper. But as she looked up, the room thirsty for whatever she was about to do, it seemed as if someone else had taken over her body. As she proudly pushed her shoulders back, an unlikely sunflower defiantly opening up, I could feel her rising voice crack me open, along with an entire congested room of heavy chests, with her song:

I sing because I'm happy. I sing because I'm FREE!

As a young father across from me unclenched his jaw, the salt water now released to baptize his cheeks.

His eye is on the sparrow . . .

Joy. A growing smile on his newly freed face.

. . . and I know He watches me.

That's who taught me forgiveness: A quiet girl finding her voice. The young father watching her who gave himself permission to finally let go. Kids with HIV at a summer camp. Adolescents trying to get out of prostitution. A gun-wielding man at a brothel. A former IV drug user trying to become literate. A recovering crack cocaine addict fighting to rebuild his life. My little brother and sister. My stepmom. My father.

And it was their lessons that finally made me into a man.

by Carlos Andrés Gómez

"I Have Been, I Am, I Want to Be"

Music swells. Overwhelming. Silence.

I have been . . .
the crybaby afraid of everything you can imagine, who was so
crippled by fear that he couldn't sleep at night.

I have been . . .
the grandson and nephew ashamed of his Spanish who would
hide from the phone when his *abuelita* called or any of his *tías*
so he wouldn't have to talk to them.

the nomad who didn't have a bed for 6 years or unpack his
room, so tired of moving after 14 of them that he didn't want
to pack up his things ever again.

I am . . .
the nerdy kid with the food allergies who can't eat wheat
gluten or yeast or bananas, peanuts, *plátanos*, or mushrooms.

I am . . .
the nutcase who does 300 push-ups at 3:38 in the morning so
that he never loses the "edge" that makes him great.

the needy guy who just wants to be touched and held by
someone and be noticed and remembered in this moment.

I want to be . . .
a great father who teaches his kids how to be strong and proud.

I want to be . . .
the senior citizen having great sex with his wife even though
their bodies are betraying them and their wrinkles are getting
wayyy out of control.

the grandfather who can give his grandson a run for his money
in basketball, even with the crippling arthritis in his swollen
hands and the pain in his right hip.

the old man at the doctor's office who sees cancer on the MRI
and laughs, to the surprise of the doctor and his wife, and says,
"I knew that motherfucker was gonna stop by for a visit at some point."

I want to be . . .
the one that always dared and dared to love and be loved.

I want to be . . .
the old man in the hospital bed with a huge smile on his face, at peace, squeezing his wife's and older sister Sarita's hands as he slowly drifts off and the heart/lung machine is turned off.

Carlos smiles.

Lights out.

Epilogue

Every artistic act is a huge leap of faith. Never have I taken a more wild jump than here. I hope that everyone I have ever loved recognizes why I had to do it, why I chose to tear myself open and so ruthlessly expose my scars and flaws and huge fuckups along the way, and why, in many instances, others had to be implicated in those stories. I know that there is a price to telling those stories, one I certainly do not bear alone.

Maybe the wisest saying I know is "the truth will set you free." When everything else around me was collapsing (or seemed to be), that was the only respite I had—that phrase. It is why I have often craved the truth like food, demanded it, shouted it out and challenged authority with it. It is why I yearned to discover more—something more profound or meaningful concealed beneath what I knew. But I have also pushed it away and hid from it. I have lied and deceived under its cloak. I have claimed to champion it, waving it like a proud banner, while having no idea what it really meant. Ultimately, though, I hope to have moved closer to unearthing more of it through these stories, and I hope they moved you, shifted something in your body in the telling.

If I achieve what I set out to do, this book will be, above all else, an affirmation for men feeling alone. It will be the quirky, awkward friend pulling a desperate teenager from the edge of a rooftop. It will be a father figure to kids like me who were vulnerable and passionate and wanted a different kind of man to look up to. Or maybe it will be a gateway, that first permission a man gives himself to be who he really is inside: artistic, brave, gay, a math nerd, a crybaby, a woman.

I also want Papi, Mommy, and Sarita to know that they are my greatest heroes, my most beloved friends, the ones who gave me the permission to be who I am, as scary and impossibly unreal as that may have been for them at times. I cannot even imagine the commitment and courage it takes to keep someone like *me* in your life.

The three of them, more than anyone else, taught me to not just think deeply but to *feel* deeply as well. Their lessons made me write this, gave me no choice, brought tears to my eyes in the nightclub when I brushed shoulders with that man who wanted to fight, make my heart ache when another young black man in my neighborhood gets shot down for nothing, made me desperate to turn all my inside hurt outward, try to share these intimate stories to maybe bring an end to patterns of destruction I can no longer stand by and watch.

And I am so desperate for these cycles to end . . .

> until fourth-graders refuse to throw the word "faggot" alongside their little-boy fists . . .

> until black men stop killing other black men over a dime bag or a scuffed shoe . . .

until gangs are not the only families ready to embrace parentless kids . . .

until fathers and sons know each other's throaty snoring and tender hearts . . .

until grandfathers can cry and sing at a family reunion, without liquor or a funeral or dementia to blame . . .

until boys can wear pink and give kisses and cry when they fall and ask questions when they don't know something . . .

until everyone can be who they are and marry who they want and share it with the world without fear . . .

until men can finally embrace their pain and scars, shed light on the demons in their past, and refuse to turn the violence outward . . . or, too often, on themselves . . .

I will continue to sing.

And not just for my father but for all the beautiful men and boys on this earth—my brothers, my friends, my cousins, my nephews, my sons, the guy at the bodega, the cop checking out my girlfriend, the old man smiling at that baby, this asshole talking too loud on his cell phone right now, and, also, most of all,

You.

ACKNOWLEDGMENTS

Grateful acknowledgment is made to the editors of the following publications where these poems first appeared:

Winning Writers: "Honest/Clean"
Rattle: "What's Genocide?"
Muzzle Magazine: "Wait"

"What's Genocide?" was featured on HBO's *Def Poetry Jam* (season 6, episode 41). Big thanks to Russell Simmons, Stan Lathan, Danny Simmons, and Kamilah Forbes.

The solo play *Man Up* was first performed in spring 2007 as part of the soloNOVA Arts Festival at PS122 in Manhattan. Big thanks to Jennifer Conley Darling, J. D. Carter, Shawn Randall, Kibibi Dillon (RIP), and everyone who helped make that possible.

Thank you, Papi. Forget all the tough years we had, you are my hero. You have been there, more than anyone else, to support me on my artistic path. I love you so much, for that and so much more.

Thank you, Mommy. You are the foundation of my blind faith, why I dare to dream and live with abandon. There is no way I would have survived this journey without you.

Thank you, Sarita. I have never encountered anyone more thoughtful, sensitive, and compassionate. You have saved my life more times than you'll ever know.

Thank you, Karin. For sticking with me and loving me through it all.

Thank you, Nico and Maya. You teach me, save me, and remind me to be present, and play every single day I am alive. I am so thankful to share this life with both of you.

Thank you, my beloved family in Florida, Colombia, and beyond—too many to name—know that you are loved more than words could ever express.

Thank you, Tamilla Woodard. You were the first person to give me permission to fully embrace this journey of deconstructing and then seeking to redefine what it is to be a man. Your genius, grace, and passion are unparalleled and absolutely breathtaking.

Thank you, Melody Guy. You are the main reason I dared to write this book. You have a combination of tenacious, gentle, and uncompromising thunder that leaves me in awe. I am so grateful to leave this project with such a mentor, guide, guru, editor, and above all, friend.

Thank you, Rene Alegria. I knew we'd get along the first moment we met—your guts, ideas, and aspirations are as big as your epic heart. You have believed and pushed and continued to believe throughout. Looking forward to what's on the horizon. . . .

Thank you, *mi hermano*—Travers Johnson. For too much to say thank you for. I knew the moment we met in the Nuyorican Poets Café that we were brothers. You have a fire, openness, and spirit that are damn inspiring.

Thank you, William Shinker, Megan Newman, Beth Parker, Megan Halpern, Lisa Johnson, Jessica Chun, Tiffany Tomlin, Melanie Koch, Alan Walker, Luara Gianino, LeeAnn Pemberton, and the entire Gotham Books, PSB, and extended Penguin family. It has been an absolute honor to share this ride with each and every one of you. I am so humbled by your continued belief and support.

Thank you, Brent. This book is as much yours as it is mine. I look forward to having each other's backs for the rest of this life . . . and the next hundred.

Thank you, Eric. You exemplify courage and compassion. You are the best there is.

Thank you, Leila. You challenge me, support me, hold me accountable, inspire me, and deepen my perspective on all things human like no one else I have ever met.

Thank you, Dave. You saved my life when I wanted to give up in eighth grade.

Thank you, beloved friends from high school, college, and beyond. Just know you are loved and cherished more than you could ever know.

Thank you, poetry family: Warren Longmire, Rachel McKibbens, Felice Belle, Mahogany Browne, Jive Poetic, Jared Paul, Adam Falkner, Jeanann Verlee, Caroline Rothstein, Obinna Obilo, Geoff Kagan Trenchard, Ellison Glenn, Angel Nafis, Jon Sands, Roger Bonair-Agard, Jamaal and Nile St. John, Lynne Procope, Rico Frederick, Shira Erlichman, Lemon Andersen, Sarah Kay, Travis Watkins, Andrea Gibson, Marty McConnell, Buddy Wakefield, Taylor Mali, Cristin O'Keefe Aptowicz, Panama Soweto, Postmidnight, Clara Nura Sala, Syreeta McFadden, Patricia Smith, Corrina Bain, Tahani Salah, Michael Cirelli, Eboni Hogan, The louderARTS Project, Bowery Poetry Club, Nuyorican Poets Café, Urban Word NYC, and of course, the Excelano Project (EP!) at UPenn. What a joy to be a part of such a community. I am better because of you.

Thank you, Spike Lee, for believing in another raw, outspoken, opinionated New Yorker.

Thank you, Kim Coleman and Eve Streger. For taking the chance. For fighting for me. For believing in me.

Thank you, Bob Krakower. Having you in my life has made me not just a better actor but also a better man.

Thank you, Jeff Perera and Jasmin Zine. Never have I met two more incredible human beings.

Thank you, longtime loyal supporters and those who just came to the party—if you've come to a show, shared one of my videos on YouTube, Facebook, or Tumblr, retweeted it on Twitter, or are holding this book right now—none of this would be possible without you. I am beyond grateful.

Thank you, Moms, Pops, Granny, Naye, Darnell, Jaime, Maurice (and Carter!). You exemplify family. You exemplify love.

Thank you, last but certainly not least: Whitney. My love. My everything.

My soon-to-be . . . wife.

DO SOMETHING

Join the movement. Share your story:
www.ManUpMoment.org

Support these great organizations:

White Ribbon Campaign
The largest effort in the world, of men working to end violence
against women.
www.whiteribbon.com

Human Rights Campaign
The largest LGBT–rights advocacy group and political lobbying
organization in the United States.
www.hrc.org

MenEngage
A global alliance of NGOs and UN agencies that seek to engage
boys and men to achieve gender equality.
www.menengage.org

Futures Without Violence
Works to prevent and end violence against women and children around the world.
www.futureswithoutviolence.org

Men Can Stop Rape
Mobilizes men to use their strength for creating cultures free from violence, especially men's violence against women.
www.mencanstoprape.org

Higher Unlearning
An online space to discuss ideas of manhood and masculinity.
www.higherunlearning.com

Voices Unbroken
A creative-writing program that works with incarcerated youth and adults.
www.voicesunbroken.org

Urban Word NYC
Offers free, safe, and uncensored writing workshops to New York City teens year-round.
www.urbanwordnyc.org

Youth Speaks (and Brave New Voices Festival)
Curates writing workshops, open mics, and the biggest teen poetry slam in the world.
www.youthspeaks.org